THE DOG OWNER'S PROBLEM SOLVER

A READER'S DIGEST BOOK

Produced by Andromeda Oxford Limited
Copyright © 1998 Andromeda
Oxford Ltd

Project Editor:	*Susan Kennedy*
Editor:	*Lauren Bourque*
Art Director:	*Chris Munday*
Senior Designer:	*Martin Anderson*
Picture Manager:	*Claire Turner*
Picture Researcher:	*Valerie Mulcahy*
Proofreader:	*Lynne Elson*
Indexer:	*Ann Barrett*
Production Director:	*Clive Sparling*
Production Assistant:	*Nicolette Colborne*

Library of Congress Cataloging in Publication has
been applied for.

Printed in Italy Petruzzi Città di Castello - PG

THE DOG
OWNER'S
PROBLEM SOLVER

JOHN AND CAROLINE
BOWER

 Reader's Digest

THE READER'S DIGEST ASSOCIATION, INC.
Pleasantville, New York/Montreal

INTRODUCTION

Mᴏʀᴇ ᴘᴇᴏᴘʟᴇ ᴛʜᴀɴ ᴇᴠᴇʀ ᴏᴡɴ ᴀ ᴅᴏɢ ᴛᴏᴅᴀʏ. Iɴ ᴛʜᴇ ᴍᴀᴊᴏʀɪᴛʏ ᴏꜰ ᴄᴀꜱᴇꜱ ᴛʜᴇ ʀᴇʟᴀᴛɪᴏɴꜱʜɪᴘ *is a happy one, but as owners and veterinarians working in a busy practice, we know how easily things can go wrong. Dog owners constantly ask us for advice, not only on medical matters, but also on how to choose and train a puppy or correct bad behavior. We are aware of the worries and concerns that are most often raised by the experienced owner as well as the first-time owner.*

The best way to deal with most dog problems is to prevent them from arising in the first place. In this book we give advice on preventing disease and identifying the illnesses and physical conditions most commonly encountered. We have also tried to help owners understand the way their dog thinks, behaves, and communicates its feelings. Practical help is given on such situations as owning a dog with small children or other pets. We also suggest ways of dealing with problem behavior once it has arisen, but in most cases it is wise to seek advice from a recognized behavior counselor, who may or may not also be a veterinarian. Your own vet can refer you to one if necessary. In addition, we have provided information on some leading dog breeds, describing the potential health problems associated with each.

In writing this book, we have been greatly assisted by contributions from colleagues at The Veterinary Hospital, Plymouth, England, whose names are listed on page 204. We are also grateful to our patients and their owners—without them, we would not have been able to pose the questions and answers, or the case studies, that are a feature of the book. Our aim has been to offer a readable, easy to use, and entertaining guide that will make owning a dog problem-free and enjoyable for you. We hope that you and your dog will enjoy many years of untroubled companionship.

Jᴏʜɴ *&* Cᴀʀᴏʟɪɴᴇ Bᴏᴡᴇʀ

CONTENTS

Choosing and Caring for Your Dog

For many individuals and families, keeping a dog as a pet offers lasting companionship and pleasure. A childhood family pet, loved and cared for since it was a puppy, can bring a lifetime of happy, treasured memories.

If you have only just decided to get a dog, the business of choosing and looking after it can seem a little daunting. This section guides you through all the stages of acquiring a pet and helps you avoid some of the potential pitfalls. It outlines the responsibilities of owning a dog, gives advice on selecting a breed that will suit your lifestyle, and tells you what to look for when choosing your puppy or adult dog.

In the pages that follow, many of the questions most frequently asked by owners of new puppies and dog are answered. What equipment do you need? How do you feed your pet? What are the best methods of housebreaking and grooming? What special adjustments should be made as a dog grows older and frailer? By providing a better understanding of your dog's care, health, and behavioral needs, this book can help you avoid some common mistakes, so as to build a satisfying and lasting relationship with your pet.

Responsibilities of Owning a Dog

WHATEVER YOUR REASONS FOR CHOOSING TO own a dog, the responsibilities of caring for it will always be the same—without you, your dog will not be fed, exercised, groomed, or receive necessary care when ill. In other words, the quality of your dog's life will depend totally on you. And you will be committing yourself to your pet's care not just for a week, or a month, or a year, but for years. The average life expectancy of a dog is 10 years, and many live to 16 or 17. So before you decide to own a dog, take a long hard look at yourself, your lifestyle, and your environment. Work out for yourself if the pleasures and companionship to be had from owning a dog are outweighed by the disadvantages. Every individual will reach his or her own conclusion, but it is better to face these questions before committing yourself to the long-term responsibility of living with and caring for a dog. Far too many dogs are abandoned simply because their owners found themselves unable or unwilling to care for them.

Your dog deserves the best health care. That means making sure it receives regular protection against the major canine infectious diseases and parasites (see pages 46–51). There are other considerations, too—how will you afford the costs of veterinary care if your dog has a serious accident or becomes sick? If you don't have money set aside, you should decide whether to take out insurance to cover your dog's medical bills. Your dog should have the benefit of a good-quality balanced diet rather than being fed on table scraps—are you prepared to pay for that, too?

Can I Afford the Time?

Ask yourself if you have enough time to devote to a mischievous puppy. Remember that it will initially need feeding four times a day, and it will not be housebroken, so you must be prepared for accidents. It will be into everything, and chew your furniture and most treasured possessions. You will need to devote a good deal of your leisure time to its training and, as it grows bigger, give it regular, adequate daily exercise. If you live in a city apartment, is there a park nearby where you can take it for walks? What about vacations and business trips? Is there someone to care for your dog while you're away, or are you prepared to pay kennel fees? All dogs require regular grooming, but for some longhaired breeds this will be a daily necessity.

Your Dog and Your Neighbors

A well-trained dog is a pleasure to keep and is a valued member of the family; a disobedient and destructive one may become a nuisance, even a danger, to your neighbors. Every state or country has its own laws and legal obligations affecting dogs (see pages 10–11). But there are a number of general rules you should observe as a matter of courtesy and good manners:

1. Keep your dog under control. When with you in the street or park, your dog should walk quietly on the leash without jumping up at every person it meets (especially children) or attacking other dogs. Off the leash, it should not rush up to strangers or children and should return immediately to you when called. Remember, not everyone you meet will be a dog lover.

2. Do not allow your pet to wander. Make sure it cannot escape from your yard or garden, and do not allow it to disappear out of sight when off the leash. Take particular care of your female dog when she is in season.

3. Clean up after your dog. When your dog defecates, make sure you always have a poop scooper, plastic bag, or supply of tissues with you to pick up the mess. Dispose of the feces hygienically, preferably in a container specially designated for the purpose.

4. Don't let your dog bark at strangers or other dogs when outdoors. This is a matter of good basic training. Training will also help you avoid some behavior problems that lead to dogs barking when left on their own at home.

▲ *Regulations in many city parks and rural areas prohibit you from allowing your dog to run loose off the leash. Always observe local laws out of consideration to other people.*

● *A stranger got very angry with me when my young puppy, Rosie, defecated on the sidewalk. She is only a baby. Don't you think he was overreacting?*

Dog feces in public areas are unsightly, unhygienic, and unpleasant. As a responsible dog owner, it is up to you pick your dog's messes up and dispose of them properly. In many localities this is an absolute legal requirement.

● *My Jack Russell Terrier, Scamp, is nearly a year old. I'm not planning to use him as a stud male. Should I have him neutered?*

There is much to be said for the early neutering of a male dog if you are not planning to mate him. It obviously cuts down on the number of unwanted pregnancies and helps limit the number of strays on the street. It can also prevent certain diseases and, if carried out early enough, may help to curb aggressive tendencies. Some people, however, are reluctant to consider neutering, as they feel it is "unnatural" and may alter their pet's personality. It is a matter that needs careful and responsible consideration. Talk it over with your veterinarian before deciding.

● *Do all dogs need to carry an identification?*

It is certainly advisable and is normally a legal requirement in most countries. An engraved disk with your name, address, and telephone number is usually sufficient, but many people consider that tattoos or electronic identification (microchips implanted in the skin) are more efficient methods.

Your Dog and the Law

MOST COUNTRIES HAVE EXTENSIVE LAWS AND regulations covering dogs. Some are embodied in federal law (in the US) or in parliamentary law (in the UK), but the vast majority fall within the jurisdiction of individual state, provincial, local, and municipal authorities. In the US dog laws often differ dramatically from location to location, or from situation to situation. When acquiring a dog for the first time, or when moving with your dog to a new area, make a point of finding out what laws affect you by calling the town, city, or county clerk and inquiring which department handles animal-control laws. State laws can be investigated at a public library.

In almost every locality it is a legal requirement for your dog to carry identification in the

▼ An unrestrained dog can cause injury to itself and others, especially if it runs loose among traffic. It is up to you to find out what the dog laws are in your locality and to make sure you comply with them.

form of a collar tag, tattoo, or microchip. Some authorities require a specific form of identification; others allow the owner to choose. Municipalities are normally responsible for collecting dog license fees. The amount of the fee may vary depending on whether or not the dog has been neutered. In the UK a collar tag with the owner's name and address is obligatory, except for working dogs, but there is no longer a statutory dog license fee.

Most cities require dogs to be kept on a leash except in designated "dog runs." Dogs may be banned altogether from entering some city parks and public buildings. Owners are usually obliged by law to clean up after their dogs. Strays are impounded and, if not reclaimed within a specific number of days, may be adopted or humanely destroyed. "Seeing Eye" or other service dogs are normally exempt from most animal-control laws, and their owners may be given reduced license fees, or the fees waived altogether.

▶ *A dogcatcher reads the information on a microchip tag inserted under the skin of a dog found wandering in the street. The owner will be contacted and may be liable to a fine for failing to confine his dog.*

Restrictions are likely to be fewer in rural areas. Dogs are allowed to run loose; if restrictions do exist, working dogs may be exempted. However, you may be liable if your dog injures farm animals or damages property. In the UK a farmer can shoot any dog worrying sheep or cattle, and there are strict penalties against allowing dogs to hunt game animals on private land.

In the US and many other countries, the law requires all dogs to be vaccinated against rabies. Many insist on the dog carrying microchip certification. In countries where rabies is not endemic, such as the UK, vaccination is not obligatory but dogs imported from abroad are subject to strict quarantine controls.

Dangerous Dogs

You may be at fault for owning a dangerous dog. Sometimes specific breeds may only be kept subject to particular conditions being fulfilled, such as the dog being muzzled in public, neutered, and not being given away or sold. In the UK Pit Bull Terrier-types and three other breeds fall into this category. Local laws may deem that attacks on domestic animals as well as people constitute a danger, and they may or may not require that a bite actually occurs before action against the dog can be initiated. A conviction will usually result in the dog being humanely destroyed. You are likely to be liable if your dog causes a street accident through your failure to control it.

Canine Protection

You will find yourself liable for prosecution if you cause unnecessary suffering to a dog or dogs in your charge—this includes neglect, starvation, lack of freedom to exercise, cruelty, and beating. Most authorities have a body of regulations concerning the ownership, operation, and inspection of breeding kennels, boarding facilities, training schools, and grooming establishments. If you intend to set up as a business, you must establish for yourself what laws and conditions pertain in your locality.

Q & A

● **Is there any limit to the number of dogs that I can keep?**

… This is likely to be determined by municipality law, so check with your relevant department. In some places keeping more than three dogs constitutes a "kennel," making you, the owner, liable to the laws, fees, and inspections regulating the ownership of kennels, even if you are not operating a business location. The welfare of the animals is an important consideration—animal protection societies such as the ASPCA and the RSPCA (in the UK) will take legal action against you if they think your dogs are being kept in crowded, insanitary conditions, or are being neglected in any way.

● **My German Shepherd, Jake, got involved in a fight with a Boxer. Both were injured. Will I have to pay the Boxer's vet bill?**

Do not admit liability, but do seek legal advice if you think action is likely to be taken. Often both parties are equally to blame in such incidents, but if you let Jake off the leash in a public place, knowing him to be aggressive, you may well be liable to prosecution. In the US injury by your dog is normally covered under your home insurance policy (in the UK owners often take out third-party insurance). However, many insurance companies are increasingly reluctant to cover certain breeds of dog against injury.

What Breed Should I Choose?

BEFORE CHOOSING A DOG, ASK YOURSELF WHY you want one. Is it for companionship, protection, exercise, for the sake of your children? If you choose a crossbred (mongrel) dog, you may have difficulty in predicting the hereditary physical and behavioral characteristics of the adult dog, but crossbreeds can make supremely reliable, friendly, healthy, and long-lived pets. If you are looking for dependable characteristics, however, choose a pedigree breed. Don't pick one on the basis of appearance alone—find out as much as you can about the different breeds and choose one that will fit in with your particular lifestyle. Some breeds are not suited to living in an apartment. Many need daily grooming. Big dogs have big appetites, so you will face large food bills. Some are not really suited to first-time owners. Weigh all the factors, then decide.

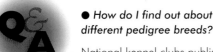

● **How do I find out about different pedigree breeds?**

... National kennel clubs publish standards for all recognized breeds, which describe their physical features. They will usually answer requests for information. Specialty dog magazines often run useful features. Your animal hospital should give you impartial advice, especially concerning behavioral and health problems.

● **I have two children ages 5 and 8, and would like to keep a dog. I work part-time, enjoy short walks, and have never had a dog before. What breed would you recommend?**

Shetland Sheepdogs, Cavalier King Charles Spaniels, and Shih Tzus are usually good with children, don't need too much exercise, and are easy to train.

● **I would like to train a dog for agility trials. I am an experienced owner. What breed do you suggest?**

Border Collies (or Collie crosses), German Shepherds, or any size Poodle are highly trainable and alert, and thoroughly enjoy the challenge of working with their owners in competitions.

	SIZE OF DOG	SUITABLE FOR FIRST-TIME OWNER	LIVING SP
GREAT DANE	5	No	5
AKITA	5	No	5
ENGLISH/IRISH SETTER	5	Yes	4
DOBERMAN PINSCHER	5	No	4
ROTTWEILER	5	No	4
WEIMARANAR	5	No	5
GERMAN SHEPHERD	5	No	5
BOXER	4	Yes	5
GOLDEN RETRIEVER	4	Yes	3
DALMATIAN	4	No	4
ROUGH COLLIE	4	Yes	3
SIBERIAN HUSKY	4	No	3
LABRADOR	4	Yes	4
BORDER COLLIE	4	No	3
CHOW CHOW	3	No	3
BRITTANY	3	Yes	4
ENG. SPRINGER SPANIEL	3	No	5
SHAR PEI	3	No	3
BOSTON TERRIER	3	Yes	2
STAFF. BULL TERRIER	3	No	2
COCKER SPANIEL	3	Yes	2
BEAGLE	3	Yes	2
BASSETT	3	Yes	2
POODLE	3–1	Yes	4–
SHETLAND SHEEPDOG	2	Yes	1
CAV. K. CHARLES SPANIEL	2	Yes	1
MINIATURE SCHNAUZER	2	Yes	2
JACK RUSSELL TERRIER	2	Yes	2
MINIATURE PINSCHER	2	No	2
W. HIGHLAND TERRIER	2	Yes	2
POMERANIAN	1	Yes	2
SHIH TZU	1	Yes	2
MALTESE	1	Yes	2
PEKINGESE	1	No	2
DACHSHUND	1	Yes	2
YORKSHIRE TERRIER	1	No	1
CHIHUAHUA	1	No	1

GOOD WITH CHILDREN	AMOUNT OF GROOMING	AMOUNT OF EXERCISE	NOISINESS/BARKING	TRAINABILITY	AGGRESSION	PLAYFULNESS/ BOISTEROUSNESS	EXCITABILITY
5	1	4	2	1	2	2	3
2	3	3	1	3	5	3	1
5	2	4	2	2	1	3	3
3	1	4	2	4	4	2	2
1	2	4	2	4	5	1	2
1	1	5	2	2	2	5	5
2	3	5	3	5	5	1	3
3	1	5	2	1	2	5	2
5	3	3	3	5	1	4	3
3	1	5	3	1	1	5	3
5	4	3	2	4	1	2	2
1	3	5	3	1	1	1	1
5	1	4	3	5	1	4	3
1	3	5	3	5	4	5	4
2	5	2	1	1	2	1	3
3	2	4	3	5	2	4	4
3	2	5	3	5	3	4	5
2	2	2	2	2	2	1	2
4	1	2	2	2	3	2	3
4	1	2	4	2	3	3	4
3	3*	2	4	3	4	4	4
3	1	4	4	2	2	3	4
4	1	2	3	1	1	1	1
3	5**	5	5–3	5	3–2	5	4
5	5	2	1	5	1	2	1
5	3	2	2	3	1	2	4
3	1**	4	5	2	3	2	4
2	1	4	5	2	4	4	5
2	1	3	4	3	3	2	3
4	2**	3	5	3	4	5	4
4	4	1	3	1	3	2	5
4	4*	2	2	2	2	3	3
4	5*	1	3	1	2	1	4
1	5	1	4	2	3	2	4
4	2	3	4	3	3	2	3
2	3*	1	4	2	4	2	4
1	2	1	5	2	5	3	4

◀ This table shows the chief characteristics of some of the most popular dog breeds. Decide which are most important to you, then use the table to find the breed (or breeds) that suits you best, bearing in mind that the behavior of any adult dog depends as much on the way it was educated as a puppy as it does on its genetic inheritance.

NOTES

5 = Highest level of characteristic

1 = Lowest level of characteristic

Size of Dog
Adult height at the withers.
5 = more than 25in (64cm)
1 = less than 10in (25cm)
Poodles straddle three categories: Standard, Miniature, Toy (see p. 179)

Amount of Grooming
* Indicates that professional grooming is optional for these breeds

** Indicates that professional grooming is advisable for these breeds

Trainability
Responsiveness to training for obedience, agility trials, and work

Excitability
Reactivity to stimuli such as noise, crowds, etc.

Taking in a Rescued Dog

RATHER THAN BUY A PUPPY FROM A BREEDER, you may decide to give a home to an abandoned dog from an animal shelter. You may successfully acquire a perfect companion, but pleasure will sometimes turn to disappointment when a dog is found to have unforeseen behavioral problems and cannot adapt to family life. There is a certain amount of luck involved, but you can improve your chances of success if you are aware of the pitfalls and have sufficient knowledge to cope with any setbacks (see pages 116–117).

Dogs in rescue centers range from small puppies to the old and sick. Every one comes to the center with a previous history. Dogs are sometimes abandoned when owners lose their jobs, divorce, move to a new location, become ill, or die. The dog itself may have fallen sick or caused allergies in a member of the owner's family. It may have been rejected because it was constantly fighting with another family pet or causing a nuisance in the home. Some dogs may have been beaten, neglected, or kept chained up alone for long periods.

Adolescent dogs (ages 6–9 months) are one of most common groups of dogs in any rescue shelter. They are frequently abandoned because their owners had failed to give enough thought to the responsibilities or practical aspects of owning a dog. Once their pet has passed the sweet puppy stage they lose interest or find they cannot control its unruly behavior. Often this is because they chose the wrong kind of dog for their circumstances or neglected its training.

Matching Dogs and Owners

Unfortunately, when owners give their dog to a shelter, they do not always admit the real reason. More than half the dogs in a rescue center are likely to have behavioral problems, ranging from nuisance barking and jumping up on people to aggressive and dangerous behavior. Many can be retrained successfully, particularly if the new owner is used to caring for dogs and is prepared to give time and patience to the task. Some rescue centers go to considerable lengths to match problem dogs to the right new home. Dogs that have had more than one previous home can be particularly difficult to place successfully.

Tell the staff at the center just what kind of dog you are looking for. Do you want a puppy or an adult? Have you kept a dog before? Do you live in an apartment or a house? Are there children or elderly people in the family? How much time do you have for training, exercising, and grooming? Ask to visit the center at least once to take the dog for a walk and get used to handling it before bringing it home. That way there'll be more successful adoptions, far fewer dissatisfied owners, and happier dogs.

▼ *Weigh all the factors carefully before you make your choice. Whatever you're looking for, the puppy or dog you pick will have an indefinable "extra" quality that says, "Please take me home!"*

Q&A...

● **What do I have to do if I take a dog from a rescue center?**

You will normally be asked to pay a small fee, and the rescue center will probably require that you have the dog neutered. It may offer reduced-cost vaccinations. If not, you must arrange for a full health check and vaccinations as soon as possible.

● **Is it better to choose a puppy or an adult?**

Only you can decide. Ideally, a puppy should be adopted before it is 10 weeks old because time spent in kennels after that age can be damaging to its development. If you choose a puppy, you are starting with a relatively "clean slate" as far as training and behavior are concerned. However, the puppy's age, parentage, and health status may be unknown, and its likely size as an adult will be difficult to predict (though big feet indicate a large adult). An adolescent or adult dog should already be housebroken but may take a longer period of time to adjust to a new home.

● **My friend got a dog from our local dog pound last week, and it has a terrible cough. She wants me to visit with my children. Is the cough likely to be infectious? Could it be passed to the children?**

The most likely causes of the dog's cough are kennel cough or distemper. Both diseases are highly infectious to dogs but do not affect humans; they can both be prevented by vaccination. It is extremely important that your friend's dog be examined by a vet to establish the cause of its cough.

Dos and Don'ts of Adopting a Dog

Do

✓ Decide if you want a puppy, adolescent, adult, or older dog before contacting the center.

✓ Consider your own circumstances. Always busy? Don't choose a dog that needs daily grooming. Getting older? Avoid an athletic type. Got a young family? Make sure the dog is used to children.

✓ Take your time. It will not help you or the dog if you make a mistake.

✓ Find out all you can about the dog's history and personality. Take it for a short walk. Watch how it behaves with other dogs and people.

✓ Have it checked over by a vet when you get it home. Make sure it has had all its shots.

Don't

✗ Choose a rescued dog simply because you think it is a cheap option. You must be prepared to give it plenty of time and patience.

✗ Rush your decision. Spend time with the dog before committing yourself.

✗ Expect to find the perfect dog the first time you go looking.

✗ Choose solely on the basis of appearance. It is just as important to see how the dog behaves.

✗ Smother your new pet with love and affection, however adorable it is. A dog with an unstable start in life can very easily become overattached. Allow it time and space to adjust to its new home.

Choosing Your Puppy

NOW THAT YOU HAVE DECIDED WHICH BREED or type of dog is right for you (see pages 12–13), you are ready to go out and find a puppy. It's best to choose one from a reputable owner or breeder known to you, or one who comes highly recommended by someone you trust. Professional organizations like national kennel clubs should provide lists of breeders in your area. Such lists, however, can tell you little about the quality or temperament of the individual dogs produced. Your local veterinary center is usually a good source of information. It should be able to supply a checklist of reliable contacts and provide a followup advice service on puppy care after you have made your choice.

Many breeders advertise their puppies in local newspapers and specialty magazines or make use of dog-finding agencies. Before acquiring a puppy from any source, make a few simple enquiries to determine the breeder's reliability. How many breeds of dog are bred at the establishment? If the answer is more than one or two, do not use them. Does the breeder show his or her own dogs in sanctioned shows? Can the puppy be returned if it turns out to have any defects or something goes wrong?

Finally, you may adopt a puppy from a shelter. This is a leap into the unknown, so make sure you consider the issues covered on pages 14–15.

▶ They all seem adorable— which do I choose? A timid puppy may be difficult to train, and a boisterous one turn out to be a handful. But your puppy's future behavior will largely depend on the education you give it once you have brought it home.

Which Puppy for You?

Once you have found a breeder, visit the litter several times to see that the mother and puppies are healthy and have good temperaments. Take time to ask questions, think things over, and develop trust in the breeder. Only when you are completely satisfied on all points should you make your choice of puppy from the litter. A normal puppy will readily approach a stranger who speaks to it in a calm, welcoming voice. Shy puppies do not, and may retreat from visitors. Normal puppies are startled by unexpected noises, but should recover quickly, so test the litter by clapping your hands or dropping a bunch of keys. Do not select a puppy that is excessively timid. It can be difficult to determine levels of dominance or submissiveness in young puppies as their mood changes from hour to hour. However, if one puppy appears consistently bolder than its littermates, it may not be the best choice for a first-time owner.

Most breeders allow their puppies to leave the litter at between 6 and 12 weeks. The ideal age is 8 to 9 weeks. While it is with its mother and littermates, the puppy is learning to communicate with other dogs and

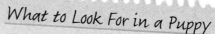

Q & A... ● *I am about to choose my first puppy. Is a male or a female easier to keep?*

Which sex you choose is a matter of personal preference. Females may be more expensive because of their breeding potential, but they are usually less assertive to their owners and less likely to show aggression to other dogs. They are generally considered easier to train as well, but there are exceptions to every rule.

● *When I went to choose a pup from a local breeder, I noticed that the litter had been separated from their mother. Because of this, a friend advised me not to take any of them. Why?*

The breeder may have separated the mother from her pups because she was behaving aggressively toward them or to visitors. Even so, the pups may have already learned bad behavior. Hand-raised puppies often lack normal behavior patterns. This can cause problems later, so if you've never kept a dog before, it's better to avoid one of these puppies.

● *I have been offered a Boxer puppy nearly 4 months old. I had been hoping for a younger one, but he is so adorable. Should I take him?*

If you are a first-time owner, you would be wise to go on looking a little longer for a puppy. By the time the puppy is 12 weeks old, it has passed the most sensitive phase of socialization and is likely to have problems adjusting to new people and situations.

What to Look For in a Puppy

✓ Do the puppies in the litter appear healthy and vigorous?

✓ Do all other dogs in contact with the pups appear healthy and friendly?

✓ Is the mother friendly and trusting or fearful and aggressive toward strangers? Timidity in the mother is a bad sign; it may be inherited by the puppies or learned though example.

✓ Are the pups being raised in an environment that provides stimulation and exposure to different objects and people?

✓ Are they being handled regularly? Early handling is of crucial importance in the puppies' socialization.

✓ Have the pups been separated from the mother? If so, when?

✓ How old is the litter? Before 6 weeks the pups are too young to leave the mother; from 12 weeks they may be too old.

behave as a member of the pack (see pages 104–107). Remove it from the litter too early, and it may never interpret correctly the signals it receives from other dogs. If it is separated from its mother too soon, it is deprived of maternal discipline, making it disrespectful both of adult dogs and humans later on. However, it is important for the puppy's socialization that it become used to handling and outside stimulation long before it is parted from its mother (see pages 108–109). A puppy that remains with the litter after 12 weeks risks becoming isolated, but the breeder can avoid this by introducing it to as many new situations as possible.

Before you go home with your puppy, ask the breeder to tell you about its diet, shots, deworming treatment, and ongoing socialization. He or she will normally stay in touch and help to sort out any problems you encounter in the coming weeks. If your pup is registered with the national kennel club, its pedigree certificate will be mailed to you later.

Your New Puppy at Home

THE ARRIVAL OF A NEW PUPPY WILL BE THE CAUSE of great excitement, especially if you are a first-time owner. The puppy will already have had more than enough for one day—removal from its mother and littermates, a strange journey, arrival in a new place, new people to feed it and care for it, a new bed, new smells, new noises—so try not to exhaust it and give it plenty of opportunity to rest. Young puppies spend a significant proportion of their day asleep.

Introduce new people and stimuli one at a time. Young children must be closely supervised and instructed not to pick up the puppy until it has become used to them. Any other family pets should be introduced carefully.

Set aside a quiet corner of the kitchen or living area for your pup to feed in. You'll need a heavy bowl so that the puppy cannot move it around (a small bowl with straight sides to prevent spillage is good), and a larger bowl for water.

Young puppies are extremely curious. Beware of dangling electrical cords, cups of hot coffee, and scattered toys. A baby gate will keep your puppy away from forbidden areas of your home. Put your most valued possessions (and your slippers!) safely out of reach of its tiny teeth.

By the end of its first day in its new home, your puppy will be ready for its bed. It does not have to be a special dog bed—if you buy one now, the puppy will only outgrow it. A simple cardboard box with a cutaway front is adequate. Line it with an old towel or blanket for comfort.

Before settling the puppy for the night, see that it has had enough to eat. Take it outside to relieve itself before you place it in its box. Leave the room quietly—do not make a big fuss about saying goodnight and ignore any protests the puppy makes, however hard it is to do so, or else it will quickly learn that whining is a successful way of attracting attention. If your puppy sleeps in your bedroom for the first few nights, don't be tempted to pick it up whenever it whimpers—you may not be able to reverse the behavior later on.

◄ *Eight-week-old Joker trots out out confidently into his new home. He's ready for a game just now, but be careful not to over-tire him. Remember a young puppy needs rest and sleep, just like a human baby.*

Your Puppy will Need

✓ **A place to eat.** Its own feeding and drinking bowls, placed in a quiet corner away from the family dining area.

✓ **A place to sleep.** A cardboard box will do, lined with washable bedding and placed in a draft-free corner. If you allow your puppy to sleep on your bed, you'll find it is a hard habit to break.

✓ **A thorough checkup** from your vet during the first week (see pages 22–23).

✓ **A collar and identity tag.** Make sure the collar is not too loose or too tight. You will need to replace it as the puppy grows, so an inexpensive nylon one is a good idea.

✓ **A short, strong leash** for walking your puppy, and a longer flexible leash for training it to respond to commands.

✓ **No sudden change of diet** in the first week. Follow the breeder's diet sheet at first.

✓ **A safe environment.** Remove all potential dangers from your puppy's path. Fence off out-of-bounds areas of your home.

✓ **A playpen or portable indoor kennel** if you have to leave it unattended for a short time.

✓ **A variety of safe toys** to play with.

▶ *A soft, old blanket and a wrapped hot-water bottle will give your new puppy something to snuggle up to and make up for the absence of its littermates.*

▼ *Essential needs are a collar, a leash (or leashes), and bowls for feeding and drinking. A few toys will keep it amused and distract its attention from your belongings.*

● *My children, who are 10 and 8, are really eager to have a puppy. I'm ready to agree, but am just a little concerned that the puppy might be under my feet all day. Do you have any advice to prevent this?*

From the time you bring your puppy home, get it used to having "time-out" sessions on its own: these will give it a chance to relax away from the noise and bustle of family life and encourage it not to demand attention endlessly. Don't make the sessions too long at first, about 15–30 minutes. A puppy playpen that folds up and can be easily moved from room to room and into the car is ideal for this purpose.

● *Should I let them choose a puppy each from the same litter?*

No. Littermates, if kept together, are often poorly socialized to outsiders. They may compete for food and attention, particularly if of the same gender, and will excite each other, making them difficult to train.

Your Puppy's Diet

MOST NEW OWNERS WORRY ABOUT HOW TO feed their new puppy. Is it getting the right diet? How often should it be fed? These concerns are quite natural. The diet you give your puppy will have a major effect on the way it behaves and how its body grows and develops. You need to make sure not only that the puppy is getting the right amount of food every day, but that the balance of protein, carbohydrates, fat, vitamins, and minerals it receives in its diet is correct. The puppy should find its food both palatable and digestible. While it is settling in, you should continue to follow the breeder's feeding instructions, but after a week or so you may wish to change to another diet. This is best done gradually to avoid a stomach upset.

A young puppy should be fed four times a day at first, lowered to three times at 12 weeks old. Because puppies are growing and developing so rapidly, their energy requirements are, in terms of body weight, about twice as great as those of a mature dog. By age 6 months, a puppy should normally have two daily meals, though some puppies may still require more frequent feeding.

▲ *A Chow puppy gets down to its meal. Try to encourage good eating manners from the start.*

Feeding a Growing Pup

AGE OF PUPPY	HOW OFTEN	WHAT TO FEED
Under 4 weeks	On demand	Mother's milk
Weaning from 4–6 weeks	3–4 times a day	Baby cereal mixed with warmed milk. Gradually add flaked meat and biscuit, or use formulated weaning food.
7–12 weeks	Breakfast	Cereal feed
	Mid-morning	A commercial puppy food (follow instructions carefully), **or** minced meat (beef, lamb, chicken) mixed with an equal amount of biscuit softened with gravy
	3–4 pm	As above
	6–7 pm	Cereal feed
At 12 weeks	Mid-morning 4–5 pm 6–7 pm }	Three daily meals of a commercial puppy food (follow instructions carefully), **or** meat and carbohydrates with added vegetables and minerals
At 6 months	Mid-morning 6–7 pm }	Two daily meals, as above. Use a commercial food formulated for the older puppy.
From 9 months	One meal (morning or evening)	Introduce adult food gradually (see page 26). Growth rates vary between breeds, so follow manufacturer's or vet's advice.

From now on, a puppy's growth rate will gradually start to slow, its energy requirements will lessen, and you should begin to reduce its daily amount of food. By 9 months old your puppy, unless a giant breed, should be ready to move to an adult diet (see pages 26–27).

Choosing the Right Diet

The easiest way of providing the right nutritional balance is to choose a good-quality commercial diet specially formulated for puppies. The manufacturer's label instruction will tell you how much to feed your pup by age, weight, and type of dog. Use this as a guide only—there is much variation between individuals. Some puppies will seize any opportunity to overeat, and a chubby puppy, however cute, is likely to grow into an obese dog. But individual dogs vary greatly in their daily requirements, so be guided also by your dog's condition and the amount of exercise it gets. If in any doubt, consult your vet. When assessing how much food your puppy is getting each day, take into account any tidbits and treats you give it between meals.

Commercial foods come in two kinds: canned and dry. Some canned brands of puppy food offer complete diets, but most of them need to have rice or biscuit added to provide carbohydrates. Dry foods are designed as complete diets, but make sure you offer your dog water to drink at the same time, as they lack the moisture of canned foods. They are increasingly popular with dog owners because they are easily stored, convenient to use, and do not smell as much as canned foods.

Some owners like to give their puppy home-prepared food (not scraps—these won't contain all the essential nutrients). It's of vital importance that a growing dog has the right balance of protein (meat, fish, or eggs) and carbohydrates, so you must know what you are doing. Add vegetables, and provide a vitamin and mineral supplement. Dairy products may be given, but full-fat cow's milk can cause diarrhea in some pups. Once they have tasted home cooking, many dogs are reluctant to change to a commercial dog food, so be warned—it's a laborious commitment for an inexperienced owner to take on, and it may last the dog's whole life.

● *Ralph, my Yorkshire Terrier pup, was a fussy eater, so I started him on ground beef and liver. Now he won't have anything else. Does this matter?*

Small breeds are often fussy eaters, but this should be discouraged from an early age, preferably by finding a commercial diet the puppy tolerates and removing the bowl after 20 minutes. Dry food can be moistened with warm gravy to make it more palatable. Ralph's diet is deficient in calcium, essential for growing bones and teeth. Start adding cereals and vegetables, and use a vitamin and mineral supplement. Gradually offer different meats and perhaps a little canned dog food. Mix any new food in well and make changes slowly.

● *The instruction on the dry-food diet I'm feeding my pup stipulates quantity according to the puppy's weight. How do I weigh him? Whenever I put him on the bathroom scales, he clambers off.*

The simplest way is to stand on the scales yourself, holding the puppy, and note your combined weight. Then weigh yourself alone and subtract that from the first total. The difference will be your puppy's weight.

Tips on Feeding

Do

✓ Feed your puppy regular meals in its own bowl.

✓ Always use a good-quality puppy food, even if it is more expensive than other brands. Ask your veterinarian's advice if in doubt.

✓ Follow the manufacturer's guides carefully.

✓ If you feed it an all-meat canned food, add two parts rice or mixer biscuit.

✓ Always provide fresh water, especially if you are feeding a dry-food diet.

✓ Make sure more than one person feeds the puppy to avoid overattachment.

Don't

✗ Allow your puppy to stand guard over its bowl. From time to time, add a tasty morsel to the bowl while the puppy is feeding. This will prevent it from becoming possessive.

✗ Feed it tidbits from the table while you are eating.

Your Puppy's Health

ABOUT TWO DAYS AFTER YOU BRING YOUR puppy home, you should arrange for it to have a health checkup. This will enable the veterinarian to identify right away if anything is wrong with it. Tragically, a major health problem may sometimes be identified, and in this case you will either have to decide to return the puppy or ask the breeder for a refund. This may be difficult to arrange at a later date.

If your puppy doesn't enjoy its first visit to the animal hospital, subsequent trips may be difficult for everyone concerned. The veterinarian will reassure and calm the canine patient, but it is a good idea to take along food treats that he or she can give the puppy at the start of and on completing the examination. This will help to ensure that your puppy has only good memories of visiting the vet's and will not show fear and resistance on later visits.

▲ *Just like a human baby, your puppy needs to have a series of routine health checks from the veterinarian during its early months to make sure it is developing normally, and to prevent disease.*

Protection Against Disease

The veterinarian may start your puppy's course of shots against the common canine infectious diseases (see pages 46–47) rightaway or suggest you make an appointment to come back in a week or so. The first shots are normally given at between 4 and 8 weeks, and are followed by one or two boosters to confer complete protection on the puppy.

Protection is not complete until about a week after the last booster has been given, and during that time the puppy should not be allowed outside the house or yard unless you are carrying it. Your vet will hand you a vaccination certificate showing what shots the puppy has been given. This should be kept in a safe place so that the dog's annual booster shots can be recorded on it.

The veterinarian will also advise you about protection against parasites (see pages 48–51). Virtually all puppies carry roundworms. These are transmitted from the mother through the

Safeguarding Your Puppy's Health

✓ Arrange for a health checkup within a week of bringing your puppy home.

✓ Ensure that it completes the full program of immunization shots.

✓ Continue with its deworming treatment.

✓ Groom your puppy regularly; check the coat for fleas, and the ears for redness and other signs of irritation.

✓ Inspect your puppy's teeth to make sure they are developing properly.

✓ Consider paying for medical insurance.

● *When Jess, my Jack Russell pup, threw up, he brought up a heap of worms that looked like spaghetti. What were they, and are they harmful to us?*

These spaghetti-like worms are roundworms, which live in the puppy's stomach and small intestine (see pages 50–51). The worms themselves are not dangerous to humans, but the adult roundworm produces hundreds of eggs that are passed in the dog's feces. After about three weeks in the environment, they hatch out into larvae. If a child were to take in some of the larvae—for example, off a sucked finger—they may, in exceptional circumstances, cause health problems. The answer is to deworm your puppy regularly and to clean up any messes it makes.

● *Woody, my 9-week-old Collie, has just started his immunization program, and the veterinarian has told me not to let him out in public areas for at least another month. Why not? Will it affect his development if I keep him home all the time?*

Until his booster shots have "taken," Woody will not have full protection against infectious canine diseases, which he can easily pick up from sniffing the places where other, unimmunized dogs have been. However, it is very important that Woody is not isolated from the outside world at this early age, so introduce him to as many stimuli as possible. Carry him outdoors to get him used to street noises and traffic, and take him in the car with you when possible so that Woody has plenty of new experiences. Encourage friends and neighbors to stop by and meet him, especially if they have small children.

▶ *Given the right start in life, your puppy should grow up fit, well, and happy. Your veterinary hospital may run puppy clinics or classes. These allow puppies to mix with others of their own age, so that they learn socialization skills, and give you the opportunity to ask advice from professionals.*

placenta before birth, and also in her milk. If their numbers are allowed to increase, they can cause serious illness. Your vet will advise you about the most suitable deworming preparation to use. Puppies should be routinely treated every two weeks until they are 12 weeks, then monthly to age 6 months. In parts of the world where heartworm is endemic, a heartworm preventive taken every month after the age of 3 months also gives protection against roundworm.

Ask for advice on antiflea protection. Itchiness and small clusters of dark specks of dirt in the coat are signs that your puppy is infested. The fleas reproduce very rapidly, so you will need to start treatment immediately. Other pets and bedding, and your carpets and upholstery, will need to be treated, too.

Check your puppy's condition everyday. Clean the sleep out of its eyes in the morning. Examine its ears and look inside its mouth. Run your fingers backward through the coat to look for fleas and lift the tail to make sure that the bottom is clean. This routine will make the puppy used to being handled and give early warning of any problems that develop. You should also groom the puppy from time to time (see pages 30–31).

Housebreaking

HOUSEBREAKING BUILDS ON THE YOUNG PUP'S natural instinct not to foul the communal sleeping area. To carry it out successfully, you need patience, persistence, and understanding of your puppy's needs. An 8-week-old puppy urinates approximately every two hours during the day. It empties its bowels three to six times a day, depending on the sort of diet it is receiving—an easily digestible diet, low in bulk, is best. It is most likely to want to relieve itself first thing in the morning, immediately after eating, on waking from a nap, and when it is excited (after visitors have arrived, for example).

When a puppy wants to relieve itself, it starts sniffing and circling around. Learn to recognize the signs. Take the puppy outside and stay with it. Praise or reward it immediately after it performs in the right place. That way, it will want to please you again next time the need arises.

If you live in an apartment, place a sheet of newspaper by the door, and teach the puppy to use that. Once it has learned to do so, take it outside and lay the paper on the ground. Praise the puppy when it uses it. After a time, stop putting the newspaper down and reward the puppy when it relieves itself outdoors without it. Let your puppy spend time on its own in a crate or indoor kennel. That way, if you have to leave the puppy alone for a part of each day, you will avoid it soiling your rugs while you are out.

Accidents

Your puppy is bound to make a mistake from time to time, but as it matures, accidents should happen less and less often. Use hot water and a biological odor eliminator to clean up after your pet. This will remove any lingering smell and discourage it from going back to the same spot again and again. Never punish your puppy if it has an accident. If you catch it in the act, shout "no" loudly and take it straight outside. Praise it lavishly if it completes the business outside.

Some puppies learn toilet training much more quickly than others, but you should expect your puppy to be reliably clean at home by the time it is 7–8 months old. If you are experiencing difficulties with housebreaking your puppy, check with your veterinarian that it does not have a physical problem. It may do better after a change of diet, especially if its present diet is high in bulk.

◄ *Housebreaking should start as early as possible. Place the puppy on a sheet of newspaper when it seems ready to go and be lavish with praise when it succeeds.*

Problems in Adults

Even a well-trained adult will have an accident sometimes. But if it occurs persistently, there is likely to be an underlying cause, either of a medical or behavioral nature. Male dogs will sometimes start lifting their legs against objects in the home—walls, tables, plant stands, even visitors' legs. This is a form of territorial scent marking, and is often a sign that the dog feels insecure, perhaps the dog's normal routine has changed, you have moved to a new home, or another dog has been introduced into the household. The behavior often ceases when the situation causing it has been resolved, but sometimes it may be advisable to have the dog neutered.

Some dogs may panic when left on their own and as a result will relieve themselves indoors. Don't punish or scold your dog if you find that it has made a mess when you return home. This is likely to worsen the problem and increase the dog's separation anxiety (see pages 132–135). The underlying causes of this problem can be complex, and you would be advised to seek professional advice in treating it.

Persistent incontinence, either of the bladder or the bowel, is often a sign of physical disease, especially in older dogs. A sudden attack of diarrhea will also cause an otherwise well-trained dog to defecate indoors. In such cases, always seek veterinary advice.

▲ *A pet door allows your dog to go outside when it feels a call of nature. Dispose of the feces hygienically, and hose down the backyard regularly.*

● My 6-month-old English Setter, Matilda, urinates on the rug right in front of us when we come home. Why does she do this?

Have you scolded Matilda harshly in the past? If so, it seems likely that she has become slightly fearful of you, and is showing her submission and deference by urinating when she sees you. Next time you return home, ignore her completely so long as she adopts a submissive posture, and wait until she is standing on all four feet before greeting her calmly without fuss. Don't show anger when she urinates. She cannot help it, and you will only make the situation worse.

● I recently adopted a Yorkshire Terrier, Jemma. She has always lived in kennels until now. She frequently soils in the house, but the vet says there's nothing physically wrong with her. What should I do?

Adopted dogs who have not been brought up as family dogs do not know that it is unacceptable to soil indoors. You will have to toilet train Jemma as if she were a puppy. Though it is more difficult with an adult, it can be done. Watch Jemma's every move, accompany her outside as soon as she shows signs of wanting to relieve herself, and encourage her with rewards and praise. If you have to leave her, put her in an indoor kennel, make sure she has relieved herself first, and don't leave her for long.

Tips on Housebreaking

✓ Learn to recognize the signs that your puppy wants to go outside. Many puppies will circle and sniff around.

✓ Do not carry your puppy outside. Go with it, but let it make its own way to the door.

✓ Use a phrase such as "there you go" when it is preparing to perform. This will encourage it to perform on command—useful when you are in a hurry or traveling with your puppy.

✓ Always praise or reward your puppy when it relieves itself outdoors.

✓ Never punish it when it has an accident indoors—it will only make it anxious.

✓ Let your puppy sleep in its crate until it goes all night without needing to relieve itself.

Feeding Your Dog

THE NUTRITIONAL REQUIREMENTS OF ADULT dogs are generally the same as those of puppies. But because they are no longer growing, they need less protein and fewer calories. There are exceptions to this. A pregnant or nursing mother will benefit from a higher protein and calorie diet. An active working dog needs more calories.

As for puppies, a great variety of commercial brands of food are sold for the adult dog. Wet foods come in cans and contain processed meats. Some need mixing with biscuit to provide carbohydrates and bulk; others have the cereal component already added, so be clear which type you are buying. Complete dried formulated foods contain only about 9 percent water and are designed to be given on their own or moistened with water or gravy. In the complete semi-moist foods, the water content is higher than in the dried foods.

▲ *Some of the prepared foods available for your dog:*
1. Complete dried food 2. Complete semi-moist food
3. Complete canned food: cereal component (pasta)
and carrot already added 4. Canned meat meal:
carbohydrates to be added by owner 5. A variety of
biscuits to be mixed with meat or fed as treats

Which kind you choose will depend on a number of factors: cost (the dried foods are cheapest), convenience (ease of packaging, bulk, and weight), and the dog's own preference. Water should always be available to your dog, but if you choose a dried food, make sure its water bowl is full at mealtimes. To feed your dog on home-cooked food involves a great deal of work and is often not as beneficial as a good-quality commercial food. If you do, it's best to obtain advice from your veterinarian to make sure your dog is getting its full balance of nutrients.

◄ *Dog treats and chews,*
high in fats and carbohydrates,
should not be overlooked when
calculating the daily calorie
intake. Chocolate is harmful
to dogs and should never
be given as a treat.

Daily Energy Requirements

BREED EXAMPLE		WEIGHT OF DOG	ENERGY NEEDED CALS	AMOUNT OF FOOD DRIED COMPLETE	CANNED COMPLETE
SMALL	Chihuahua	4½lb/2kg	230	2¼oz/65g	8oz/230g
	Miniature Pinscher	11lb/5kg	450	4½oz/132g	1lb/450g
	Shetland Sheepdog	22lb/10kg	750	7½oz/220g	1½lb/750g
MEDIUM	Staff. Bull Terrier	33lb/15kg	1010	10½oz/297g	2⅛lb/1kg
	Springer Spaniel	44lb/20kg	1250	13oz/368g	2¾lb/1.25kg
	Chow Chow	55lb/25kg	1470	15⅛oz/432g	3¼lb/1.5kg
LARGE	Labrador	66lb/30kg	1675	1lb/493g	3¾lb/1.7kg
	Doberman	77lb/35kg	1875	1⅛lb/552g	4lb/1.9kg
	Rottweiler	88lb/40kg	2070	1¼lb/609g	4½lb/2kg

Amounts are guidelines only. Individual needs vary, depending on the dog's age and lifestyle

Feeding the Right Amount

Since fewer dogs today lead working lives and have less opportunity for exercise, it is not surprising that the most common nutritional disorder in dogs is obesity. Have your dog weighed regularly and adjust the amount of food you give it to make sure it is neither too fat nor too thin. Use your own eye and judgment—a healthy dog does not carry unnecessary weight on its body, nor does it tire easily or get out of breath—but ask your vet's advice if you are uncertain what your dog's correct adult weight should be.

Use the manufacturers' label instructions, but remember that breed, temperament, and lifestyle are all important in assessing how much to feed your dog. Lazy types tend to need fewer calories than nervous or excitable ones, and put on weight more easily. A Labrador, for example, will burn up fewer calories than an Irish Setter of the same size. As a rule, neutered dogs need to eat less. It is harder to get your dog to lose weight by dieting than it is to prevent it from becoming overweight.

▶ *It is traditional to feed a dog once a day, but two smaller meals are less stressful to the digestion. Avoid feeding just before or after exercise.*

● *I feed my 1-year-old terrier-type dog, Flint, dried food twice a day. He rarely cleans his bowl in one sitting, but comes back several times during the day to finish it. Does this matter? He is otherwise fit and healthy.*

Like humans, dogs have individual eating habits. Some are greedy, others less so. As long as Flint is eating the right amount of a balanced food for his size and age, and is not putting on or losing weight, you have no reason for concern, but ask your veterinarian to check Flint over to make sure there is no health problem.

Your Healthy Dog

IMPORTANT THOUGH IT IS, A BALANCED DIET is just one aspect of caring for your dog's all-round health and happiness. Just as essential are good early education and training to prevent the development of behavior problems in the adult dog (see pages 108–113), the regular provision of strenuous daily exercise, and plenty of mental stimulation in the form of activity toys and inter-relating games.

As a responsible owner, you should take your adult dog once a year to the animal hospital to receive its booster shots against the major infectious diseases (see pages 46–47). It is usual at this annual visit to have your pet thoroughly examined by the vet, to have it weighed, and its health records updated. Take this opportunity to raise any concerns you may have regarding your dog's development and behavior. Your vet will be happy to give advice on general health matters such as effective parasite prevention, neutering, mating, and breeding.

▲ Adult dogs need plenty of sleep. Provide a comfortable bed in a quiet, draft-free corner of the house. It should be large enough for the dog to stretch out on, and easy to keep clean.

How Much Exercise?

The key to canine fitness is exercise. It's also good for the owner and can often be combined with an activity such as jogging. Ideally, your dog should have two or three walks a day, one of which should last at least 30 minutes. Allow some time for your dog to run off the leash, if you can. It will benefit from the freedom to explore and will travel three to four times farther than you do. But only do this if you are certain of being able to recall your dog on command, and if the park or open country is free of dangers and distractions such as cars, animals, children, joggers, bicyclers, and ball players.

Some breeds of dogs have higher activity levels than others and will become difficult to live with if their exercise is neglected. Medium-to-large dogs like Border Collies, Boxers, and Dalmatians fall into this category, but size is not always a guide to the amount of activity needed. A small energetic breed like a Jack Russell requires more exercise than a large but lazy Great Dane.

◄ Alert and ready to go. A fit, healthy dog responds eagerly to an invitation for a walk or game. A bored dog quickly turns its energies to more destructive activities.

FLYBALL

▲ *Agility trials are an excellent way of channeling the energies of an active dog, and provide lots of healthy fun for you and your pet.*

Q&A

● *How can I tell if my dog is unwell or in pain?*

... As a general rule, dogs tolerate pain better than humans. If your dog seems unusually restless, or is depressed and lethargic and has a "hangdog" expression, with ears and tail down, you should suspect something is wrong.

● *How are deworming tablets given?*

Nearly always as tablets that can be crushed up and mixed with food. It can be difficult to get dogs to swallow tablets or capsules whole. One way of doing so is to coat the tablet with butter, which disguises the smell, and which most dogs like.

Routine Needs of the Adult Dog

✓ Plenty of exercise. Most healthy dogs require two or three walks every day.

✓ A balanced diet (see pages 26–27).

✓ Fresh, clean water always available—make sure the bowl isn't empty, especially in warm weather.

✓ Regular grooming, taking care to check for sore places, lumps, and bald patches.

✓ An annual visit to the vet for booster vaccinations and an overall examination.

✓ Regular preventive treatment against parasites (see pages 48–51).

✓ Companionship. A dog, especially a young one, should not be left alone for long periods.

✓ A bed of its own, where it can be quiet during the day and sleep at night.

Grooming

THE MAIN PURPOSE OF GROOMING IS TO REMOVE dead hair and debris from your dog's coat. It is also a chance to look for ticks and fleas and to check the general condition of the coat and skin. This should be clean and supple, with no signs of excess scaling or greasiness; any unusual lumps, bumps, or bald patches should be examined by your veterinarian right away. Above all, grooming is an important social activity, a time to build up your relationship with your dog.

Dogs' coats come in a variety of textures and thicknesses. Long, silky coats require the most work. Always comb the coat of a longhaired dog after walking in long grass or brush, especially if you live in a tick-infested area.

Get your puppy used to the grooming routine as early as possible. Even longhairs have only a

short, fluffy coat at this stage, so the whole job can be completed in a few minutes. If you wait until the full adult coat has developed, the dog will be suddenly subjected to a long, unfamiliar experience, which it may not enjoy. Regular grooming will accustom your puppy to being handled and having its eyes, ears, and mouth looked at. This will make trips to the vet easier.

Basic Grooming

1. Comb out any tangles from the coat. Use a fine-toothed comb for long, feathery hair on the ears, around the neck, and under the tail. Look out for, and remove, ticks and burrs.
2. Comb out dead hair from the dense undercoat, especially if the dog is molting (shedding its hair). Nearly all breeds molt twice yearly.
3. Using an appropriate brush for the thickness of your dog's coat (coarse, dense hair requires a firm bristle brush, silky hair a softer one), brush the entire coat, working back from the head.
4. Follow the direction of the hair growth down the back, across the flanks, and down the legs to the feet. Do not neglect the underparts.
5. Watch out for flea dirt (small dark specks on the skin), particularly when grooming around the base of the tail.
6. Clean the area around the bottom and check that the anal sacs are not inflamed.
7. Use scissors to tidy the hair around the ears, eyes, muzzle, and bottom.
8. With a dampened cotton ball, wipe away any mucus in the corner of the eye.

Make teeth cleaning a part of your grooming routine. Your vet will advise you. Do not bathe your dog more than is necessary. Use a mild baby shampoo or special shampoo for dogs. Avoid a medicated type, especially

▼ *Regular grooming sessions help to strengthen the bonds of closeness between owner and dog.*

▲ *If the dog's nails grow too long, shorten them with a sharp pair of clippers. Care is needed to avoid the "quick," the living tissue at the center, so ask a professional to show you how.*

if your dog loves rolling in mud and filth and needs frequent baths.

Poodles need clipping every few weeks by a professional groomer. Longhaired and wirehaired breeds need occasional thinning (stripping) to remove the dead hair, using a finger and thumb or a serrated knife. Many owners prefer to leave this to a professional groomer.

Ears and Feet

Pluck excess hair out gently from the ear canals to prevent wax building up, increasing the likelihood of ear infections (see pages 86–87). This is a particular problem in poodles. Some dogs produce excess amounts of wax, and their ear canals should be cleaned regularly with a special solution available from your vet.

Ease out thorns, grass seeds, and other debris from between the toes and pads of the feet. If left, these can work their way into the skin and cause considerable pain.

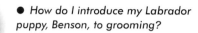

● **How do I introduce my Labrador puppy, Benson, to grooming?**

... Choose a time when Benson has just been fed and exercised and is calm. Place a nonslip bathmat on a low table and stand Benson on it so he cannot slip. If possible, get someone to help you by steadying his head with one hand and placing the other under his body. Use a soft brush at first and take care not to hurt the puppy, or he will learn to resent and fear grooming sessions. Keep the sessions very short at first and gradually build up to longer sessions from there. Always praise him at the end and reward him with a tidbit.

● **My Old English Sheepdog, Monday, hates being groomed. He just won't stand still long enough to complete the job, and his coat has become very matted as a result. What should I do?**

These dogs have tremendously thick, long coats and looking after them is a fulltime job. It might help to have Monday's coat clipped back regularly by a professional groomer to a more manageable length of about 1¼in (3cm). It will take you less time to groom Monday, and he should tolerate it better.

● **Is it necessary to groom my Boxer puppy, Arabella? Her coat is so short it doesn't seem worth the bother.**

Even Boxers molt in the spring. Brushing Arabella regularly will reduce the amount of hair she sheds on the furniture. Boxers suffer from quite a lot of skin problems, so use the grooming sessions to check for any unusual lumps or sore patches.

▼ *A selection of grooming aids for your dog. From left to right: nail clippers, scissors, and a thinning knife; fine- and wide-toothed combs; bristle and wire brushes. The pimpled rubber glove is used on shorthairs.*

Traveling with Your Dog

IF YOU TAKE THE TIME TO GET YOUR DOG USED to the car, with luck it will adjust to it quickly so every journey does not become an ordeal. Place your young puppy inside the car for short periods of about 10 minutes. Settle it on a familiar blanket with some of its toys. Stay with it at first, then leave it on its own. The next stage is to have the puppy in the car with the engine running. If this causes no problem, then you are ready for the first journey.

Make sure the puppy has relieved itself. If possible, choose a time when it is feeling sleepy. Try to keep your journeys short at first. All dogs should be restrained within a moving car. The easiest way is to settle your puppy or dog inside a portable kennel or traveling crate. This is then placed securely on the back seat of a sedan or in the back of a hatchback or station wagon. Dog guards and harnesses can also be used.

On long journeys stop approximately every two hours to allow the puppy to stretch its legs and have a drink. Provide it with toys and chews to occupy it during the journey. A bored puppy

can cause an astounding amount of damage to a car, particularly when it is teething.

Many puppies suffer from motion sickness the first few times they travel. They will look miserable, begin to salivate profusely, then throw up. Keep journeys short and have a window slightly open. Most grow out of it fairly quickly, but if your dog remains a persistent sufferer, your vet can prescribe sedatives and antiemetics.

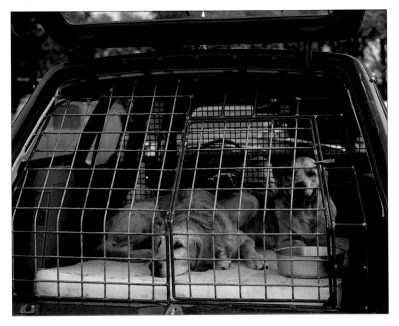

▲ *The wind in its face. Many dogs love the sensation of car travel. Do not let your dog ride without a restraint or allow it in the front of the car, where it can distract the driver.*

◄ *A dog guard stops your dog from jumping or clambering from the back of a station wagon into the passenger section. This car has tailgates too, so that the dogs cannot leap out into the road. They have their own space to relax in during the journey.*

▶ *A special harness will secure a dog safely on the back seat of the car.*

Dogs cannot control their body temperature as efficiently as humans. If confined inside the car in hot weather, they can rapidly develop heatstroke. Shade the windows from the sun and carry a waterspray to cool your dog down if it becomes overheated. Never leave a dog in a parked car in sunshine, even for a short time.

Flying with Your Dog

To transport a dog by air, it is usually necessary to arrange for it to travel in the pressurized cabin of the baggage compartment. Some domestic airlines may arrange for a small dog to travel with you as hand baggage. Always check all regulations well in advance. The airline will specify what type of container the dog must travel in and may lay down other rules. Some will only fly snub-nosed breeds such as Boxers, Bulldogs, Pekingese, and Pugs if they are certified free of respiratory problems. For international journeys you will need an international certificate of vaccination and a current health report signed by your veterinarian. Precise requirements vary, so you should contact the consulate of the country to which you are traveling for information well ahead of your date of departure. Some countries that are rabies-free, such as Great Britain, Australia and New Zealand, impose strict quarantine rules on all animals entering the country.

● *I recently took charge of a 5-year-old Springer Spaniel, Jasper. He goes crazy in the car when I drive him to the park for his walk, barking and leaping around. His previous owner did not have a car. What can I do?*

Jasper has learned to associate the car with going for a walk, an activity he loves. Try giving him a toy or chew to take his mind off the journey. If that fails, put Jasper in the car for short periods without taking him anywhere. Once he reacts calmly to being in the car, take him for a short journey. If he becomes excited, put him on the floor so that he can't see out. Use a car harness to secure him. Alternatively, it may help to put him in a covered traveling crate.

● *My Airedale, Freddie, is a real nuisance in the car. He barks at strangers, even when we are halted at traffic intersections. How do I get him to stop?*

Car-guarding is a form of territorial behavior. You can prevent it by having a water pistol ready, and when Freddie barks or growls at a passerby, aim a jet of water at him. Reward him if he allows someone to walk past the car without barking at them. Reduce the stimulation of the journey by placing him so that he cannot see out the window. If he continues to show aggression, obtain professional help.

Travel Arrangements

- ✗ Never have an unrestrained dog in the car: portable kennels or crates, travel containers, dog harnesses, and guards are all available.
- ✗ Never leave a dog in a parked car in direct sunshine.
- ✓ Make sure your puppy or dog has relieved itself before starting on a journey.
- ✓ Stop at intervals to give your dog exercise and a drink of fresh, cool water in a bowl.
- ✓ On long journeys make sure you have food for the dog, but avoid overfeeding.
- ✓ Opening the window a little may help to prevent motion sickness. Seek medical advice if the problem is persistent.
- ✓ When flying, contact the individual airline well in advance for information and to make sure there's space available, especially if you've a large dog.

Going on Vacation and Moving

A PROBLEM MOST OWNERS HAVE TO FACE IS how to care for their dog when they go on vacation. Sometimes the dog goes, too, and this obviously works well if you are traveling by car, not going a great distance, and are camping or staying in a rented apartment or cabin (so long as dogs are welcome: check before you book). Bed and breakfasts, and less often hotels and motels, occasionally allow dogs to stay with you in the room. Much less frequently, you may discover one that provides kenneling facilities. Even when it is said that "dogs are welcome," you may find that the dog cannot be left unattended in your room, so always check the situation first.

If you cannot take your dog with you, and you have several pets to care for, the most stress-free solution is to have a friend or dog-sitter move into your home. It helps if the sitter has met the animals beforehand. Alternatively, a friend or family member may be willing to have the dog stay with them during your absence, but this is quite a responsibility to take on.

● *My 5-year-old Poodle, Flame, is going into a kennel for the first time in her life. I am worried she may panic. What can I do to reassure her?*

Send her with something familiar—her usual blanket, one of your old shirts, some toys. If you can, arrange for Flame to spend a morning or a day in the kennel first so that she gets to know the owners and surroundings. When you finally leave her, she'll know that you haven't abandoned her but will be coming back.

● *The house we are moving to has got a large, fenced yard. At present we live in an apartment. Will it be safe to let Ross, our 4-year-old Cocker Spaniel, run around on his own, or will he try to escape? You often read stories of dogs that have gotten lost and turned up months later at their old home.*

Dogs love the freedom of a backyard, and provided you check the fences regularly to make sure they are secure, Ross should not come to any harm. Don't let him outside without his identity tag and collar. Then, if he does escape, he can quickly be returned to you.

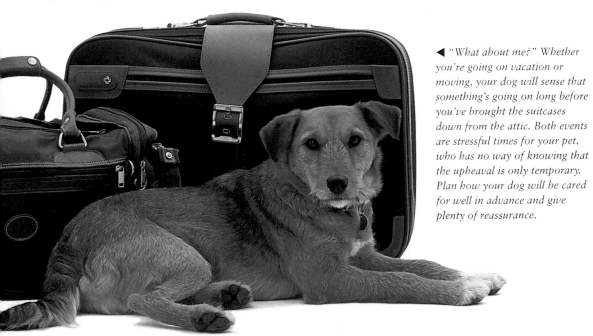

◀ *"What about me?" Whether you're going on vacation or moving, your dog will sense that something's going on long before you've brought the suitcases down from the attic. Both events are stressful times for your pet, who has no way of knowing that the upheaval is only temporary. Plan how your dog will be cared for well in advance and give plenty of reassurance.*

◀ *An owner leaves her West Highland White Terrier at a kennel. She investigated the place earlier and knows he will be in good hands. His own bed and blanket, as well as some favorite toys, will provide extra comfort.*

Vacation Care Checklist

✓ Check if your dog is up to date with its booster shots.

✓ Have it inoculated against kennel cough (should be done 2–3 weeks beforehand) and treat it for fleas.

✓ Tell the kennel staff what your dog likes to eat. Sudden changes can cause stomach upsets.

✓ Make a written note of any medication it is currently receiving, including its regular deworming treatment (if on a daily or monthly tablet).

✓ Pack its sleeping blanket and some familiar toys for comfort and reassurance.

✓ Leave the name of your vet in case of emergencies.

✓ Provide a contact telephone number for yourself or other family member or friend.

For many people, however, the only option is a boarding kennel. Owners often fret that their dog will be unhappy and pine in unfamiliar surroundings, but the majority of dogs settle in with very little fuss. Be sure to visit first. If you do not like what you see, go elsewhere. The buildings should be clean and well ventilated; to avoid infection, the dogs should be accommodated in separate rooms or cages (unless they usually live together at home). If kept outdoors, the sleeping areas should be warm and draft-free, with heating provision in cold weather. There should be a secure run or enclosure for exercise. Many kennels arrange for the dogs to have a daily walk.

Moving

Moving into a new home is every bit as stressful for your dog as for yourself. Plan well ahead about how you will care for your dog. You may decide to book your pet into a kennel or arrange for it to stay with friends for a few days. If you prefer to keep your dog with you, do everything you can to ensure its daily routine remains as normal and undisturbed as possible.

Make sure that you exercise the dog as early as possible on the day of the move—you may not have an opportunity later on. Find somewhere safe where you can leave the dog while your home is being packed up, with a friend or neighbor, or shut away in a quiet room with its own things for reassurance.

Do not bring the dog into the new home until the furniture is moved in and things have calmed down a little. As soon as you can, show the dog where its bed is going to be so that it has its own space, with its familiar things, to retreat to. Reassure it and take it round the new home. It will soon grow used to seeing all the old furniture and objects in new surroundings, especially as the people who live there have not changed.

The Older Dog

WHEN IS A DOG OLD? IT IS COMMONLY HELD that a dog lives 7 years for every year that we do. However, this serves as only a very rough guide when calculating a dog's age. Dogs grow up very rapidly in their early years of life, and then slow down. A one-year-old dog is similar to a 15-year-old human teenager. At age 6 it is approximately 40 years in human terms. By 12 it is elderly, and at 15 it is equivalent to an 80-year-old.

Small breeds such as terriers and poodles tend to live longer than large ones. They are still fully active at 13 and 14 and will often survive to 16 or 17. Giant breeds such as Great Danes and Wolfhounds begin to slow down by 5 years and rarely live to more than 8 or 9. Naturally, there are exceptions to these rules. For example, the small Cavalier King Charles Spaniel lives only 9–13 years on average because of its genetic predisposition to heart disease.

Older dogs have a tendency to become overweight. Because they have fewer interests to distract them, they attach even more importance to eating. But because they are less active, they need fewer calories. Obesity in the older dog is highly damaging to joints, muscles, heart, and lungs, and increases the risk of diabetes and tumors. Have your dog weighed regularly (at least every 6 months), so that any weight gain can be spotted promptly and the diet "fine-tuned" to suit the dog's requirements. There are several ways of cutting down on calories. You can give less of the usual food, or you can switch to a lower calorie food and give the dog the same amount. If it becomes very greedy, feed it more often, but give it smaller portions. Weigh the food carefully, and don't just dole it out, so that you can be sure it is getting its daily quota and no more.

A healthy diet for the older dog should include less protein than before, but it should be of high quality (red meat, fish, poultry). It should contain more fiber (bran, vegetables, etc.) to prevent constipation and be low in fat and salt for a healthy heart. It is a good idea to switch to a specially formulated commercial diet for the older dog. Keep an eye on how much your dog is drinking, as excessive thirst can be a first sign of ill health in old age.

Age-related Conditions

Gray hair, reduced vision or hearing, slight stiffness in the morning, less eagerness to play, and increased sleep are all normal signs of old age. Some older dogs become quite irritable, especially when disturbed by younger dogs or children. Make sure your pet's wish for peace and quiet is respected. If its behavior changes rapidly, consult your veterinarian without delay.

Do not force an older dog to take prolonged or strenuous exercise, but provide shorter, gentler strolls more often to help keep old legs supple. Stiffness in old age usually results from osteoarthritis, with degenerative changes in the joints. Relieve the symptoms by restricting exercise, putting the dog on a slimming diet, and providing a soft mattress. Aspirin can help pain in mild cases, but check with your vet first, who may prescribe anti-inflammatory drugs.

Needs of the Older Dog

- ✓ **Food** should be tasty and digestible but contain fewer calories. A high-fiber, low-sodium diet can be helpful.
- ✓ **Grooming** is even more important now that your dog's spine is becoming less flexible and it cannot groom itself. Use a softer brush as your dog's coat gets thinner and its skin less robust.
- ✓ **Bedtime comfort** can be provided by a thicker mattress, which will be easier on arthritic joints.
- ✓ **Massage** stiff joints, especially first thing in the morning, to keep your dog active.
- ✓ **Exercise** in moderation. Your dog will tell you when it's time to come home.

● *I've noticed that my 13-year-old Yorkshire Terrier, Twinkie, has a milky-looking eye. Is this normal?*

The eyes of older dogs often appear cloudy due to changes in the lens and retina that occur in old age. But cloudiness could also indicate a developing cataract. Yorkshire Terriers have an inherited propensity to cataracts, so seek advice from your veterinarian as soon as possible.

● *My Boxer, Henry, who is nearly 10, is spending more and more time asleep. Is something wrong?*

Older dogs spend increasing amounts of time asleep. As 10 is a good age for a Boxer, there's probably nothing to worry about, especially if Henry is showing no other signs of ill health.

● *My crossbreed, Tinka, is visibly aging. Where can I find out how best to look after her?*

Many veterinary hospitals run geriatric clinics you can go to for advice on the particular needs of the elderly dog and regular checkups.

▲ *Old friends together. With loving care, dogs can maintain their enjoyment of life well into old age, but they often appreciate the chance to take things a bit more slowly.*

Breathlessness in an older dog, combined with a reluctance to exercise and a cough, could indicate incipient heart and lung failure. Superficial lumps and bumps on the skin often increase in number and size. Most of them are simply fatty lumps and warts, but always get them checked by the vet. An elderly dog may need to urinate more frequently, especially if it is drinking more. It will have less warning of when it has to go, so remember to let it outside more often.

Tooth decay and periodontal disease are common in old age, and a painful tooth or sore gums may lead to a sudden loss of appetite. Other signs are bad breath, discolored teeth, and bleeding gums. Regular teeth brushing throughout your dog's life is the best protection you can give.

Death of a Pet

AS AN OWNER, YOU MUST BE READY TO FACE THE eventual death of your beloved pet. However much you think you have prepared yourself, when the time comes to say good-bye, you may find yourself overwhelmed by the intensity of your grief, even if it is not the first such loss you have sustained. People who have never owned a dog are often unable to understand what you are going through. However, feelings of acute loss are perfectly normal. Don't hide them away, but allow them to come to the surface.

A great number of pets do not die naturally, but by euthanasia—being put painlessly to sleep. Most dog owners and vets believe that this is an ethical and compassionate way to end the life of animal that is terminally ill, in continuous incurable pain, or has lost essential body functions and has no hope of resuming an active life. No vet likes to lose a patient, and treatment will be given as long as it is having positive effects. Sometimes an owner may refuse further treatment for his dog and request euthanasia. If the vet is reluctant to do this, owner and patient may be referred elsewhere.

A Peaceful Transition

Once the decision to euthanize the dog has been made, many owners feel that they cannot bear to watch the procedure. The veterinarian will always respect such feelings. However, the dog will feel happier and calmer if someone it knows is present. It will also help to alleviate the owner's later distress if he or she has seen for themselves just how peaceful the transition was.

While the dog is held gently in a sitting or lying position, his right foreleg is lifted for the vet to inject an overdose of anesthetic into the vein. The dog is normally completely at ease, as sitting and giving a paw is a familiar activity. A sedative may be given first if the dog is upset or if the procedure is awkward for the vet. Usually the dog is completely unaware of the injection and falls asleep in five to ten seconds. Breathing ceases

● My 9-year-old Boxer, Ruffles, died three months ago. I still cry for him every day. My sister says I am being silly. What do you think?.

Anyone who has ever owned a dog will understand how you feel—it is perfectly normal for you to be still grieving. A new puppy may help ease the process, but only if you feel ready for it. It won't mean you have forgotten your old friend.

● Pigalle, my elderly Cavalier King Charles Spaniel, has heart disease. Her symptoms are getting worse, and friends tell me I should have her put to sleep, but I really hope she will die in her sleep one night. What should I do?

Overcome your fears and consult your vet. He or she may be able to help Pigalle, but if not, euthanasia is the kindest option. She can't enjoy quality of life, and death from heart failure is often painful.

Assessing Quality of Life

To decide whether euthanasia is necessary or not, your veterinarian, in discussion with you, will assess whether the basic needs of the dog are being fulfilled. Ask yourself the following questions:

✓ Does the dog have freedom from uncontrollable pain, distress, and discomfort?

✓ Is it able to walk and balance?

✓ Can it eat and drink without pain or vomiting?

✓ Is it free from painful inoperable tumors?

✓ Can it breathe freely and without difficulty?

✓ Can it urinate and defecate without difficulty or incontinence?

✓ Is it able to see or hear?

If the answer to any of the above is "no," and all possible treatment has been exhausted, then the dog is no longer capable of leading a normal life without suffering. Euthanasia should be gently carried out.

within one or two minutes, and the heart stops shortly after this. The transition is smooth and without trauma, perhaps with an occasional spasmodic twitch. There can be no kinder way of bringing an end to your pet's suffering.

Your vet will be able to advise you about disposal of the body and may offer facilities for cremation and burial. Many owners choose to inter their dog in a pet cemetery, with an appropriate headstone, but others prefer a favorite spot of the backyard or garden. This can usually be arranged, but make sure you observe the legal and hygienic requirements.

Afterward, expect to grieve; it is only natural. If you have children, be honest with them about what has happened to the dog and explain why it was necessary. You may find it

▲ *This old dog still has a sparkle in his eye, but in time illness and the processes of aging will reduce his quality of life. The moment of saying good-bye to a faithful friend is one that every owner has to face.*

helpful to talk to sympathetic friends (especially other dog owners) or to the vet or animal nurse a few days later. Whatever you do, don't blame yourself for the dog's passing—if the decision was carefully considered under expert advice, you have made the correct choice. Don't rush to replace the lost pet unless you are certain that this is the right decision. On the other hand, don't resist having another dog because you think it would be a betrayal of the last one. It certainly won't be. Every dog is an individual and should be valued for his or her unique qualities.

YOUR DOG'S HEALTH

HOWEVER MUCH CARE YOU GIVE IT, YOUR DOG
is likely to suffer at least one illness during its life.
Early recognition of a problem by the owner and
prompt veterinarian attention are the keys to good health
and a long, active, and happy life for your dog. As a dog
cannot explain its symptoms, it is important that you take note of
any physical or behavioral changes that occur and describe these
accurately to the veterinarian. To help you know what to look for,
and to give you a better understanding of your dog's health, this section
starts by describing the dog's basic anatomy. It then lists the most
common diseases and parasites of the dog.

The section concentrates on the medical problems that owners
are most likely to encounter. The starting point is the particular
symptom, or group of symptoms, that alerts their concern that
something is wrong. All the likely causes of that condition are
discussed, followed by advice on prevention and possible
courses of treatment. You'll also find advice on whether to
have your dog neutered, on breeding, and on first aid.

Structure of the Dog

THE DOG IS A SUPERBLY DESIGNED MACHINE. The skeleton acts as a protective cage for the internal parts of the body such as the brain, heart, lungs, liver, and spinal cord, and the powerful muscles, attached to the skeleton, give it formidable strength and mobility.

Dogs show greater extremes in size and shape than possibly any other animal species. Selective breeding by humans has played a great part in this, though miniature and dwarf breeds are to be found in nature. The number of bones are always the same, but they vary tremendously in size and proportion. A dwarf breed such as the Dachshund has much shorter limb bones and, proportionally, much bigger joints than does a large dog, illustrated below.

Canine joints are quite similar to our own. The knee joint in the hind limb is usually referred to as the stifle, and the ankle is the hock. Joint abnormalities, especially of the hip, sometimes develop during growth. Back problems tend to occur most often where the different types of vertebrae meet, such as the midback, and are most common in the dwarfed breeds.

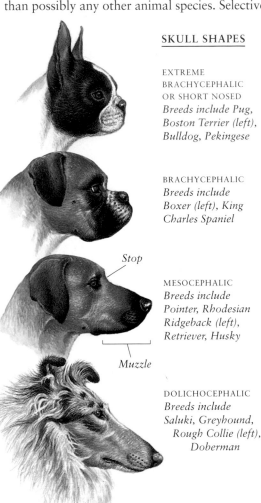

SKULL SHAPES

EXTREME
BRACHYCEPHALIC
OR SHORT NOSED
*Breeds include Pug,
Boston Terrier (left),
Bulldog, Pekingese*

BRACHYCEPHALIC
*Breeds include
Boxer (left), King
Charles Spaniel*

Stop

MESOCEPHALIC
*Breeds include
Pointer, Rhodesian
Ridgeback (left),
Retriever, Husky*

Muzzle

DOLICHOCEPHALIC
*Breeds include
Saluki, Greyhound,
Rough Collie (left),
Doberman*

▲ *Selective breeding has had a role in developing the four basic shapes of skull. Short-nosed dogs are more likely to have respiratory problems, but a dog with a long muzzle may suffer from diseases of the nose.*

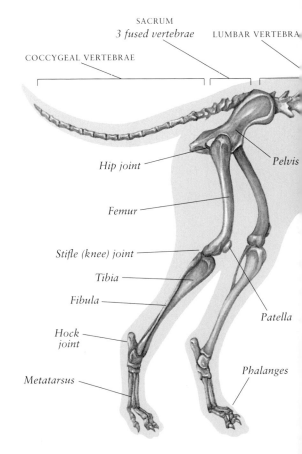

SACRUM
3 fused vertebrae LUMBAR VERTEBRA

COCCYGEAL VERTEBRAE

Hip joint

Pelvis

Femur

Stifle (knee) joint

Tibia

Fibula

Patella

Hock
joint

Metatarsus

Phalanges

● *How do bones grow?*

During the first few months of life, the long limb bones grow from plates near each end, called growth plates. They are made of soft, growing tissue, which is converted first into cartilage and then into bone away from the growth point. These areas are prone to damage, resulting in short or bent limbs. Large, rapidly growing breeds such as Rottweilers and German Shepherds are especially vulnerable to growth deformities. For this reason they should not be heavily exercised during the first 6 months of life. The growth plates close at maturity.

● *Are there any advantages to docking tails?*

Not really—the major reasons for docking (or shortening) dogs' tails are tradition and fashion. Docking does avoid tail injuries, but these are not common in dogs kept for companionship. Vets see more cats with tail injuries than dogs, but cats are never docked. The tail has a part to play in balance, but its most important function is as a means of communication. Vets and their professional associations regard tail docking as a cruel and unnecessary deprivation.

● *Why do some breeds of dog have such a high incidence of hip malformation?*

Hip dysplasia, the commonest cause of hip disease in dogs, occurs during growth. The ball of the hip remains too loose in the socket, causing excessive wear to the joint, which fails to form properly. It frequently occurs in large and giant breeds of dog because their size and rapid growth expose the developing joints to a great amount of strain. In addition, there is a genetic tendency to hip dysplasia in certain breeds (see Breed Profiles, pages 150–199).

DOG SKELETON

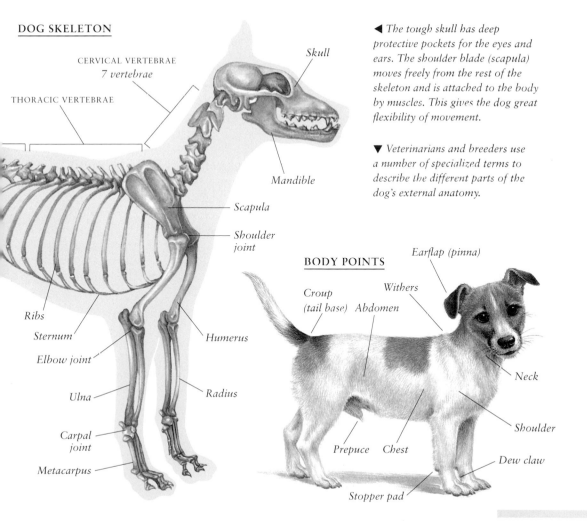

CERVICAL VERTEBRAE
7 vertebrae

THORACIC VERTEBRAE

Skull

Mandible

Scapula

Shoulder joint

Ribs

Sternum

Humerus

Elbow joint

Ulna

Radius

Carpal joint

Metacarpus

◀ *The tough skull has deep protective pockets for the eyes and ears. The shoulder blade (scapula) moves freely from the rest of the skeleton and is attached to the body by muscles. This gives the dog great flexibility of movement.*

▼ *Veterinarians and breeders use a number of specialized terms to describe the different parts of the dog's external anatomy.*

BODY POINTS

Earflap (pinna)

Croup (tail base) Abdomen

Withers

Neck

Shoulder

Prepuce Chest

Dew claw

Stopper pad

Getting the Most from Your Vet

YOUR VET WILL PLAY AN ESSENTIAL ROLE IN THE care of your dog from puppyhood to old age, and you should choose one as carefully as you would your own doctor. The recommendations of friends, neighbors, and fellow dog-walkers are always an excellent way to begin. If you have recently moved into a new neighborhood, your previous vet may be able to make suggestions.

The veterinary hospital should not be too far away: an hour-long drive with a sick dog is not desirable. The level of the facilities offered will vary, depending on the size of the practice, and will be a factor in the fees. Large hospitals provide a wider range of specialist services such as surgery, ophthalmology, cardiology, radiology, dentistry, dermatology, and behavior therapy. Visit the facility and ask to have a look around. You may have more contact with the support staff than with the vet(s), so ensure that they are equally friendly and helpful, both to you and your dog. Ultimately, the most important thing is that you feel the vet is taking good care of your animal. It is important that both you and your dog like and trust the vet.

When Going to the Vet

Do
- ✓ Be ready to answer questions about your dog's general health and any specific problems.
- ✓ Have your dog's record cards or other relevant documentation with you.
- ✓ Take any samples that the vet requests in a clean, sealed container.

Don't
- ✗ Ask someone to go in your place. You know most about the dog's symptoms.
- ✗ Forget to bring a leash and muzzle if your dog is likely to be aggressive.
- ✗ Call your vet at night or over the weekend unless it's an emergency.

Don't Wait for a Crisis

Make an appointment for a routine checkup without waiting for your pet to fall sick—it is best for the vet and the dog (especially a young puppy) if the first examination takes place without the pressure of an emergency. The vet will examine and weigh your dog, and take notes for future reference. Most veterinary centers today have computerized record keeping. At the first visit the vet will take the opportunity to discuss deworming and vaccination programs with you. Many proprietary drugs for flea control and deworming, as well as prescription medicines, can be dispensed only if your dog is under the direct care of a veterinarian. This is for the animal's own benefit.

If you have to make an emergency appointment, explain to the receptionist, the nurse, or veterinarian on duty exactly what the problem is. You will be given immediate advice for dealing with the emergency and advised whether or not the dog needs to be seen right away. If it is outside normal working hours, you may be asked to go to a different location—check before you leave home.

It is always better to take your dog to the vet than have the vet come to you, as the facilities for diagnostic tests or emergency surgery are not portable. However, it may be necessary to arrange a home visit if the dog cannot be moved or if there are several animals to be treated. Try to avoid night and weekend calls unless it is absolutely necessary.

You will normally have to wait to see the vet. This can upset even a calm dog, so have a muzzle handy. If the receptionist has warned you to bring along a urine or feces sample, make sure it is in a clean, sealed container. Your vet will be able to give you a special collection kit for the purpose, though any clean food container will do. After the visit, make sure that you understand any instructions for giving medication and that you know if a follow-up visit is needed.

▲ *A Yorkshire Terrier allows a vet to examine her eye without fuss. If the first puppy checkups are handled well, subsequent visits to the veterinarian need not become stressful occasions for the dog.*

Q&A

● *How often should I take my dog for a checkup?*

... For healthy adult dogs, an annual visit for booster shots is a reasonable interval. Puppies, old, and chronically sick dogs should be seen more often. Regular checkups make it easier to spot the early onset of some diseases. Small changes that you have not noticed can be obvious to the vet. It also means that your vet gets to know you and the dog.

● *Why does my vet want to see Cassie a second time for her ear infection, when he has already prescribed medication to clear it up?*

Dogs cannot tell you if they are still experiencing pain, so vets nearly always arrange a return visit to make sure the condition has disappeared. If any infection is left, the problem will almost certainly recur within a few weeks. It is better to be sure—a prolonged ear infection may require surgery to repair the damage.

● *My dog has to have a simple operation requiring a general anesthetic. What is involved?*

Anesthesia is very safe these days. You will probably be asked to bring the dog to the animal hospital first thing in the morning, having withheld food overnight. The dog will be sedated prior to receiving the anesthetic drugs, which are normally injected into a vein in the foreleg. The dog is unconscious in seconds, and a breathing tube is put down the windpipe and connected to an anesthetic machine. The dog's breathing and heart rate are monitored throughout the operation. Afterward, it is taken to a recovery ward and kept warm and comfortable. Recovery rates vary, but most dogs are allowed home the same day.

Infectious Diseases

DOGS ARE SUSCEPTIBLE TO A NUMBER OF VIRAL diseases that are transmitted from animal to animal and spread with devastating speed. Nearly all can be prevented with vaccination programs. Though many people know them only as the diseases that their dogs need regular shots against, they remain a very real threat in most parts of the world. No owner can afford to be complacent about these diseases. The first vaccinations should be given at between 6 and 8 weeks of age. Boosters will be required, and all dogs should have annual shots thereafter for life.

Distemper is a frequently fatal virus disease that usually affects puppies up to a year old. It is spread by droplets released into the air when the dog coughs or sneezes, and is highly contagious. A cough develops, and there is a discharge from the eyes and nose. Pneumonia, vomiting, and diarrhea usually follow. The infection sometimes responds to antibiotics, but affected dogs often develop fits, paralysis, or chorea (a spasmodic twitch) and have to be put to sleep. The pads of the feet often become thickened and hard, hence the disease's alternative name of hard pad.

Infectious Canine Hepatitis (ICH) is caused by a virus that attacks the liver. In severe forms of the disease, the dog goes off its food completely, becomes very depressed, and collapses. Death is almost inevitable and can occur very suddenly. ICH is transmitted in urine and can be picked up by a dog sniffing at a fencepost or other spot on which an infected dog has urinated.

Leptospirosis affect dogs in two forms: L. canicola, which causes acute kidney disease, and L. icterohaemorrhagiae (Weil's disease), which affects the liver. Both are able to cross between species, including humans. Dogs sometimes pick up Weil's disease from rat's urine when swimming in ponds or rivers.

Canine Parvovirus (contagious enteritis) causes vomiting and diarrhea, often with hemorrhage. It has a sudden onset, and death often follows as a result of dehydration unless prompt action is

▲ *This sad young puppy with crusting around his eyes and nose has distemper. Though the disease is not always fatal, affected dogs often have to be put to sleep.*

▲ *Any area of land used by dogs will be infected with viruses passed on in urine and feces. Protect your pet by keeping up to date with vaccination programs.*

● *My dog, Paddy, is 5 now and very robust. Do I really need to have him vaccinated every year? After all, I don't have regular vaccinations myself. Isn't this just a way for vets and drug companies to make money?*

Scientific evidence points overwhelmingly in favor of annual vaccination. You should take into account that dogs are exposed to a lot more disease than humans. They sniff at everything, with their noses and mouths only inches off the ground. Many viruses and bacteria are passed in urine and feces, and are concentrated in all the places that dogs investigate most actively. Prevention really is better than cure.

● *My friend's Labrador puppy died from distemper only about four weeks ago. She is heartbroken and wants me to bring my own Labrador, Glen, to visit. He is 2 years old and has been regularly vaccinated. Is it safe for me to do so?*

Perfectly, even if Glen was not protected by his vaccinations. Distemper is spread by direct contact between dogs. The virus cannot survive for long outside the affected dog, so all risk of infection will have disappeared by now.

● *Six months ago Lucy, my Fox Terrier, spent a few days in a kennel. I had her protected against kennel cough before she went. I am thinking of taking Lucy to a country show next weekend, when there will be lots of other dogs around. Will her kennel cough protection still hold good?*

No, it wouldn't be safe to rely on it. The nose drops against bordetella normally give up to 6–9 months' protection, so if Lucy is to enter a high-risk area toward the end of this period, you would be well advised to give her new protection.

taken to replace lost fluids intravenously. Infected dogs pass on the virus in their feces. It can remain active in grass or soil for more than a year. Most public areas used by dogs are heavily infected with parvovirus.

Rabies, a virulent viral disease found in animals such as dogs, cats, foxes, bats, and skunks, is spread in saliva when an infected animal bites another. The virus travels up to the brain and affects the central nervous system. Symptoms take between 10 days and 6 months to develop, and death normally follows within 10 days of their appearance. Rabies is endemic in most of the world. Exceptions are Japan, Australia, New Zealand, United Kingdom, Ireland, Scandinavia, Spain, and Portugal. Dogs entering these countries from abroad must show proof of vaccination, and are subject to quarantine laws in some.

Kennel cough is the name given to a group of bacterial and viral infections that cause persistent coughing. Generally nonfatal, they spread rapidly among dogs in crowded conditions. A vaccine against the parainfluenza virus is usually included in annual booster shots. Nose drops to prevent bordetella should be given 2–3 weeks before a dog goes into a kennel.

Infectious Enteritis is caused by any of a number of bacterial and viral infections that produce severe diarrhea and vomiting. There are no effective vaccines. The most significant infections are campylobacter and salmonella, and both can be passed to humans. If diarrhea is persistent, the vet will take fecal and blood samples to establish the cause of the infection, and prescribe intravenous fluids and antibiotics as appropriate.

What You Should Do

✓ Take your puppy to be vaccinated when it is between 6 and 8 weeks old.

✓ Follow up with booster shots as recommended by the vet.

✓ Keep your puppy off the ground in public areas used by other dogs until the primary vaccination course has taken.

✓ Make sure your dog is vaccinated every year.

✓ Keep an infected dog in complete isolation for as long as the vet indicates.

✓ Protect your dog against kennel cough 2–3 weeks before it mingles with other dogs in a crowd (i.e., at a public show, or when placing it in a kennel).

✓ Some viruses (e.g., parvovirus) can be carried on skin and clothing. Take all necessary precautions to avoid cross-infection.

✓ If you suspect your dog has a contagious disease, warn the animal hospital beforehand and leave the dog in the car until the vet is ready to see it.

Common Parasites

DOGS ARE HOSTS TO MANY KINDS OF PARASITES. Some are insects that live on or close to the skin and feed on the animal's blood. They cause skin irritations and patches of hair loss, and if present in large numbers can take so much blood from the host dog that it becomes severely run down and anemic. Parasitic worms live in the gut and other parts of the body. They can cause symptoms such as abdominal pain, diarrhea, anemia and weight loss. Some parasites of the dog can infect humans and are a potential hazard to your family's health. For all these reasons, it is important to make prevention a routine part of caring for your pet. Don't wait until the dog is showing signs of infestation before treating the problem.

Which type of parasite poses a threat to your dog depends to a very large extent on where you live. Your vet is the best person to advise you on what preventive measures you should take. Anti-flea preparations and deworming treatments are available in various forms, and he or she will know which of them is best suited to the individual needs of your dog.

External Parasites

Fleas are the best-known parasitic inhabitant of the dog and the commonest cause of itchy skin (see pages 52–53). The life cycle of the flea takes about 3 weeks, but the eggs and larvae can remain dormant for long periods in cool weather. Only the adult flea lives on the dog, feeding on its blood. A female can lay 50 eggs a day. These fall off the dog into the environment and hatch in two to five days in warm weather. The larval and pupal stage are spent off the dog, but the adult flea needs a host to feed on. To control fleas effectively, eggs, larvae, and cocoons must be destroyed as well as adult fleas. This means treating not only the dog, but bedding, rugs, soft furnishings, and all other pets. The most effective treatments are available by prescription from your vet. They include sprays, topical lotions, and pills that prevent fleas from breeding. **Lice** are small insects, barely visible by eye. They mostly infest neglected, run-down dogs or puppies, and attach their eggs ("nits") to the dog's hairs. Antiflea treatments usually kill lice, too.

THE LIFE CYCLE OF THE FLEA

◀ *Fleas take about 3 weeks to grow from eggs to adults. Most of the life cycle is spent in the environment, not on the dog.*

▼ *Small and fast-moving, fleas are difficult to spot in the dog's coat. Tiny black specks of flea dirt are a reliable sign of their presence.*

Pupa

Adult flea

The pupa forms within the cocoon and hatches into an adult

Cocoon

Adult flea finds host dog to feed on. Female lays eggs on dog

Eggs drop to the ground. After 2–12 days, a larva hatches from each egg

Eggs

Larvae

External Parasites

PARASITE	SITE & SYMPTOMS OF INFESTATION	PREVENTION & TREATMENT
Fleas	Heat stimulates egg laying on coat. Eggs hatch in environment and adults find host to feed on. Bites can cause severe allergy	Check dog regularly for flea dirt. Treat all pets and soft furnishings in the house with good-quality antiflea preparations
Lice	Spend whole life cycle in dog's hair. Irritation. Causes anemia in severe cases	Killed by most antiflea treatments
Ticks	Attach themselves to the skin. Drop off after feeding. Localized irritation. A tick's saliva can transmit other diseases, e.g., Lyme disease	Check the dog's coat daily and use an antitick wash, spray or topical treatment. Kill and remove any ticks
Mites	On or burrowing into the skin. Sarcoptic mite causes scabies (very itchy and highly contagious; can be passed on to humans.) Demodex mite causes a non-itchy mange with widespread hair loss. Harvest mites attack the feet in the fall	Check skin, coat, ears, around eyes, elbows, and anal region regularly. Use special treatments for mites, available from your vet

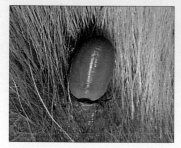

Tick

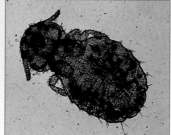

Dog louse

Harvest mites

Ticks resemble tiny spiders, to which they are related. They live on vegetation and get caught up in the dog's coat as it brushes past, attaching themselves to its skin. As they feed, their bodies swell up with sucked blood and look a little like small peas. Some ticks carry diseases that affect humans as well as dogs, such as Rocky Mountain spotted fever and Lyme disease. The latter, carried by the deer tick, causes flulike symptoms, a rash, joint inflammation, and lameness. The Scrub and Bush tick, found in warm coastal areas such as southern California and Australia, can cause paralysis in the host. If you live in a tick-infested area, search your dog's coat daily and use a protective wash or topical treatment regularly. The tick is less likely to pass on the disease during the first 72 hours, before it has become fully swollen with blood.

Mites are tiny creatures related to ticks and spiders. Several commonly infest dogs, burrowing into the skin and ears. Treatment is usually by antiparasitic washes, sprays, or injections.

● *How can I tell if my dog has fleas?*

Comb back the dog's undercoat with your fingers. If any tiny black specks show up against the skin, pick them up on a damp sponge or cotton ball. If the specks (flea dirt) smear and turn red, fleas are present.

● *The vet has recommended giving my dog monthly flea tablets. How do they work?*

They contain a drug that enters the dog's bloodstream. When a female flea ingests it with her meal of blood, it makes her sterile, and any eggs she lays fail to hatch. The dog suffers no ill effects from the drug. Treat all household dogs and cats. Spray and vacuum carpets in your home as well, so that all dormant eggs and larvae are destroyed.

● *What's the best way to destroy a tick?*

Kill the tick with rubbing alcohol. Using fine tweezers or your fingers, pull the dead tick away from the skin. Do not squeeze the tick, as this releases more poison into the dog. Special tick-killing preparations and tick-removing tools are available from your vet.

Internal Parasites

Roundworm (above)

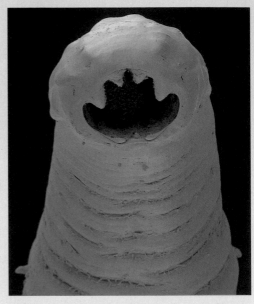

Tapeworm (left) and head of a hookworm (above)

PARASITE	SITE & SYMPTOMS OF INFESTATION	PREVENTION
Roundworm	Intestine and lungs. Inflammation, diarrhea, pain	Regular deworming from 14 days old. Stool (fecal) tests at annual checkup
Tapeworm	Intestine. Diarrhea, vomiting, weight loss	Good antiflea control. Avoid raw meat and offal. Stool (fecal) tests at annual checkup
Hookworm	Intestine. Inflammation, diarrhea, blood in feces, weight loss, anemia	As part of regular worm prevention. Stool (fecal) test at annual checkup
Whipworm	Intestine. Diarrhea, blood in feces, poor coat, weight loss, anemia	As part of regular worm prevention. Stool (fecal) test at annual checkup
Heartworm	Heart and lungs. Cough, weight loss, weakness, abdominal swelling, anemia	Daily/monthly tablet. Stool (fecal) tests at annual checkup. Start prevention 2 weeks before visiting an endemic area; continue for 90 days after

Internal Parasites

Parasitic worms are picked up from the environment. Most live inside the intestine. It is important that your dog be given adequate protection against them and that you learn to recognize the symptoms of worm infestation. Dogs living close together in cities and suburbs are often more heavily infected with internal parasites than country dogs.

Roundworms (Toxocara canis) are the most common internal parasite in dogs. They are round and white, and can grow to 8in (20cm) long. They are usually noticed in the feces, but sometimes the dog vomits up a coiled heap of the worms. Thousands of microscopic eggs are laid inside infected dogs and passed out in their feces. After three weeks the eggs can infect other dogs, particularly puppies, who swallow them. The eggs then hatch in the intestine, and the larvae migrate across the bowel wall, through the liver, and into the lungs. Some are coughed up, swallowed, and taken into the intestine, where they develop into mature worms. All females should be treated during pregnancy and while feeding their young. Routinely deworm puppies every 2 to 3 weeks until they are 3 months old, and then once a month until they are 6 months old. Continue to deworm adult dogs every 6 months. If your dog is receiving regular protection against heartworm (see below), there is no need to give a separate roundworm preventive.

Tapeworms have flattened, segmented bodies and small pointed heads that imbed themselves in the dog's intestinal wall. Several kinds affect dogs. As the common dog tapeworm (Dipylidium caninum) grows in the intestine, segments break off at the end and pass through the gut to lodge in the fur around the dog's anus. At this stage the segments are mobile and full of eggs. They dry, resembling a grain of rice, and then burst. The eggs are released and are eaten by flea larvae where they remain. If, while grooming itself, a dog swallows an infected adult flea, the tapeworm egg then hatches and grows in its intestine. Tapeworm infestation can have serious effects in young, sick, or old animals. Stool tests will show if a dog is infected. Sometimes tapeworm segments are found around the anus or in the dog's bedding.

Hookworms and **whipworms** are common intestinal parasites in dogs. In tropical areas the Ancylostoma hookworm is a particular threat. The eggs can live for years on the ground. The larvae burrow their way through the skin, especially on the feet, causing severe irritation. The adult worms bury themselves in the wall of the gut. There is blood loss and diarrhea, with consequent weight loss and anemia. Puppies are infected through the their mother's milk. If you live in an infected area, your vet will suggest a full-protection treatment.

Heartworms are small parasitic worms living in the heart and arteries that supply the lungs. The dog becomes infected with the larvae after being bitten by an infected mosquito. They enter the circulation and develop to maturity in the heart. As the adult worms grow in number and size, pressure increases in the right side of the heart and the dog eventually develops heart failure: the full symptoms can take years to develop. Heartworm disease is difficult to treat. If you live in a part of the world where it is endemic, your pet must receive regular protection.

▶ *Large numbers of worms living in the dog's heart interfere with the flow of blood to the lungs, eventually causing heart failure.*

Q&A...

● **Why do puppies have roundworms?**

Roundworm larvae can remain dormant in body tissue. When a female becomes pregnant, hormone changes awaken these dormant larvae and they migrate to her intestine, where they mature. Others travel through the placenta to enter the embryos, so the puppies are born infected. Puppies can also take in larvae when nursing.

● **Can a dog catch tapeworm from another, for example, by sharing the same bed?**

No, there has to be an intermediate animal host. In the case of the common dog tapeworm, it is the flea. This is an additional reason for making sure your dog has regular antiflea treatment. Other tapeworms are picked up from eating infected raw meat, or from small animals the dog hunts such as mice, lizards, and rabbits. Make sure you give your dog only cooked meat, and keep it from eating dead carcasses.

● **Is it true that heartworm is spreading?**

Yes. It was formerly confined to warm, humid areas such as the southern states of the US, South America, the Mediterranean, Africa, and parts of Australia, but now extends beyond that range. It is present in nearly every state of the US and also found in Canada. It is probably spread by infected dogs moving with their owners to new homes. It may be that new strains have developed that can survive in colder temperatures.

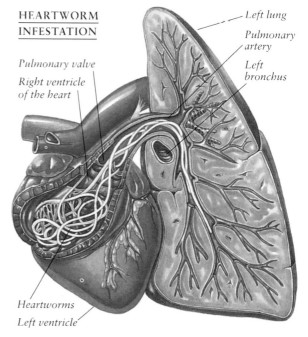

HEARTWORM INFESTATION

Pulmonary valve

Right ventricle of the heart

Left lung

Pulmonary artery

Left bronchus

Heartworms

Left ventricle

Itchy Skin Conditions

◀ *All dogs scratch themselves from time to time. It's part of normal canine life. But if your dog seems unbearably itchy, and scratches, rubs, chews, or shakes its skin in a torment of agony, it's time to see the vet.*

IT CAN BE VERY DIFFICULT TO PINPOINT THE cause of skin irritation. A dog that suddenly becomes itchy in early summer, for example, could be a victim of flea infestation, or reacting to a pollen allergy. To help find the cause, your vet needs to know the answers to a lot of questions. Did the itching start suddenly? Is only one part of the body affected, or is the dog scratching and shaking its whole body? Have you noticed any telltale black specks on the dog's skin that could indicate the presence of fleas? Have you or anyone else in the family noticed bites on themselves? Has the dog eaten anything new or been in contact with an unusual household product? Have you started walking it in a new area? Is the dog otherwise in good health?

Bites and Stings

Many skin irritations are caused by parasites that live on and in the coat and skin: fleas, mites, ticks, and lice (see pages 48–49). A dog that is grooming, licking, and scratching more than usual, especially around its rump and hindlegs, may have a strong allergic reaction to fleabites. Fly and mosquito bites usually clear up without

intervention, but if the dog scratches and breaks the skin, the place can become infected. Sometimes infected bites cause "hot spots," areas of moist, painful infected skin that the dog keeps irritating. In rare cases the dog may develop multiple itchy swellings—an allergic response to the bite that requires urgent veterinary attention.

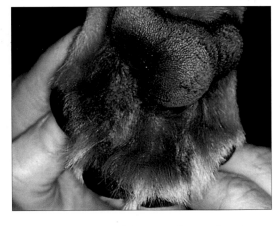

▲ *An allergy has caused this area of raw, inflamed, itchy skin on a dog's foot. Paws are a common site for such allergies. So are the ear flaps and the hairless skin of the groin.*

Some Causes of Skin Irritation

Signs	Main area affected	Possible cause*	Action
Black specks (flea dirt), scratching or chewing, patchy baldness, ulceration	Rump, hindlegs, and tail base	Fleas	Various forms of insecticidal preparation to disrupt fleas' breeding cycle. Treat all in-contact pets and environment.
Intense itching, red rash	Ears, elbows, hindlegs	Sarcoptic mites (scabies, or sarcoptic mange)	Contagious. Treat all in-contact pets and environment with an acaricidal (mite-killing) preparation.
Head shaking and scratching, black waxy discharge	Ears	Ear mites	Contagious. Treat all in-contact pets with acaricidal drops.
Itchiness and dandruff-type appearance to coat	All over body	Fur mites (Cheyletiella)	Contagious. Treat all in-contact pets and environment with appropriate insecticide.
Inflamed skin, persistent licking and chewing of affected site	All over body, particularly ears, paws, hairless skin of groin	Allergy	Allergy shots, topical washes, and various anti-inflammatory agents.
Localized reddened swelling, violent scratching, which may lead to infection	Any part of body	Insect bite	Anti-inflammatory drugs
Area of moist, smelly skin, painful itching	Any part, particularly face and neck	Wet eczema or "hot spot"	Antibiotic and/or anti-inflammatory drugs
Hive-like raised lumps, acute itchiness	Any part of body	Hypersensitivity reaction	Anti-inflammatory drugs

*Laboratory tests are usually necessary to establish precise cause.

Other Causes of Itching

Allergic reactions to substances such as foods, pollens, dust and dust mites, and chemicals often cause persistent irritation. Usually, the allergy starts in the young dog. Large patches of skin become inflamed, and the site becomes increasingly sore as the dog licks and gnaws it. Bacterial infections also cause itching. The folds of the skin (particularly on the face of short-nosed dogs) and feet are frequently affected.

The vet will probably need to carry out a number of tests before a diagnosis can be confirmed. These tests could involve taking skin scrapings, plucks of hair or brushings from the coat, and blood tests. If the veterinarian suspects an allergy, he or she may inject a small amount of a suspected allergy-causing substance into the skin, and wait for a reaction. Treatment will depend on the diagnosis. Meanwhile, make sure you are using an effective antiflea treatment. The best way to ease your dog's discomfort is to sponge the affected area of skin with cold water.

● I've noticed dandruff-like specks in my puppy's fur recently. My son, who plays with Brendan a lot, has developed a rash on his hands. Could they be connected?

A mite infestation called Cheyletiellosis, commonly called "walking dandruff," is the most likely cause of both. The mite will bite humans, especially on parts of the skin in contact with the dog's coat. Your vet will be able to detect the mites with the aid of a magnifying lens. Treatment requires the use of an acaricide on the puppy and in the environment. Your son's rash should clear up easily with medical attention.

● My German Shepherd, Nero, keeps rubbing his bottom on the ground. What could be causing it?

There could be several causes of severe itchiness in this area, but one possibility is impacted anal sacs. These are the two scent glands that help dogs recognize each other. Get your vet to examine Nero. If they are impacted, they will need regular emptying to avoid infection. The sacs can be removed surgically if they are a persistent source of problems.

Non-itchy Skin Conditions

AREAS OF SCALING AND DISCOLORATION, SPOTS, growths, and rashes may appear on your dog's skin without it showing obvious signs of irritation. They are usually, but not always, accompanied by hair loss, which may be the first sign that something is wrong. Skin problems of this kind will rarely resolve themselves without medical attention. As with itchy skin conditions (see pages 52–53), it can be difficult to diagnose non-itchy skin diseases without laboratory tests.

Your vet will want to know if the condition has spread or altered since you first noticed it. Has there been any itchiness before or after it first developed? Have you, a family member, or any other pets, shown similar symptoms? What do you feed the dog, and have you made any recent changes to its diet? Is it otherwise healthy?

Ringworm

Ringworm, a highly contagious fungal infection of the skin, hair, and hair follicles, can be picked up from the soil or other animals and passed by contact from animals to humans. Despite its name, it is not a worm and the fungus does not always grow in a ring. It often appears first on the head and limbs, but once the dog is infected, can spread rapidly all over the body. To see if the fungus is present, the veterinarian may shine an ultraviolet lamp on the area in a darkened room, as sometimes it will fluoresce. Samples of affected skin and hair will be taken for microscopic examination. In some cases, an attempt is made to grow cultures of the fungus from them. Treatment is given as fungicidal shampoos, lotions, or ointments, or as tablets. It may take several months for the condition to clear up completely.

Mange

A mite (Demodex canis) that lives in the hair follicle causes the scaly skin and patchy, local hair loss known as demodectic mange. All dogs are believed to have the mite as part of the skin's normal flora, but if the immune system is suppressed (in very young, elderly, or sick dogs), the mites start to multiply, causing symptoms. Usually in young dogs, a single site only, often on the head or paws, is affected. It may clear up without treatment. The patches are not itchy unless infected by bacteria or fungi. Mange tends to be more generalized in other dogs and is more difficult to treat. Dips, baths, and the elimination of other medical problems are all helpful.

Principal Non-itchy Skin Conditions

SIGNS	POSSIBLE CAUSE*	ACTION
Usually round, hairless area of scaly skin, may be slightly raised at edge	Ringworm	Treat with antifungal tablets, lotion, ointment, or washes
Scaly skin and patchy hair loss. Usually localized in young dogs, but more generalized in older dog	Demodicosis (demodectic mange)	Acaricidal washes, immune stimulants, elimination of other medical problems
Areas of blackened skin, hair loss on flanks	Hormonal disease (see pages 56–57)	According to underlying hormonal problem
Scaling, crusty patches, baldness, poor quality coat	Nutritional disease	Change of diet
Multiple symptoms	Autoimmune disease	Immune system modulators
Variable: patch of inflamed skin; large, nodular growth	Skin cancer	Appropriate to particular cancer

*Laboratory tests are usually necessary to establish precise cause

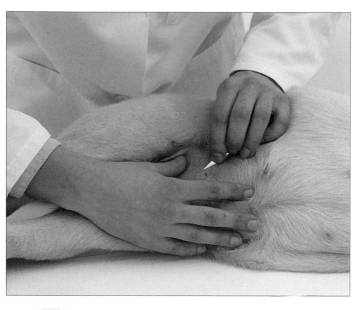

◀ *To help establish the cause of a skin problem, the vet removes a tiny piece of skin with a scalpel for microscopic examination.*

Other Skin Diseases

Nutritional deficiencies caused by a poor diet may lead to scaling, skin crusts, baldness, and a dull coat. The areas around the eyes, ears, muzzle, and paws are most often affected. It may be treated by supplementing or completely changing the dog's diet, usually with success.

For some reason, a dog may start to produce antibodies against parts of its own skin. Autoimmune disease is difficult to detect since the symptoms mimic those of others. Diagnosis is by blood tests and a skin biopsy. Drugs can be given to stop the dog producing the antibodies, but a complete cure is rarely achieved. Such drugs can have side effects, so your dog will need regular checkups for the rest of its life.

Skin cancers also appear in various forms, ranging from small patches of slightly inflamed skin to large, nodular growths. Consult your vet immediately if you notice an abnormal growth or any change on your dog's skin. A biopsy will establish if the growth is benign or malignant. If it is cancerous, the vet will advise you about the future outlook and treatment.

Q&A

● *Is it true that dogs get sunburn?*

Yes. Exposure to the sun can cause ulceration and inflammation, most usually to the nose but also to any bald or white-haired part of the body. Some of the lesions are considered precancerous, so consult a veterinarian if you suspect a problem. Sun blocks should be applied under veterinary supervision.

● *My St. Bernard, Jacob, has developed an area of hardened, thick skin on his elbow. Recently it has become cracked. What should I do?*

This sounds like a callus, a thickening of the skin over a pressure point such as an elbow. They are quite common in the heavier, larger breeds. Usually harmless, they sometimes become infected, so seek your vet's advice. Increase the thickness of your dog's bedding and apply a pressure pad to the sore area.

● *My Labrador, Barney, has been prescribed acaricidal washes for demodectic mange. How long will he have to have them for?*

They are usually given weekly and should be continued until at least two tests have failed to find any parasites. Mange can take many months to treat, and in some cases it may be possible to do no more than keep the symptoms under control.

▶ *The scaly patches of skin on this dog's foreleg are caused by overgrowth of the tiny Demodex mite that lives in the hair follicles.*

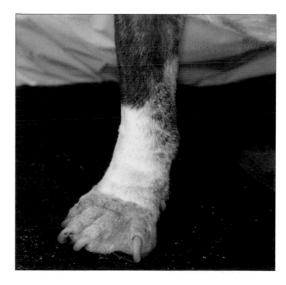

Hair and Coat Problems

HAIR LOSS IS A NATURAL PART OF THE DOG'S hair cycle. Hair does not grow everywhere at the same time or pace, so a dog may be shedding it (molting) on one part of its body while growing it in another. The growth-and-loss cycle of hair is influenced by many factors, including seasonal changes in temperature and sunlight, hormones, or diet. Females occasionally shed more after they come off heat, during pregnancy, and when they are nursing pups.

If your pet begins to shed hair heavily, this is not necessarily a reason for concern in itself. Some breeds with double coats, such as German Shepherds, sometimes shed their dense undercoat in tufts, which may cause alarm the first time you see it but is perfectly normal. Thin patches of hair occasionally appear on the flanks of certain breeds, such as Doberman Pinschers, English Bulldogs, and Airedale Terriers, during seasonal shedding. Very often the skin will be darker than usual at this time, but the problem will usually improve without treatment. It will normally recur. The season of hair loss varies

with individual dogs, though commonly the coat thins during the warmer months and regrows in the cooler months.

Very often, however, total or partial hair loss (alopecia) is an indication of another underlying disease, so it's always advisable to consult your veterinarian if you discover a bald patch on your dog, or if its coat begins to look sparse. The vet will want to know if there are other symptoms accompanying the hair loss. Patchy baldness accompanied by excessive chewing and scratching is very often a sign of parasitic infestation or an allergy (see pages 52–53). If the skin is scaly or discolored but there is no apparent itchiness, ringworm, demodectic mange, or another skin disease may be suspected (see pages 54–55).

Hormonal Disorders

Thinning of the coat is sometimes a symptom of a hormonal disease, such as hypothyroidism (underactivity of the thyroid gland) or hyperadrenocorticoism (Cushing's syndrome). The hair may fall out easily, often forming symmetrical

▲ The appearance of a bald patch in your dog's coat is often the first sign of an underlying skin problem. The vet may need to run a number of diagnostic tests, including skin scrapes, coat brushings, hair plucks, and blood tests before a precise diagnosis can be reached.

Cleaning a Contaminated Coat

If your dog's coat becomes accidentally contaminated with a harmful substance, muzzle it immediately to prevent it from licking the area. If the underlying skin is burned (in the case of a chemical spill), sponge the area carefully with cold water to remove all traces. Cover it with a damp, clean cloth and contact your vet right away.

PAINT, VARNISH	Allow to harden, then cut away the hair with scissors. Do not use paint solvent or thinner as they can damage the skin
OIL	Cover the affected area in a vegetable cooking oil, or smear with a hand-cleaning jelly. Wash it off with warm, soapy water (liquid detergent will do) and rinse thoroughly
TAR	Cut away contaminated hair, or rub with vegetable cooking oil and treat as above

bald patches on the flanks, and the skin in the affected areas may turn black. There are usually other symptoms as well. A dog with low levels of thyroid hormone, for example, will often search out warm places to lie in, show reluctance to exercise, and put on weight. Diagnosis is made by blood tests and, occasionally, skin biopsies. Treatment depends on the underlying cause.

Lick Granuloma

Sometimes a dog licks an area of its body, usually on the feet or lower limbs, so frequently and obsessively that a bald patch appears and the skin becomes ulcerated and sore. The licking itself may be caused by behavioral or psychological problems such as boredom, or the dog may have a specific skin disease such as an allergy or bacterial infection. If left untreated, granulomas can sometimes be very slow to heal. The problem is how to persuade the dog to stop licking the area. The majority of dogs will have no difficulty in removing a bandage, so the vet may recommend that the dog wear an Elizabethan collar (see below). Topical medication can usually control the itchiness, but treatment is dependent on the underlying cause.

● *My Doberman Pinscher, Thor, suffers from seasonal hair loss. Will it help if I brush or shampoo his coat, or will it simply make his condition worse?*

It's unlikely to make much difference either way. Brushing and shampooing certainly won't do him any harm, but it won't do anything to restore growth. The cause of seasonal hair loss is as yet unknown, and there is no specific treatment for the condition.

● *I've noticed that my Dachshund, Tonto, is developing bald patches on his ears. Is this a cause for concern?*

Dachshunds, especially males, often begin to lose hair on both ears when they are about a year old. By the time the dog is 8 to 9 years old, the ears may have become completely bald. There is nothing that can be done to reverse the symptoms—you and he will have to live with it, just as men have to put up with baldness. However, other diseases such as an allergy could be responsible for Tonto's baldness, so you should have the veterinarian examine him as soon as possible.

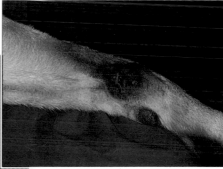

▲ *A skin allergy has caused this dog to lick and gnaw its foreleg so much that a lick granuloma, a bald area of ulcerated skin that is very slow to heal, has developed.*

◀ *An Elizabethan collar, formed from a stiff piece of plastic or cardboard folded into the shape of an old-fashioned megaphone, is an effective way of preventing your dog from worrying away at a lick granuloma or other irritated patch of skin.*

Coughing

As with humans, dogs cough when the sensitive linings of the windpipe (trachea) and the tiny airways of the lungs (bronchioles) are irritated. Coughing clears the airways of accumulated fluid or mucus and expels inhaled foreign matter. Some coughs develop rapidly and become harsh and frequent; others start more slowly, are soft and less frequent, but may persist for days or even weeks. Both should be investigated. The vet will want to know when and how the cough began and ask you to describe it—is it "chesty," "throaty," harsh, gentle, dry, or moist? Does the dog appear to cough more at night, or when it is drinking? Are there other symptoms such as loss of appetite? Does the slightest exertion leave the dog exhausted?

Respiratory Infections

Infection is one of the most likely causes of coughing. A group of bacterial and viral infections known as "kennel cough" can inflame the lining of the upper airway

▼ *Bordetella vaccine is sprayed into a dog's nose as protection against kennel cough.*

(the larynx and windpipe). A sudden harsh, dry, and unproductive cough develops, as if something is stuck in the dog's throat. The coughing fit may result in gagging or retching, and sometimes the dog will bring up white, frothy mucus. Kennel cough is highly contagious. If your dog shows any of these symptoms, isolate it from all contact with other dogs and consult your vet. To avoid the risk of infection, dogs should always be inoculated against kennel cough before being placed in kennels or shown in public. (See Infectious Diseases, pages 46–47.)

Fortunately, kennel cough is not serious. Apart from the cough, most dogs with the illness seem unaffected by it. If a dog is in obvious distress, refuses food, or appears lethargic, or if the infection lasts more than a week, the vet may carry out tests for specific bacterial or viral infections and X-ray the lungs.

Once an infection becomes established in the lungs rather than the upper airway, pneumonia, a serious and potentially life-threatening condition, can develop. It sometimes occurs after liquid has been inhaled, so take special care when administering fluid medicines to your dog. Signs to look for are a deep, moist cough that brings up fluid and harsh, labored breathing. The chest may make a bubbling sound when you put your ear to it (these noises are easily heard by the vet with a stethoscope). The dog is reluctant to move around and seems obviously ill. If you suspect your dog has pneumonia, lose no time in contacting your vet, who may prescribe antibiotics.

▲ *A vet listens to a dog's chest with a stethoscope as part of his diagnosis. A persistent cough is often one of the first signs of heart disease.*

Chronic Coughing

Persistent coughing in an older dog, particularly one of the small breeds, may be a symptom of chronic bronchitis or chronic airway disease caused by irritants such as cigarette smoke or house dust. As the airways become narrowed and clogged with mucus, the cough, which is normally of a dry, harsh nature, intensifies. By this time, the disease cannot be cured, but drugs can alleviate the symptoms. You can help by cutting down on smoking and by vacuuming the dog's environment more frequently.

A persistent dry cough and fatigue may be signs of congestive heart failure. In advanced cases of heart disease, coughing and breathlessness will increase as the lungs fill with fluid. The presence of parasites such as heartworms, lungworms, and roundworms, and fungal infections, can also affect a dog's lungs and breathing, causing persistent coughing.

▶ *A normal heart and lungs. In congestive heart failure, the heart enlarges and presses against the lungs, compressing the airways. In advanced stages of heart disease, the lungs fill with fluid.*

● *My Cocker Spaniel, Ella, had a malignant breast tumor removed eight months ago. Though she seems fine, she has developed a soft cough. Should I be worried?*

Sadly, this may be a sign that the malignancy has spread to Ella's lungs. A cough is often the only initial sign. It generally becomes more persistent and may be accompanied by weight loss and other signs. Your vet may take an X-ray and will discuss with you what is best for Ella if another tumor is found. Unfortunately, secondary lung tumors are almost invariably incurable.

● *For the last few weeks, my 9-year-old Miniature Poodle, Pepe, has been waking me up at night with coughing fits. He sometimes coughs when drinking and has little stamina during exercise. My vet told me last year that he had a slight heart murmur. Does this mean it's getting worse?*

It is a possibility. Degeneration of the heart valves is common in poodles and other small breeds. The murmur your vet heard was caused by blood leaking back into the heart through the faulty valves. X-rays may show that the heart has enlarged in the attempt to pump blood around the body and is now pressing against the lungs, causing Pepe's cough. The degeneration of the valves cannot be halted, but prescribed drugs will relieve the coughing and fatigue.

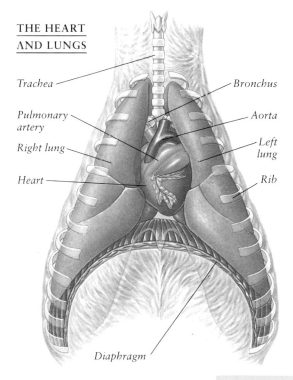

THE HEART AND LUNGS

Trachea

Pulmonary artery

Right lung

Heart

Bronchus

Aorta

Left lung

Rib

Diaphragm

Breathing Difficulties and Choking

NORMAL BREATHING FOR A HEALTHY DOG IS between 10 and 30 breaths per minute—with large dogs at the low end of the scale and small dogs at the high end. It is a good idea to familiarize yourself with what is normal for your dog. A sudden change may signal that all is not well. If your dog is having real difficulty in breathing, it may appear reluctant to settle or will lie on its front (sternally), holding its head and neck in an upright position.

Panting (fast, shallow, open-mouthed breathing with a lolling tongue) is triggered by changes elsewhere in the body, usually in response to excitement, panic, sudden pain, shock or heatstroke. Such panting is normal after a dog has been exercising hard, or in hot weather. It will be exaggerated in an overweight or old dog. Sometimes, however, panting can be a sign of anemia or internal bleeding. If your dog has frequent fits of panting, consult your vet. Prolonged panting in a visibly distressed dog is an emergency—do not delay in getting help.

Rapid breathing without accompanying panting is a sign that the dog's chest cannot expand or that the lungs are not inflating with each breath. The cause may be obvious, such as fractured ribs after a car accident, but rapid breathing can be a sign of congestive heart failure (see pages 58–59)

▲ Dogs with flat, "squashed" faces are prone to anatomically related breathing difficulties. These can often be corrected by surgery.

and also occurs with lung tumors and in the later stages of pneumonia.

Deep, labored breathing, or wheezing, which is sometimes accompanied by a harsh vibrating noise known as stridor, is a sign that the dog's airways are obstructed. If the onset is gradual, the most likely cause is a persistent condition such as an elongated soft palate. This is a hereditary problem in flat-faced breeds such as Bulldogs, Boston Terriers, and Pugs. The owners of these dogs often become alarmed when their pet begins to snort and cough, and even appears to choke, especially after exercise. It occurs because the soft palate in these breeds descends much further than normal into the throat and may intermittently obstruct the flow of air into the larynx. Surgery will often correct the condition. Other causes of labored breathing are tracheal collapse, resulting in narrowing of the windpipe, found most frequently in miniature breeds such as Yorkshire Terriers, and paralysis of the larynx, caused by weakening muscles. This is most common in older, larger dogs.

If Your Dog is Choking

Do

✓ Open the dog's mouth and pull its tongue free.

✓ If the dog is asphyxiating, give it air by breathing into its nose.

✓ Call your vet for advice or drive straight to the nearest emergency animal hospital.

Don't

✗ Attempt to remove a trapped ball by reaching with your hand into your dog's throat.

Breathing difficulties are sometimes caused by infections of the throat and upper airway, such as tonsillitis or kennel cough (see pages 46–47). An affected dog may have fits of harsh, unproductive coughing and appear to be gagging, so that the owner often believes it has something stuck in its throat.

True Choking

Dogs love to chew and can easily swallow toys and splintered fragments of wood, bone, or plastic. If an object becomes trapped or stuck at the back of the throat, the dog chokes and panics, and will paw frantically at its mouth, trying to dislodge the object. As it becomes starved of air, its tongue and gums begin to turn blue.

Treat this as an emergency (see First Aid and Emergencies, pages 98–101). Open the mouth, pull the tongue out, and call your vet for assistance, or take the dog to the nearest emergency animal center. You should not attempt treatment yourself unless immediate help is not available. To free a ball, use the Heimlich maneuver—grab the dog at its waist and squeeze, elevating the abdomen—or press on the throat from the outside and try to push the ball up and out over the back of tongue.

True choking can also occur if the dog has difficulty in swallowing and pieces of food remain stuck in the pharynx, or are regurgitated into the throat from the esophagus as the result of a condition known as megaesophagus (see page 69).

Q&A...

● *My neighbor told me I shouldn't throw a ball for my dog in case he chokes on it. Can this happen?*

Yes, it can. If the ball is not big enough to lodge between the upper and lower jaw, it may pass through them and be swallowed, either deliberately (dogs do this) or accidentally. A ball in the pharynx cannot move up or down. It acts like a ball valve, closing off the airway, and the dog can suffocate rapidly. Always make sure any ball you throw to your dog is too big to swallow.

● *My 4-year-old Spaniel, Megan, gets out of breath after anything more than a short walk. Even going upstairs to bed makes her puff. I've been trying to walk her more to lose weight. What else can I do?*

Take Megan for a checkup to ensure she has no medical problem such as congestive heart failure. If obesity is her only problem, you must reduce her calorie intake to lose some weight. Ask your vet to recommend a commercial low-calorie diet.

● *My 12-year-old Golden Retriever, Zorro, becomes breathless as soon he goes outside for exercise. He stops and heaves for breath, and seems upset. Is it just old age?*

No, Zorro may have an obstruction that is preventing him from getting oxygen when he needs it, possibly caused by paralysis of the larynx. This condition can worsen, so have the vet examine him.

▼ *Your dog may like to pick up sticks and chew them. Discourage the behavior. Sticks can easily splinter and cause injury.*

THE AIR PASSAGES

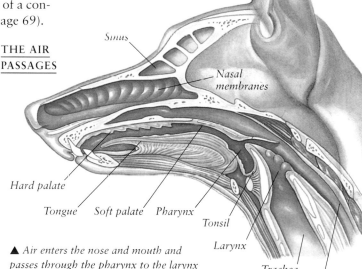

Sinus

Nasal membranes

Hard palate

Tongue   *Soft palate*   *Pharynx*

Tonsil

Larynx

Trachea

Esophagus

▲ *Air enters the nose and mouth and passes through the pharynx to the larynx at the head of the trachea (windpipe). Food passes down the esophagus.*

Sudden Weakness and Collapse

IT CAN BE VERY FRIGHTENING IF YOUR DOG suddenly collapses. There are two kinds of collapse: a faint, when the dog goes limp and falls over; and a seizure, when the dog becomes rigid and jerks involuntarily (see Seizures and Convulsions, pages 64–65). It is not easy to tell the difference if you are seeing this for the first time.

If your dog collapses, it is important that you remain calm. Usually the collapse will last only a matter of seconds, no more than a minute or two at most. Don't try to move the dog, but make sure its breathing is unobstructed by pulling the tongue out and to one side. If the dog is having a seizure, make the room dark and stay as quiet as possible. Allow the dog time to recover, reassure it, and then call your veterinary hospital. They will advise you if it is necessary to bring the dog in right away for treatment.

Dogs quite often faint for no apparent reason, and very few instances of collapse are fatal in themselves. Sometimes, however, particularly if the dog has a series of attacks, the collapse may be caused by one of a number of serious diseases. For this reason any sudden collapse should be

▼ *After a collapse, cover your dog with a coat or jacket to keep it warm. The dog will need plenty of reassurance as it recovers and may be wobbly on its legs for a while.*

● *My 8-year old Cavalier King Charles Spaniel, Pugwash, has been coughing for several months. Last week he coughed so hard he collapsed, but recovered quickly and now seems quite well. Should I tell the vet?*

Yes. Cavalier King Charles Spaniels tend to develop heart disease in middle or old age. One sign of this is coughing, which triggers fainting as you describe.

● *Last week Bruno, my 10-year-old Boxer, became wobbly and fell over. He presses his head against the wall for an hour or so every day and looks confused at times. Could he have a brain tumor?*

This is quite possible, but brain tumors are difficult to diagnose as they rarely show up on X-rays. Take Bruno to the vet to discuss what to do. Blood tests may help clarify whether some other problem (such as kidney disease) is causing his behavior. Your vet may refer Bruno to a specialist who can carry out tests such as MRI or CT scans.

● *If my dog faints, what should I do?*

Lay the dog on its right side in a comfortable position. If its gums and tongue appear bluish and the dog is unconscious, ensure a free airway by pulling its tongue as far out of its mouth as seems comfortable. Get someone to call the vet for advice. Meanwhile, attempt artificial respiration if necessary (see pages 98–99).

◀ Place an unconscious dog in a recovery position on its right side. Check for a heartbeat by feeling the left side of its chest behind the elbow and give first aid if necessary (see pages 98–99).

reported to the vet. The dog should be examined as soon as possible to make sure it shows no continuing ill effects. The vet is likely to ask a number of questions about the nature of the collapse (see box). If someone else was with the dog at the time, make sure he or she goes with you to the veterinary hospital as their description of events will provide important information in discovering the cause of the collapse. If it is the first, and remains the only, collapse the dog sustains, it is quite likely that no further treatment will be necessary.

What To Tell Your Vet

Try to write down as many details as you can remember about your dog's collapse, especially if it has already had previous episodes. Your information will help the vet identify the cause of the problem.

- How long did it last? This is surprisingly difficult to estimate but is vital information.
- Was anything usual about the dog's behavior prior to collapse? Was it whining or barking, looking subdued, dazed, or wobbly?
- What was the dog doing? Exercising or eating, for example, or did the attack occur immediately on waking?
- Was it a single episode, or one of a series? If the latter, how frequent are the attacks?
- Did the dog appear to lose consciousness and go limp?
- Was there any movement or muscle activity during the collapse?
- Did it recover immediately? Did it appear restless, excited, or distressed?
- Is the dog taking any medication?
- Could it have had access to a source of poison such as rat poison?
- Has it recently been in a car accident, been kicked or bitten, or hit its head?

Some Causes of Collapse

Fainting occurs when the brain becomes starved of oxygen or essential nutrients such as glucose. It may be caused by poor circulation resulting from the heart's failure to pump blood efficiently. Obstruction of an airway (see Breathing Difficulties, pages 60–61) that hampers the flow of oxygen into the lungs will have a similar effect on the brain. A dog is more likely to faint after it has been exercising heavily or after a prolonged bout of coughing.

A convulsive fit may signal a brain disorder such as epilepsy (see pages 64–65). The dog will normally take longer to recover than after a faint. Some metabolic disorders of the liver and kidneys, and diabetes mellitus (see page 75), can also cause convulsive-type collapses and lead to coma if untreated. A sudden internal hemorrhage may bring about collapse in a dog that has been recently injured. Occasionally, a tumor in the spleen or liver may rupture after the dog has done nothing more active than jump down from a chair. The collapse is the first sign that the tumor exists.

Seizures and Convulsions

DOGS FREQUENTLY TWITCH AND YELP IN THEIR sleep. This is perfectly normal: the dog is probably dreaming of chasing rabbits or the mailman. It is very different from the uncontrolled muscular movements that a dog makes when it is convulsing. The dog's body becomes rigid, and it makes paddling movements with its legs and jerks involuntarily. The spasms may affect the whole body. The dog is usually unaware of these movements and cannot be roused out of them (as it can from normal sleep). Most fits occur when the dog is quiet and resting, as opposed to being brought on by exercise.

It is deeply upsetting to observe your dog having a fit the first time it happens. Your pet is probably unaware of the fit and is unlikely to be experiencing pain. Stay as calm as you can. Do not try to touch or move the dog. Make sure everyone nearby stays quiet, turn off the TV or radio, and stop any other noise. Cover the windows and switch off any lights. If it is outside, try to shade the dog from glare. Move any piece of furniture the dog could damage or injure itself against. Most fits only last about 2 or 3 minutes, but the time can seem endless while you stand helplessly by. Try to make a note of the exact length—this is important information for the vet. As soon as the seizure is over, your dog will

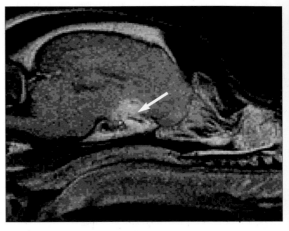

▲ *A magnetic resonance image of the brain of a 9-year-old Boxer reveals the presence of a tumor (indicated by the arrow). Seizures can be a symptom of a developing brain tumor.*

demand reassurance and comfort. It may seem to be a little disorientated for a while afterward, and sometimes it will experience temporary difficulty in seeing. Often the dog will be hungry or thirsty.

It is important to call your vet as soon as possible. If the fit seems severe, you may be asked to bring your dog in for immediate examination. In any event, you are well advised to arrange a visit

Characteristic Signs of a Seizure

STAGE 1: AURA	STAGE 2: ICTUS	STAGE 3: POST-ICTUS
Early onset	**The fit itself**	**After the fit**
• The dog seems dazed or confused.	• The body becomes rigid ("tonic phase").	• The dog seeks comfort and reassurance.
• It wobbles or loses direction when walking.	• The dog paddles with legs ("clonic phase").	• It is hungry and thirsty.
• It may become aggressive.	• It has spasms or tremors over whole or part of body.	• It appears slightly disorientated.
• It may become very hungry.	• It urinates and/or defecates.	• It may have temporary difficulty in seeing.
• It whines or barks for no obvious reason.	• It salivates excessively.	
• It may be quiet and subdued.	• It may lose consciousness.	
• It may seek out its owner.		

● *My 4-year old Collie, Bonnie, convulsed last week. The vet could find nothing wrong and said that it may have been a single episode. She wanted to do some blood tests. How are they likely to help?*

An epileptic fit is caused by a temporary malfunction within the brain. After the dog recovers, there is nothing to show what caused it. Sometimes a dog will have one fit, and no treatment is usually given at at this stage. Blood tests will establish if any other disease is responsible for the fit. The vet should certainly do them if Bonnie has another fit.

● *My 15-month-old German Shepherd female, Zara, has been found to have hereditary epilepsy. She started treatment four months ago and was doing very well, but has had four fits in the last two weeks. She is in heat at the moment, and I'm keeping her home. Could this be related to the fits?*

It is more than likely that the change in hormone levels due to Zara's being in heat is causing her fits to recur. You may need to increase her daily medication slightly for a short time. Discuss this with your vet. It may be advisable to have Zara spayed before she comes in heat again so that this problem can be avoided and you don't risk passing epilepsy on to any offspring.

within the next few days. The vet will question you about the dog's behavior before, during, and after the fit, so it can be helpful to note down as much as you remember while it is still fresh in your mind (see box on page 63). Seizures can be caused by any number of things, including infections such as distemper, poisoning, a head injury, encephalitis (inflammation of the brain), a brain tumor, and liver and sugar disorders. "Worm fits," associated with heavy worm infestation in puppies, and milk fever in nursing females can also cause fits. Tetanus, rare in dogs, produces muscular spasms that can be mistaken for a fit.

Living with Epilepsy

When fits occur repeatedly over a period of time, the dog may be diagnosed as having epilepsy. Epileptic fits originate in the brain. They have three rapid stages, the aura (early onset), ictus (the fit itself) and post-ictus (recovery period), each with its distinct signs (see box). The fits may or may not increase in frequency and severity over time. It is thought that epilepsy is inherited in some breeds including the German Shepherd, Boxer, Irish Setter, Labrador Retriever, Golden Retriever, Beagle, Cocker Spaniel, and Poodle. The seizures usually start in young adulthood (between 6 months and 3 years of age).

Epilepsy can be controlled with an anticonvulsant drug such as phenobarbital. This is normally given as a daily tablet. Treatment does not usually start until blood tests have ruled out all other causes of the fits. Unfortunately, in a small number of cases of inherited epilepsy, it proves impossible to establish a balanced medication program and the dog's fits may begin to grow in frequency and severity. The owner is then faced with the sad task of deciding whether it is kinder to euthanize the dog than allow its life to continue in these circumstances.

◀ *German Shepherds are one of the breeds of dog in which epilepsy appears to be inherited. Dogs with the disease should never be used for breeding.*

Loss of Balance

It is quite common for an older dog to lose its sense of balance partially: it may go weak in the legs, its head may tilt, or the body may lean or roll to one side. It is alarming when this happens, particularly if there is no warning, and it is important that you consult your vet as soon as possible. Meanwhile, take care that your dog does not harm itself, and keep it on a leash outside the house.

The problem is likely to be caused by one of several diseases of the ears or brain that can disturb the mechanism of balance. Balance is controlled by the organs of the inner ear (the semicircular canals, utricle, and saccule) adjacent to the cochlea. They can tell which way is up and detect movements of the head. They send this information via the vestibular nerve to the cerebellum, the part of the brain that coordinates posture and movement. When the brain tells the body to get up, the cerebellum checks out the position of the body and coordinates the appropriate movements of neck, body, and legs.

Signs of Loss of Balance

- Dog leans, rolls, or falls to one side.
- Dog circles to the same side as it walks.
- Dog's head tilts to the left or right.
- Rhythmic horizontal or vertical flickering of the eyeballs (nystagmus).
- Paralysis and drooping of the facial muscles, accompanied by saliva dribbling.
- Repeated shaking of the head and/or scratching of the ear(s).
- Squint of the eyes (strabismus).
- Vomiting.

▶ *A dog suffering from vestibular disease has a head tilt to the left.*

The most common reason for balance loss in dogs is vestibular syndrome. An animal with this condition has difficulty in keeping upright and leans to one side. The cause is unknown, and the condition usually clears up gradually of its own accord, though the dog may be left with a permanent slight tilt of the head.

Middle-ear infections are another cause. There may be accompanying paralysis of the facial and eye muscles. One side of the face will droop and saliva dribble from the side of the mouth. In inner ear infections (quite rare in dogs) the head may tilt by as much as 90° or more, causing the animal to spin, particularly when stressed. It may be unable to get up and will circle to the affected side when walking. Ear infections are treated with antibiotics and, possibly, surgical drainage. Facial paralysis and eye changes may be permanent, but the dog's sense of balance will normally improve.

Brain damage resulting from a skull fracture, tumor, drug intoxication, or stroke (this is less common in dogs than in humans) can also cause loss of balance. Accompanying symptoms may include seizures, sudden collapse, or depression. The dog may exhibit obsessive behavior, repeatedly banging its head against the wall or walking in a circle. If the seat of the problem is in the cerebellum, coordination of movement will be affected, indicated by tremor, a high-stepping walk, and a straddling stance. The prognosis and treatment will vary, depending on the nature of the underlying disease.

Apparent Loss of Balance

There are several conditions that can, in their early stages, look like damage to the ear–brain balance mechanism. It is important, therefore, to have your vet examine your dog as soon as possible to eliminate these causes. Provide as much information as possible about your dog's behavior. Anything you can tell the vet about the onset of the dog's symptoms will aid diagnosis.

▲ *This healthy dog climbs a ladder easily, but some diseases can cause a total or partial loss of balance.*

▶ *The organs of balance are located in the inner ear. Sound waves, transmitted from the ear drum by the bones of the middle ear, are converted to impulses in the cochlea and then conveyed to the brain.*

THE EAR

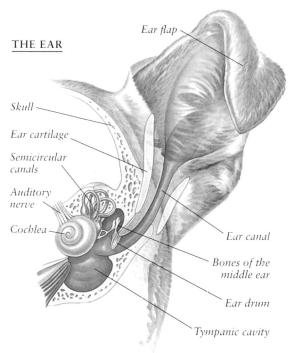

Ear flap

Skull

Ear cartilage

Semicircular canals

Auditory nerve

Cochlea

Ear canal

Bones of the middle ear

Ear drum

Tympanic cavity

● *My 10-year-old Rough Collie, Buddy, keeps falling over to his right side. It started quite suddenly. The vet prescribed some tablets and says Buddy should recover, but I'm not sure what's wrong. Can you help?*

This sounds like vestibular syndrome, a disease of older dogs where balance is disturbed. There is usually no obvious cause, but the prognosis is good in most cases, so I'm sure your vet is right to say it will clear up. As Buddy becomes used to his "sloping world," he should stop falling over, and the other symptoms of head tilt and imbalance will then gradually subside.

● *My English Setter, Charlie, is being treated for a middle-ear infection that has made him lose balance. What can I do to help him?*

Charlie will be feeling acute distress (just as a human would) that his sense of balance has disappeared. Rest and reassurance are Charlie's most important needs in the initial stages. You may have to assist him to walk—a soft, wide sling around his chest behind his front legs may help as he is probably very heavy—and move him into position so that he can relieve himself. Keep him away from stairs and other dangerous places. As Charlie's mobility improves, steady him with a hand on each side of his back and encourage him to walk slowly. If he tries to rush or turns corners too fast, he is likely to fall over.

Muscular weakness and collapse after a bout of severe vomiting and diarrhea, for example, may make the dog appear to lean to one side when it tries to walk. A number of diseases of the nerves and muscles can have a similar effect.

Joint stiffness in an older, arthritic dog may often be worse in one leg than the others. This can make the dog appear to wobble, and the owner may think its balance is affected. The stiffness and stumbling will be worst when the dog first gets up, and then gradually wear off.

Spinal cord diseases can cause one-sided partial paralysis of the legs. In certain diseases the gait is likely to be wobbly (a condition known as ataxia). It is seen in "wobbler syndrome," a disease that affects Dobermans in particular and is caused by unstable vertebrae in the neck. Intervertebral disk problems in Dachshunds, causing weakness or paralysis of the hindlegs, will display similar symptoms.

Partial or total blindness that causes a dog to bump into things can sometimes look like a loss of balance.

Sedative drugs, including anticonvulsants prescribed for epilepsy, can make a dog wobbly and unbalanced. Dogs also appear uncoordinated when recovering from general anesthesia.

Vomiting

AS ANY OWNER KNOWS, DOGS ARE NOT FUSSY about what they eat. Scavenging brings them into contact with all kinds of unsuitable foods, from the spoiled contents of garbage cans to carcasses and filth. Vomiting is a natural response to an unsettled stomach, and an occasional episode need not cause alarm—especially if it can be traced to a source such as rotten apples lying under the tree. Along with scavenging, overeating is one of the most common reasons why dogs vomit. Motion sickness is another; it is never a good idea to feed a dog just before a journey.

You may notice several signs before your dog vomits, such as excess drooling, licking of the lips, and repeated swallowing. Always try to be aware of what your dog has been eating, and if it vomits, look to see what it consists of. If it's undigested food from its bowl, your dog has probably just eaten too fast. This may be typical canine greediness, or it may be a sign that the dog feels threatened—perhaps by the arrival of a new pet or an unfamiliar person in the house. Modifying the dog's feeding regime should overcome this. Food that is brought up undigested is said to be regurgitated, rather than vomited up. It will be mixed with saliva and compacted so that often it looks like a sausage.

When to Call Your Vet

A vomiting dog can often be treated at home (see box), but contact your vet at once if the vomiting is repeated, is accompanied by severe diarrhea, or if the vomit is flecked with blood (like coffee granules), the dog has a bloated stomach,

▼ *This owner is raising the food bowl while her Setter eats. This can help prevent gastric bloat, a problem in some deep-chested dogs. Vomiting is often an early sign.*

● *I have a 4-month-old Irish Setter, Rusty. She is a lovely dog and very active, but she keeps bringing up her food, usually within half an hour of eating. What do you think the problem could be?*

Rusty could have a condition known as megaesophagus, which is hereditary in Irish Setters. The esophagus (food pipe) is dilated, which means that food cannot pass down into the stomach but comes back up—Rusty isn't actually vomiting but regurgitating her food. In Irish Setters the condition is usually diagnosed when the puppy is first weaned onto solid food, but it's also seen in other breeds later in life. You should consult your vet at once to check for complications associated with this condition and to discuss the options for treatment. Careful long-term monitoring is likely to be essential.

● *About two or three times a year we keep our in-laws' dogs when the family goes away. All the dogs get along fairly well together, but Moocher, our 6-year-old crossbreed, gets very anxious about his food. He eats so fast he throws up. This goes on for about a week after the other dogs have gone home. Can we do anything about it?*

Try feeding Moocher separately from the other dogs. Take him into another room and speak reassuringly while putting his food down. Hold him back for a few minutes to let him see that there is no competition. You may also wish to give him smaller portions and give them more often. When the other dogs visit again, ensure that they are fed separately from Moocher.

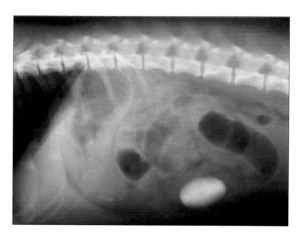

▲ *This X-ray shows a pencil eraser lodged in a dog's intestine (visible as white object, bottom right). Sometimes a swallowed object will obstruct the gut, causing vomiting and diarrhea.*

seems fevered, or is distressed. Even if the problem turns out to be fairly simple, prolonged vomiting can lead to dehydration, with serious consequences. But the vomiting may be a symptom of a major underlying problem—the dog may have gastroenteritis, an ulcer or tumor, or an obstruction of the gut, for example.

Dogs that are heavily infected with gastrointestinal worms may vomit because the worms are blocking part of the digestive tract. It is more common in puppies than adults. A blockage of the gut caused by a swallowed foreign body or a buildup of uneliminated waste due to constipation may have the same effect. Canine distemper, parvovirus, and infective enteritis (see pages 46–47) can all cause severe vomiting. The first two can be prevented if you keep up to date with your dog's vaccinations.

Vomiting and diarrhea may be symptoms of acute gastric bloating caused by excess gas. This is a serious condition requiring fast action, so consult your vet without delay. Deep-chested breeds such as Boxers, Irish Setters, and German Shepherds are prone to gastric torsion, in which the gas-filled stomach twists, causing rigidity and pain. Minimize the risk of bloating by waiting at least an hour after feeding before exercising your dog. If your dog swallows a lot of air when eating, spread its food across the bottom of the bowl so that it has to take smaller bites.

Treating Vomiting at Home

Try this if your dog has vomited only once and does not have other symptoms such as diarrhea or a bloated stomach. Consult your vet.

1. Withhold all food for 12 hours.

2. Restrict access to water—only a cupful approximately every 2 hours. Never give a vomiting dog milk.

3. Rest the dog and keep it warm.

4. After 12 hours, if vomiting has not recurred, give the dog a bland meal of an easily digestible protein and carbohydrates—cottage cheese, boiled chicken, or white fish mixed with boiled rice in a ratio of one part protein to four parts rice. Feed small amounts every four hours. If the dog does not vomit again, gradually return to the normal diet over the next two days.

Diarrhea and Other Bowel Problems

DIARRHEA IS JUST ABOUT THE MOST COMMON reason for taking your dog to the vet. It is often caused by nothing more than overindulgence, over-rich food, or a sudden change of diet. Travel and heavy worm infestation can also disrupt bowel functions. Stress, seen most often in working dogs or those whose owners are frequently away from home, is another possibility. The best way to avoid diarrhea is to ensure that your dog is in overall good health by deworming it regularly and giving it its annual vaccinations, and by preventing it from scavenging.

If your dog has mild diarrhea and shows no other obvious symptoms, try treating it with the home remedy suggested for a vomiting dog (see pages 68–69). Don't let the dog become dehydrated. The large amounts of water lost through diarrhea must be replaced in frequent, controlled amounts. Too much water given all at once will only lead to vomiting. Take care that the dog doesn't drink from puddles and other unclean sources.

If other symptoms are present, especially vomiting and listlessness, you should contact your veterinarian without further delay. Diarrhea and vomiting together may be indications of a variety of illnesses, including canine distemper and parvovirus, infective enteritis, accidental poisoning, and gastric torsion. Look for indications of blood with the feces. A small amount of fresh red blood is not unusual if the dog has been repeatedly straining to pass feces, but the presence of dark, digested blood suggests damage to the gut lining, possibly due to a stomach ulcer or a tumor bleeding into the gut. It calls for urgent medical examination and treatment. You should also seek advice from your veterinarian if the dog seems exhausted and depressed, if the diarrhea lasts more than a few days, or if it stops and then recurs again.

▲ A dog scavenging among garbage gets hold of an old bone or other item of decayed food and picks up the organisms that cause diarrhea.

◀ Emergency treatment for fluid loss resulting from acute diarrhea is given as a solution of salt and glucose fed orally through a syringe.

With acute diarrhea, the most urgent require-ment is to replace lost fluids and restore the dog' body chemistry. Food should be withdrawn fo at least 12 hours and fluids given by mouth or intravenously. The vet may prescribe prepared powders, containing salt and glucose, that you add to a measured amount of water and admin-ister directly into the dog's mouth through a syringe. Antispasmodic drugs to calm the move-ment of the bowel, anti-inflammatory medicines, and antibiotics may also be given.

The diagnosis and treatment of chronic diar-rhea can be more difficult. Blood tests, examina-tion of fecal samples, and X-rays may have to be carried out. Endoscopy may be necessary to look at the bowel wall and take a biopsy, and your dog may have to stay in the veterinary hospital for further tests and treatment.

Flatulence and Constipation

As with humans, flatulence becomes a common affliction of older dogs as they begin to lose mus-cle tone in their bowels. It is more likely to dis-tress the owner than the dog. Slightly old meat or leftovers, milk and milk products, raw vegeta-bles, beans, and soybean products are known to produce excess gas in dogs, though their effect varies greatly between individuals. Gas may also occur if the dog eats greedily and gulps in air. Try feeding it from a wide, shallow dish so that the food is not piled up and the dog is forced to take smaller mouthfuls.

Constipation can cause intense discomfort to dogs. Inactive dogs, older dogs with less muscle tone, and male dogs with enlarged prostates are particularly likely to be sufferers. Lack of dietary fiber may also be a significant factor. Ask your veterinarian for information on diets, and make sure that your pet has 30 minutes' gentle exercise about an hour after eating. This will aid digestion and improve the dog's overall muscle tone.

▶ *Charcoal biscuits (at left of picture) can help reduce flatulence. A fiber-rich diet will prevent constipation. High-fiber mixer biscuit and bran (at right) help. Raw vegetables such as carrot are also an excellent source.*

● *How can I change my dog's diet without causing diarrhea?*

A… The best way is to introduce the changes gradually over three or four days, mixing the new food with the old in increasingly larger proportions.

● *My 4-year-old Collie, Sheba, suffers a lot from diarrhea. My friend tells me she has a food allergy. Is this likely?*

True food allergies are uncommon in dogs and difficult to confirm since it is necessary to demonstrate an immune-based response to something in the diet. Many vets prefer to use the term "dietary intolerance." This simply means that the dog is unable to tolerate a particular food. Chronic diarrhea may be a sign that this is the case. Ask your vet for advice about investigating Sheba's diet.

● *Is it true that soybean causes flatulence in dogs?*

Soybean, a source of protein in many commercial dog foods, contains raffinose, which seems to be indigestible to some dogs, reacting with bacteria in the gut to produce excess gas. It may be worth eliminating it from your dog's diet if there's a problem.

● *Sandy, my Cocker Spaniel, suffered badly from constipation in his last years, due to an enlarged prostate gland. Is there anything I can do to prevent my new puppy suffering the same problem?*

Constipation is commonly associated with diseases of the prostate gland. Prostatic diseases are related to testosterone, produced by unneutered males, so neutering your new dog will help to eliminate the cause.

Increased Appetite

DOGS ARE NATURAL SCAVENGERS AND rarely pass up the chance of a quick snack—certain breeds such as Beagles and Retrievers are renowned for their enormous appetites and nonselective feeding habits. The old saying that dogs will eat only what they need is simply not true—the fact that approximately one-third of dogs in the US and UK are overweight bears witness to that. Of course, owners frequently contribute to the problem by giving their dogs much food of much higher palatability than would be naturally available—a bit like offering your kids an unending diet of cookies and potato chips. Occasionally, however, a dog's increased appetite is not caused by greed but by one of a number of medical problems. The dog may eat indiscriminately, or develop an unusual or undesirable eating habit. Veterinarians call this "polyphagia."

Ruling Out the Obvious

There may be a perfectly simple explanation for your pet's increased appetite. If your dog is getting more exercise than usual, it will be burning up more calories and therefore require more frequent refueling. It is natural for a pregnant female, or one that is feeding puppies, to eat more. Is your dog still growing? Puppies and young dogs need to eat more than inactive elderly dogs. Are you underfeeding your dog? Check with the manufacturer's guides to see if you are giving roughly the correct amount of food for the dog's weight, keeping in mind that individual requirements vary enormously. Is the dog a healthy weight for its size or breed? Ask your veterinarian to weigh your pet and advise you. It is important to know if a hungry dog is gaining or losing weight. Needless to say, dogs on weight-reduction programs are likely to be hungry.

▲ Beagles have a reputation for greed and can sniff out food anywhere. If you have a dog with a boundless appetite, take special care to guard against obesity.

If you have ruled out all the obvious causes, then you should seek further advice from your veterinarian. Intestinal worms (see pages 50–51) are common causes of increased appetite, and your vet can carry out a simple test to establish whether they are present in the dog's stools, or feces. Prepare for this by taking a sample with you. If worms are ruled out, the vet will look for disorders of eating and swallowing that leave hunger unsatisfied. You may be asked if there has been a recent alteration in the appearance of your dog's stools, since this can be an indication

● *My German Shepherd, Tara, has developed some unpleasant eating habits—she demands food even after we have fed her, steals food from the kitchen, and even eats her own feces. How can I stop her doing this?*

A dog with these habits may have a behavioral problem (see pages 142–143), but if Tara is losing weight as well, she could be seriously ill. German Shepherds are prone to a disease called exocrine pancreatic insufficiency (EPI), which means that the food passing through the gut is not digested properly. The feces are often bulky, pale, and greasy, and may smell offensive. Since they contain undigested food, the dog—who is hungry all the time—will return to them to satisfy its appetite. The condition can be treated, with varying degrees of success, by putting the dog on an easily digested special diet with enzyme supplements.

● *Mitzi, our Yorkshire Terrier, used to have a small appetite. Since we acquired a new puppy, however, she has started gobbling her food down as quickly as possible. She even steals food from Tim's bowl. She is becoming a little plump. Why is she eating so much, and how can we stop it?*

Mitzi seems to be perturbed by Tim's arrival. It may be that she is worried that Tim is going to eat her food and is playing a dominant role by eating the pup's food. Very rapid eating is not good for Mitzi's digestion and may lead to flatulence. Try separating the dogs at mealtimes and remove the bowls after about 20 minutes, even if some food remains in them. If Mitzi is fed on canned food, you could try to slow down her rate of eating by pressing it firmly down into a wide tray with a fork. Another tip is to switch Mitzi to a commercial brand of food that is not so much to her liking, as this will make her less greedy and stop her from gobbling her food so fast.

of abnormal bowel function. The dog is unable to digest or absorb its food properly and is left permanently unsatisfied.

Disorders of the adrenal gland and pancreas, including sugar diabetes, may affect appetite, so it's wise to take a urine sample with you as well. Kidney disease can cause protein loss and muscle wasting, leading the dog to eat more. Some medicines have the effect of increasing appetite, so be sure to inform the vet if your dog has received any recent treatment.

Abnormal Signs

A sudden increase in appetite may have an obvious cause, such as an unusual spurt of activity, growth (in a young dog), pregnancy, or underfeeding. If the dog's eating habits have the following characteristics, there may be an underlying medical problem:

● The dog demands food at unusual times of day and is unsatisfied when its meal is finished.

● It eats less selectively and sometimes ingests inedible matter. This is called "pica."

● It eats more rapidly than normal, clearing its bowl as quickly as possible (this may be competitive, if sharing mealtimes with another dog).

● It eats feces—either its own or other animals', such as cows, sheep, or horses. This unpleasant habit is called "coprophagia."

▼ *"More please." If your dog is always hungry, and you are feeding the right amount of a good quality diet for its size and age, it may have a medical problem.*

Increased Thirst

DOGS MAY BECOME THIRSTY FOR ANY NUMBER of natural reasons. They pant to keep cool, losing water from their lungs in the form of vapor. This fluid must be replaced, so it is not surprising that thirst increases on a hot day, especially in heavy-coated dogs. A dog shut in a car or unventilated room on a hot or sunny day dehydrates very rapidly and must be given water to replace lost body fluids. After a long, exhausting chase, a dog will drink plentifully to replace the water it has lost trying to keep cool while running about. A pregnant female, or one that is nursing puppies, needs a higher intake of fluids than normal. A change in diet may have a marked effect on your dog's thirst. Some canned foods contain as much as 80 percent water, while dried ones may have as little as 9 percent. Foods that contain a lot of salt to improve palatability will obviously make your dog thirsty. Never try to prevent your dog from drinking fresh water unless your vet has specifically instructed you to do so. It could endanger its health.

Is There Something Wrong?

Increased thirst frequently accompanies illness in a dog. After a bout of vomiting and diarrhea, for example, a dog needs to drink greater amounts than normal to replace the body fluids it has lost. Surprising amounts of fluid can be lost through a bleeding or seeping wound, or a surface burn. Dogs being treated with certain drugs, such as steroids or diuretics, will also drink more. In all such cases, your veterinarian will have advised you to give your dog plenty to drink as part of its recovery program.

Sometimes, however, you may find no obvious reason for a sudden increase in your dog's thirst. Always consult your veterinarian, as the condition needs thorough investigation. It will help diagnosis if, before your visit, you make a note of the amount of water your dog has drunk during the previous 24 hours. If possible, take a urine sample with you. Collect a small amount

Signs of Increased Thirst

- Frequent visits to the water bowl.
- Drinking takes longer.
- The dog doesn't stray far from the water bowl. It may even fall asleep with its muzzle on the rim!
- The water bowl is always empty and needs frequent refilling.
- The dog may drink from unusual places, such the toilet bowl, rain puddles, or the bird bath.
- It urinates more frequently.

▼ *Dogs will often stop on warm, sunny days to lap from a stream or puddle, or even from a garden hose. The cause of the dog's thirst isn't hard to find. But there could be a major problem if the drinking never stops and your dog's water bowl is always empty.*

● **The vet has asked me to record how much my dog drinks over 24 hours. How do I do this?**

Fill the water bowl to a set level in the morning (make a mark on the side in some way). Over the next 24 hours, keep filling it to this level from a measured jug and make a note of how much you are adding. The total will be the amount your dog has drunk during that period.

● *My elderly Collie, Todd, is always drinking. He is hungry, too, but is looking thin. His tummy is swollen and his eyes look cloudy. Could he have diabetes?*

With this combination of symptoms, it is a very strong possibility. You must have your veterinarian examine Todd as soon as possible. The clouding of the eyes sounds like cataracts, one of the changes brought about by diabetes. It is irreversible, so the sooner the condition is diagnosed and treatment starts the better. Diabetes really isn't as frightening as it sounds. The animal hospital will show you how to care for Todd and administer his daily injection of insulin. Sometimes medication is given by mouth.

● *When Nell, my Shetland Sheepdog, became very ill and started drinking a lot, the vet advised me to have her spayed. Why was this?*

Your vet most probably found that Nell was suffering from pyometra, a life-threatening disease of the uterus that is accompanied by fever and a heavy thirst. It usually starts soon after the female's season ends. She vomits, becomes dehydrated, and collapses. There may be an unpleasant vaginal discharge. Spaying is normally the most successful treatment, though the condition can sometimes be treated medically.

in a clean, empty food container, or use a special scoop you can obtain from your veterinarian.

Your dog may be drinking a lot as the result of a fever (especially if it is accompanied by vomiting and weakness) or metabolic disorder. For example, if the kidneys are not functioning properly, the dog will drink more in order to replace the fluid that it is losing through excessive urination (see pages 76–77). Conversely, some dogs suffer from a psychological abnormality that makes them drink a lot, and so they urinate a lot. Some types of malignant tumor increase thirst by raising the levels of calcium in the blood, which leads to abnormal fluid loss.

Increased thirst is also a symptom of a number of hormonal diseases such as Cushing's syndrome (a disorder of the adrenal gland), diabetes insipidus (which affects the pituitary gland), and diabetes mellitus (sugar diabetes). In the latter, the pancreas fails to produce insulin, the hormone that controls the level of glucose (sugar) in the blood. It is relatively common in dogs, affecting as many as one in 100. Left untreated, the dog will become progressively ill, stop passing any urine, become comatose, and eventually die. The disease can be controlled with a daily injection of insulin, a carefully regulated diet, and measured amounts of exercise.

Urinary Problems

DISEASES OF THE URINARY TRACT ARE COMMON in the dog. There are a number of different causes, but the symptoms can be very similar, so it is important to give the vet an accurate description of what you have observed.

By far the most common urinary problems are bacterial infections in which the bladder lining becomes inflamed (cystitis): the dog feels as if it needs to pass urine most of the time, but will strain to do so and manage to pass a small amount only. It will have considerable discomfort, and males who normally lift their leg may adopt a squatting posture. Very often the urine is tinged with blood. Alternatively, the dog is likely to have an accident in the house. Dogs with diabetes are especially prone to urinary tract infections as the raised levels of glucose in the urine provide a breeding ground for bacteria.

Stones formed of crystallized salts may develop in the bladder and grow quite large. They often give rise to infections. Sometimes a stone moves into the urethra. In a male this can create a potentially life-threatening situation, as a large stone can completely block the flow of urine, causing acute kidney failure. Obstruction is less common in females as their urethras are not so narrow. Some breeds seem to form stones more readily than others. They include Dalmatians, Cocker Spaniels, Miniature Poodles, Shih Tzus, Dachshunds, and Yorkshire Terriers.

The symptoms of urinary obstruction are similar to those of cystitis. A vet can sometimes feel the stones if they are very large. X-rays and ultrasound will confirm the diagnosis. Special diets may be fed to try to dissolve the stones, and associated infections will be treated with antibiotics. The vet will usually attempt to "flush" a stone lodged in the urethra back into the bladder. If this fails, however, an operation may be needed to remove it.

Masses (benign and malignant tumors) in the bladder and urethra may also show symptoms of cystitis or lead to urinary blockage. A biopsy is necessary to determine the nature of the mass.

THE URINARY SYSTEM

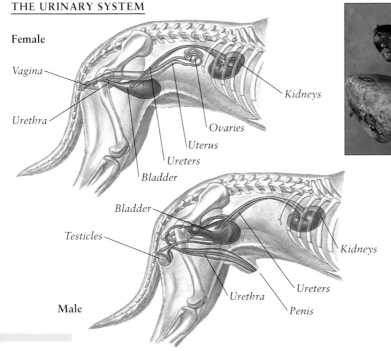

Female

Vagina

Urethra

Kidneys

Ovaries

Uterus

Ureters

Bladder

Bladder

Testicles

Kidneys

Ureters

Urethra

Penis

Male

▲ *Stones formed of crystallized mineral salts from a dog's bladder, approximately ¼ – ½ inch (8–16mm) in length.*

◄ *The kidneys filter waste from the blood. Urine then passes through the ureters to the bladder and is expelled through the penis or the vagina.*

Signs of Urinary Problems

Seek your vet's advice if your dog develops any of these symptoms.

- Blood in the urine. The urine is red or contains streaks of blood. Clots of blood may be seen. There may be bleeding when the dog is not urinating.
- Strong-smelling and/or dark-colored urine.
- Increased frequency of urination.
- Dog strains to pass small quantities of urine.
- Tries to pass urine without success (seek immediate help).
- Increased volume of urine (usually in association with increased thirst—see pages 74–75).
- Dog relieves itself indoors.
- Dog leaves a wet patch on getting up.
- Dog urinates when excited or after sudden movement.

● How do I collect a urine sample from my dog?

... Keep the dog indoors until you are sure it is ready to go. Collect the urine in a clean, shallow container such as a cookie sheet or pie tin, then transfer it to a clean jar or sample container (the vet can supply a special collection kit). A full tablespoon should be enough.

● My Scottie, Braveheart, has had an operation to remove bladder stones. Is there anything I can do to prevent new ones forming?

Try increasing his water intake so that he produces a greater quantity of urine to flush any developing crystals through his bladder. Diet can also be a factor. Your vet should be able to give you further advice following analysis of the stones.

● My 2-year-old Irish Setter, Saffron, was spayed several months ago. Since then I have noticed damp patches on the rug when she gets up from sleeping. Why is she doing this?

This requires investigation by your vet. Spayed females occasionally develop a leaky valve at the neck of the bladder (perhaps as a result of low estrogen levels). Sometimes an operation to pull the bladder forward in the abdomen will help, or the leakage can be controlled by long-term medication.

Urinary Incontinence

There are many possible causes of urinary incontinence (passing urine without being aware of it). It is more common in females than males and is often due to faulty control of the valves that regulate the flow of urine from the bladder to the urethra. Abnormalities of the bladder and vagina can also be responsible. Incontinence may occur in diseases affecting the nerves of the spinal cord, such as intervertebral disk disease, and in males with a prostate gland disorder.

Kidney Disease

The kidneys' filtering function can be disrupted as the result of chronic disease. Symptoms are slow to develop; they include an increased volume of urine and increased thirst. As the kidneys start to fail, toxic wastes accumulate in the body and the dog becomes progressively sicker, with symptoms of lethargy, loss of appetite, loss of weight, and bad breath. Long-term infection may lead to chronic kidney failure, resulting in degeneration and scarring of the kidneys, congenital defects, or cancer. In most cases the condition is irreversible, though medication and a low-protein diet may help control symptoms.

Acute kidney failure may follow from infectious disease, urinary obstruction, poisoning (including snakebite), or severe accidental injury. The urine may be discolored or contain blood clots, and the dog will vomit and have pain in the mid-back. If your dog suddenly stops urinating entirely, the problem can be life-threatening. You must take the dog to the vet immediately.

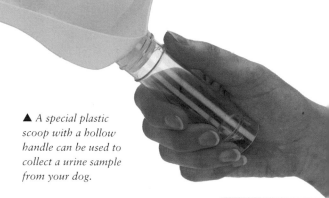

▲ *A special plastic scoop with a hollow handle can be used to collect a urine sample from your dog.*

Tumors and Cysts

TUMORS AND CYSTS ARE LUMPS (MASSES) THAT form anywhere in or on the body. If you find one, do not immediately assume that your dog has cancer. The majority of lumps are harmless, but they should always be investigated as soon as possible to be sure.

Tumors occur when cells in the body begin to divide and proliferate in an uncontrolled manner, producing a swelling or lump. Since every cell has the potential to start tumor growth, tumors can develop in any tissue or body organ. Malignant tumors grow very rapidly, forming irregularly shaped masses. They are aggressive, invading the surrounding tissues, and can spread through the lymphatic system or bloodstream to other parts of the body. This is called metastasis.

Benign tumors grow more slowly. They push aside normal tissues and are not invasive. The most common type, known as lipomas, develop in the fatty layer below the skin. They can often be left untreated, but may have to be removed if they grow very large or begin to cause the dog obvious discomfort.

Cysts are sacs of fluid or semi-solid (chalky) matter contained in a membrane. They may not alter shape or size for several months, or even years, and can usually be moved around beneath the skin with the fingers. They are often left untreated unless they become infected, cause discomfort, or become filled with fluid, when drainage may be necessary. In very rare cases, cysts may change into tumors.

Spotting Tumors Early

It is much easier to spot tumors on the skin or in the mouth than those inside the body. When grooming, run your hands over your dog's body and feel for lumps. Surface cancers may become inflamed, ulcerate, bleed, and change size rapidly. Breast tumors are most common in unspayed females over 6 years of age who have had no litters. They are rare in females spayed before coming in heat for the first time. About half of mammary tumors are benign, but it is important to identify the nature of the tumor as soon as possible. Even if malignant, tumors that are caught early can be treated before they spread.

If malignancy goes undetected, or if treatment is not successful, new tumors called "secondaries" develop in organs such as the lungs or liver. Treating these is much more difficult. The vet will discuss with you whether it is kinder to let nature take its course or to bring an early end to your pet's suffering (see pages 38–39).

◀ *This crossbred terrier has a hugely swollen mastocytoma, a type of skin tumor, on its neck. Mastocytomas are often, but not always, malignant. Some grow slowly, but others develop much more aggressively.*

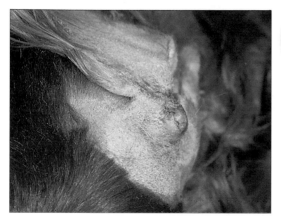

▲ *This cyst has developed in a Setter's ear. It will be surgically removed. Some cysts can be left if they are not causing the dog discomfort.*

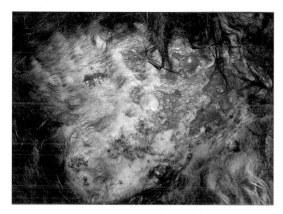

▲ *Squamous-cell carcinoma (malignant skin cancer) on the chest of a dog. Skin cancers are common and easier to detect than cancers of internal organs.*

● *Duke, my 8-year-old Bulldog, is putting on a bit of weight. About a year ago I felt a lump about the size of a golfball on his chest between his front legs. It hasn't grown any larger since then and doesn't appear to hurt him at all. What do you think it is?*

It is unwise to let a lump go this long without examination by the vet. However, from what you say about Duke's weight and age, and the length of time he has had the lump without noticeable change, it is most probably a lipoma—a harmless collection of fat cells. These are very common in dogs and can occur anywhere on the body. They normally cause problems only if they become very large or interfere with the normal movement of a limb.

● *Do dogs get leukemia?*

Yes, they do. Tumors of the white blood cells cause very serious illness. Symptoms include fever, enlargement of the lymph glands, and possibly the spleen and liver. Diagnosis is by blood tests and biopsy of the lymph nodes. Unfortunately, in most cases, there is no cure.

● *Should I examine Sally, my female Collie cross, for breast lumps?*

Yes, if she lets you do so, especially if she is more than 6 years old. Mammary (breast) tumors can be felt in their early stages as firm, irregularly shaped lumps, the size of a pea or smaller. They do not move easily. Detection before the disease has spread to all five sets of mammary glands greatly improves the chances of successful treatment for the dog.

Pathology Tests

No "lump" can be accurately diagnosed without pathology tests on the structure of the affected cells. The tissue for testing is removed in one of several ways. Fine-needle aspiration may be used to investigate surface tumors. A needle is passed into the center of the tumor and a sample of the cells withdrawn by suction. This is a straightforward test, and the dog may not even need sedating. In a biopsy a piece of the tumor is removed to see how the cells are arranged. It can be done with a large, hollow needle (tru-cut biopsy), a biopsy punch that removes a circle of tissue, or by surgically excising a sample of the tissue. In the majority of cases the dog will be sedated or

anesthetized. In an excisional biopsy the vet removes the tumor in its entirety in order to examine it microscopically.

In addition to the biopsy, the veterinarian will probably also arrange for blood tests and X-rays in order to check the dog's general health and to see if the tumor has spread. Once the biopsy has established the nature of the tumor, the vet can determine the course of treatment to be followed. Surgical removal may be indicated, but surgery is not the only method of dealing with a malignant tumor. Other treatments include chemotherapy, cryosurgery (freezing the tissues), and radiation therapy, either used alone or in combination with one another.

Lameness

LAMENESS MAY COME ON SUDDENLY. YOUR DOG is out exercising when it falters, comes to a stop, and is unable to put weight on one of its legs. Sometimes the symptoms develop more gradually. The dog has difficulty in moving on waking but loosens up during the day, and it may be some time before you realize that the problem is not getting any better. Any information you can give the vet will make diagnosis easier, so keep a note of which leg is affected (the dog may be so excited in the consulting room that this is not immediately apparent) and of the way it is walking. A stiff, hopping gait suggests damage to an upper joint. A dog that is reluctant to put weight on a leg may have a fracture. If it has a damaged foot, it will place the paw gingerly to the ground.

Often there's no need to look far for the cause of the lameness—a fall, jump, or collision that resulted in a fracture, sprain, or heavy bruising is clearly responsible. The fine-boned breeds such as Chihuahuas, Italian Greyhounds, and Maltese dogs are particularly prone to broken bones.

Before attempting to examine the affected leg, have someone restrain the dog for you. If the dog

LUXATION OF THE PATELLA

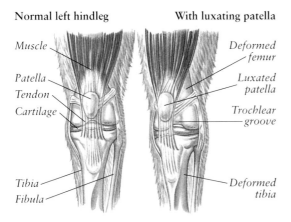

Normal left hindleg

Muscle
Patella
Tendon
Cartilage
Tibia
Fibula

With luxating patella

Deformed femur
Luxated patella
Trochlear groove
Deformed tibia

▲ *The patella or kneecap, a small oval bone, normally slides up and down in a groove in the femur, but in cases of luxating patella it moves out of position.*

seems fractious, apply a tape muzzle. Beginning at the paw, carefully and methodically examine the pads, between the toes, and the nails themselves (a broken claw can sometimes cause lameness). Look for cuts and bruises and for signs of heat, pain, or swelling, working your way carefully up the leg. If you have reason to suspect a serious injury, especially one affecting the back, don't attempt to examine the dog yourself but call your vet immediately for advice.

Non-accidental Injury

Developmental abnormalities of the bones and joints during growth (in the juvenile and young dog) and arthritis (most common in the older dog) are major causes of lameness. The breed is also a factor. The giant breeds are prone to hip dysplasia, growth-related bone pain, bone tumors, and torn ligaments, while small breeds with short, bandy legs are more likely to suffer from dislocating kneecaps (luxating patella).

The vet will probably decide to take an X-ray. This usually means anesthetizing the dog so that the limb can be manipulated and placed in the uncomfortable positions required. Samples of joint fluid may be taken at the same time for laboratory analysis. If diagnosis proves difficult, the dog may be referred to a specialist for nerve tests and advanced imaging techniques.

Many causes of lameness, such as fracture, dislocated joints, or developmental malformations, can be surgically corrected. Anti-inflammatory, pain-killing drugs (the aspirin family) are often given to relieve symptoms. In all cases, the vet will prescribe rest, or at least advise that exercise be restricted until the injury is healed. It should then be reintroduced slowly to avoid possible recurrence. The vet may also recommend gentle physiotherapy to restore movement to the limb or limbs. Obesity is often a major contributory factor to lameness, especially in the older dog. If your dog is overweight, the vet may suggest that you put it on a slimming program.

Some Causes of Lameness

Osteochondrosis (OD): A disease of the cartilage that occurs most often in large, fast-growing dogs such as Rottweilers and German Shepherds. It can affect all the joints, especially the elbow and shoulder, causing pain and lameness. Often requires surgical correction.

Panosteitis (growing pain): Most common in large breeds during their rapid growth phase. Can be treated with anti-inflammatory drugs and dietary restrictions.

Hip Dysplasia: Congenital abnormality of one or both hips. Develops during puppy's growth period but may not be apparent until early adulthood. There is a characteristic bunny-hopping gait and stiffness on getting up. Affected dogs may develop arthritis in later life.

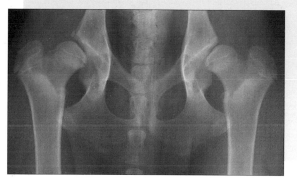

▲ *An X-ray of a 6-month-old German Shepherd shows severe dysplasia in both hips. The head of the femur should normally be smooth and well fitting.*

▲ *A cart allows a dog without use of its hindlimbs to exercise. Appliances like this are helpful in some circumstances but must be used carefully to avoid discomfort in a chronically disabled dog.*

Luxating Patella (dislocating kneecap): An inherited defect in several smaller breeds. Sometimes causes acute lameness. The kneecap often goes back into place of its own accord or clicks back into position if the leg is massaged. If the problem recurs, surgery may be needed to fix the kneecap in its groove.

Torn Ligament: The cruciate ligament of the knee joint is prone to rupture. Affects large, heavy breeds.

Perthes Disease: A degenerative disease of the hip joints of small breeds. Requires surgical correction.

Arthritis: Inflammation of the joints caused by infection, auto-immune disease, or gradual degeneration of the bones and ligaments. Painkillers and anti-inflammatory drugs can help.

Spinal Damage or Disease: Disk disease (most common in dogs with long backs), spinal injuries, or wobbler syndrome (a disease of the neck vertebrae) may cause stumbling, weakness, stiffness of the limbs, or even paralysis. Do not move the dog, and seek urgent help.

Lyme Disease (Borreliosis): Most commonly manifests itself as lameness about a month after exposure to infection. Joint pain is treated with antibiotics and anti-inflammatory drugs.

Bone Tumor: Affects large or giant breeds especially. Very painful. Weakened bone may fracture.

● *Otto, my 2-year-old Rottweiler, has to have an operation to replace his cruciate ligament. What does this involve?*

The anterior cruciate ligament of the knee is liable to rupture in some large breeds at a surprisingly young age. In dogs weighing more than 20lbs (9kg), the forces on the joint are such that the ligament will not heal. A graft made from the tissues up the side of the leg is used to replace the damaged ligament. Recovery takes about 3 to 6 months, and exercise should be severely restricted. It is not uncommon for the ligament in the opposite joint to rupture subsequently.

● *When Hannah, my Cairn, started hopping and yelping, I thought she had broken her leg. Her lameness turned out to be caused by a cyst between her toes. Is this common?*

Skin complaints in the feet quite often cause lameness. Sometimes the root of the problem can be difficult to find, especially if the foot is well covered in hair and the dog is in pain. Cysts on the feet may be caused by an infection or by the presence of a foreign body.

Paw Problems

DOGS ARE AT CONSIDERABLE RISK OF CUTTING a paw after stepping on broken glass, a discarded drink can, or other garbage. An injured paw often bleeds very profusely at first. Keep yourself and the dog calm; place a pressure bandage on the wound to try and stop the flow of blood (see First Aid and Emergencies, page 98). Do not attempt to remove any piece of glass or other embedded object yourself as this may cause further bleeding and/or damage. Take the dog immediately to the vet or emergency center. Most cuts will need stitching under a general anesthetic. Cuts affecting the tendons and the pads of the feet can be slow to heal, and strict rest and immobilization of the affected foot may be necessary. Antibiotics are given to clear up and prevent infection.

A broken or cracked claw is painful and causes lameness and irritation. The dew claws (the extra claw on the inside of the leg) seem particularly susceptible, perhaps because owners have a tendency to forget about them and let them grow too long. The damaged nail will need removing to ease pain and prevent the dog from causing

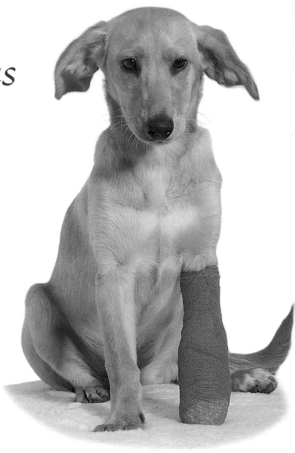

▲ *An injured paw is often slow to heal. You should try to prevent the dog from putting weight on it, but this can be difficult in an active dog.*

▲ *A vet removes a grass seed trapped between a dog's toes. The dog gnaws the site to relieve the irritation, and the seed's serrated barbs push it deeper into the skin.*

further injury by licking the site. If the nail bed has not been damaged, the claw will regrow though it is often misshapen. Occasionally dogs suffer from nail disease in more than one foot. Bacterial, viral, and fungal infections are possible causes, as are cancers. Diagnosis can be difficult and a biopsy is often required.

When an object such as a splinter or grass seed gets caught between the toes, it will sometimes penetrate the skin of the foot and then move deeper into the tissues. The dog's body reacts to this by surrounding the offending object with inflammatory cells. These eventually form a cyst or abscess—a painful, irritating swelling that sometimes ruptures to release the foreign body, together with pus and blood. All cysts require veterinary treatment. If it is particularly painful, the dog may need to be sedated or anesthetized.

● *How do I deal with a splinter in my dog's paw?*

A ... Get someone to hold the dog for you while you examine the paw. If you can see the splinter easily, remove it with a pair of tweezers and then soak the paw in warm, salty water for a few minutes. Apply an antiseptic and dry the paw gently and thoroughly. If the splinter is deeply embedded, have the vet remove it.

● *Our dog's claws are brittle and crack often. How should we look after them?*

Knocks and blows incurred when the dog is digging or scrambling can cause claws to crack. Overlong claws seem to be particularly susceptible, so keep them trimmed and clean. You can relieve the pain of cracked nails by gently soaking them in warm water and lifting away any loose pieces. Make sure you are giving your dog a balanced diet—this will help strengthen claws.

● *This fall we noticed that Patti, our Labrador Retriever, was licking and chewing her paws excessively. On examination, we could see some small, moving orange specks. What were they?*

They were probably the parasitic larvae of the harvest mite. These emerge in the late summer and fall, especially in woodland and grassy areas, and attack the feet of dogs and other animals, causing localized itching. This can be very severe in hypersensitive dogs. Treatment involves applying topical antiparasitic agents and (occasionally) anti-inflammatory drugs to relieve the symptoms.

Once the foreign body has been removed, antibiotics will clear up the problem in most cases. Sometimes an interdigital swelling may turn out to be a tumor. These should always be biopsied. Most will require surgical removal.

Excessive Licking

Aside from the lameness, the most obvious sign of damage to a paw or paws is constant licking and chewing. When only one foot is affected, the problem is likely to be localized (for example, a small cut or a cyst). But if more than one foot is involved, there is a strong probability that the dog has a generalized skin allergy (see Itchy Skin Conditions, pages 52–53). A range of tests may be required, possibly including blood tests, hypersensitivity tests, skin scrapings, fungal cultures, and biopsies.

Acral lick dermatitis, which usually affects one foot only, occurs when a dog excessively licks a particular area of skin (usually just above the paw), making it bald. In time the skin becomes ulcerated, thickened, and pigmented. There are many possible causes of this behavior, including boredom, localized pain and injury, parasites, and allergies. Diagnosis can be very difficult, and a full history is needed. Treatment depends on the cause and may range from administering topical ointments or creams to taking steps to alleviate behavioral disorders.

Routine Care of the Paws

Routine care and examination of the paws play an important part in the prevention of disease. Many dogs seem to have sensitive feet and resent them being felt and prodded. But if regular checking begins in puppyhood, these problems are less likely to develop.

● **Look for damaged claws,** foreign bodies, and swellings between the toes, cuts on any part of the paw, and bare patches of inflamed, crusty skin. Have a veterinarian examine your dog if you discover any of these problems.

● **Check the paws after exercise** for cuts, scratches, ticks, thorns, and other debris, especially if the dog has been walking or running over rough ground.

● **Always dry wet paws** carefully after swimming, exercising in wet grass, or bathing, as a precaution against infection.

● **Prevent the dog from licking** a sore or irritated paw by using an Elizabethan collar (see page 57) or covering the foot with a bandage.

● **If chemical contamination** to a paw or paws is suspected, prevent the dog from licking, as above. Sponge the area carefully with cold water and consult your veterinarian.

● **Trim the claws** regularly. Overlong claws are more susceptible to damage and can cause the dog discomfort.

▶ *In an extreme case of neglect, this dog's claws have grown so long it can no longer walk.*

Mouth and Teeth Problems

A PUPPY'S FIRST TEETH EMERGE AT ABOUT 3–4 weeks, and by the time it is 6 weeks it should have its full quota of 28 temporary teeth. These begin to fall out at about 4 months, when the first permanent teeth, the incisors at the front of the mouth, start to emerge. Over the next two months they will be followed by the premolars and molars, used to shear meat off bones and to crush and break up food, and then by the canine teeth, the long, deep-rooted teeth used in defense and attack. Teething in puppies is less traumatic than in humans, though there may be occasional soreness of the gums and the puppy will want to chew a great deal. Provide plenty of hard, safe chews for it to gnaw on, rather than your shoes and furniture.

Sometimes a dog will retain one or several of its deciduous (baby) teeth after the permanent teeth have begun to emerge. Consequently, as the permanent teeth come through, they are forced to grow out of position, and this can cause long-term dental problems. The retained teeth must be removed as soon as possible under anesthetic, so consult your veterinarian if you think your puppy has this problem. The cause of retained deciduous teeth is unknown, though it appears to be hereditary in some breeds.

Q&A

● **How often should I have my dog's teeth looked at by the vet?**

When you take it for its annual vaccinations. If your dog has a history of mouth disease, your vet may recommend dental examinations every six months. Mouth lesions may occur as part of a generalized illness, so your vet will often examine the mouth during a routine clinical examination to establish the cause of ill health.

● **Can you re-implant a dog's tooth that has been knocked out?**

Yes, if the root hasn't been fractured and it is treated quickly. Pick up the tooth by the crown (the white end) without touching the root, and place it in a container of cool milk. This will prevent the delicate tissues around the root from drying out while you rush the dog to the vet. After the tooth has been replaced in the jaw, the pulp will probably die, but root-canal treatment can be given when the tooth is secure in the jaw again.

● **How do I set about brushing my dog's teeth?**

Start by gently cleaning the front teeth with a brush fitted on your finger until your dog is used to the procedure; then you can tackle the ones at the back with a long-handled brush. Canine toothpastes contain enzymes that destroy plaque, plus antibacterial and antiviral agents. If your dog refuses to cooperate, use chews impregnated with enzymes instead.

Some Common Conditions of the Mouth

Signs	Possible cause	Action
Bad breath. Reddened and receding gums. Difficulty in chewing. Drooling (saliva may be blood-tinged). Signs of mouth pain (pawing at mouth, rubbing head on ground)	Periodontal disease	Descaling to remove plaque. Tooth extraction in extreme cases. Use of longterm oral hygiene preparations
Too many teeth (especially obvious in the dog's canine teeth). Abnormally angled teeth. Inability to close mouth fully. Reddened gums	Retained deciduous teeth	Removal of retained teeth under anesthetic
Swelling of face. Difficulty in chewing. Signs of mouth pain	Abscess	Antibiotics. Tooth extraction if necessary
Bad breath. Lump in mouth. Bleeding from mouth	Mouth tumor	Treat as urgent problem. Biopsy or removal

▲ A baby canine (left) retained behind the permanent tooth.

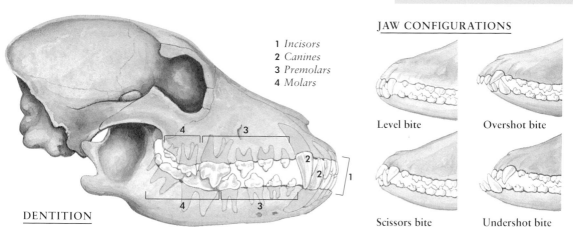

1 *Incisors*
2 *Canines*
3 *Premolars*
4 *Molars*

JAW CONFIGURATIONS

Level bite

Overshot bite

Scissors bite

Undershot bite

DENTITION

▲ *An adult dog has 42 teeth. In a level or scissors bite the upper and lower incisors meet exactly or very closely. In an overshot or undershot bite they do not align. The latter is "normal" in breeds such as Bulldogs.*

The Importance of Oral Hygiene

Many owners assume that bad breath, yellow teeth loaded with tartar, and red, inflamed gums are normal in a dog, but they can be prevented with good oral care. Examine your dog's mouth from an early age as a matter of routine. If you wait until the mouth is painful, the dog will not tolerate you or anyone else coming near the source of the problem. Regular brushing prevents periodontal disease, the commonest mouth disease in dogs. A buildup of bacterial plaque on and around the teeth leads to inflamed gums (gingivitis). The gums ulcerate, and the plaque mineralizes to form tartar or calculus. Infection spreads rapidly into the periodontal space between the bony socket and the root of the tooth, destroying the bone that holds the tooth in place. This causes the dog severe pain, and the tooth eventually falls out. The process often occurs simultaneously in several teeth.

Caries (bacterial decay) is less common in dogs than humans, though some breeds such as the Labrador Retriever appear to have a hereditary weakness in the enamel that can lead to its formation. Sugar in the diet and lack of oral hygiene does the rest. As with our own teeth, early decay can be treated by drilling and filling the tooth. In extreme cases, however, extraction may be the only option.

In a young dog, if a tooth is fractured or lost as a result of accidental injury, the vet may be able to restore the end of the tooth, leaving the pulp alive. The tooth may then continue to grow. Neglect of a fractured tooth may cause infection, leading to the formation of a painful abscess in the bone at the end of the tooth root.

A common complaint of the gums (especially in Boxers) is a lump called an epulis. It is harmless and is easily removed. However, many other mouth tumors are malignant. Early treatment is necessary if complete removal is to be successful. It is essential that veterinary advice be sought as soon as possible if you notice a lump or lesion in your dog's mouth.

▼ *A dental chew is a painless way of keeping your dog's teeth free of plaque.*

Ear Problems

IN THE WILD, HEARING IS A VITAL PART OF AN animal's survival kit, enabling it both to find its food and avoid predators. Ears are also used for balance (see pages 66–67) and play an important part in communication. In the dog, they come in a variety of shapes, from the small, erect ears of the German Shepherd to the large, pendulous flaps of the Basset Hound.

Dogs with long, floppy ears have a particular tendency to ear problems, but they are common in all dogs. Signs to look out for are vigorous head shaking, scratching of the ear, loss of hair on the earflaps, crusting, swelling, redness, discharge, odor, head tilting, and loss of balance. Allowing an ear problem to persist for long can make subsequent treatment more difficult, and may even lead to deafness, permanent loss of balance, or chronic irritation.

The ear consists of an outer, middle, and inner section (see page 67). The vet will try to discover which part of the ear is involved and whether the problem is confined to the ear or is part of a more generalized disease. The dog may have to be sedated or anesthetized to allow all the ear to be examined. X-rays may sometimes be required to look at the middle and inner ears. Diagnostic tests also include skin scrapes, allergy testing, fungal and bacterial cultures, and biopsies.

The skin of the outer ear is a common site for allergies (see pages 52–53). It becomes very itchy and inflamed and, combined with the humidity of the ear, produces an ideal environment for bacterial and fungal growth. A buildup of wax in the ear, which can lead to secondary infections, is also often related to food allergies. In all such cases the vet will usually run hypersensitivity tests to establish the cause of the allergy and decide appropriate action.

Loss of Hearing

Owners do not always realize their dog is going deaf. Suspect a problem if your dog is failing to respond to noises that normally provoke its interest or has difficulty in locating sources of sound. Special hearing tests for dogs are now available in many animal hospitals. A straightforward and completely curable cause of deafness is a buildup of wax in the ear canals. Excess

Common Ear Problems

SIGNS	POSSIBLE CAUSE	ACTION
Sudden onset, severe head shaking and scratching	Foreign body in ear, e.g., grass seed	Dog will be sedated or anesthetized to aid removal of object
Sudden onset, severe head shaking, discharge, odor, pain (head rubbing)	Acute infection	Topical antibiotic, antifungal, and anti-inflammatory drugs
Intense scratching, a black, waxy discharge	Ear mites	Acaricidal (mite-killing) agent in both ears. Highly contagious; treat all in-contact pets
Sudden onset, swelling in one or both ears, no pain	Hematoma due to trauma, e.g., head shaking or scratching	Drainage, treatment of underlying cause, e.g., ear mites
Inflamed, itchy skin, possible hair loss	Atopic allergy, possibly with secondary bacterial and/or fungal infection	Antibiotics/anti-inflammatories to alleviate symptoms. Hypersensitivity tests to find cause
Severe, permanent head tilt	Middle and/or inner ear disease (see pages 66–67)	Dependent on cause

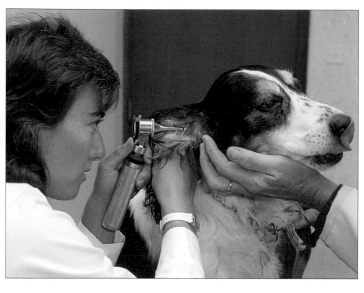

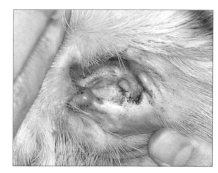

◀ *An otoscope, an illuminated tube with a magnifying lens, is used to examine a spaniel's outer ear.*

▼ *Reddened, sore skin around the ear canal is the sign of a severe infection that is causing considerable discomfort.*

hair in the ear canals helps the wax accumulate, so it should be removed regularly. Some dogs, particularly German Shepherds, tend to produce excess wax. Cleaning once a week with a special cleansing agent will help prevent this. Consult your vet. Some products can cause irritation. If this occurs, stop their use immediately.

Deafness is also caused by disease or damage to the ear drum or to the middle and inner ear. Some breeds of dog, particularly Dalmatians, have an hereditary tendency to deafness. As in humans, deafness sometimes occurs in

old age. It is usually gradual in onset, the ability to hear low-frequency noise remaining longest. If you suspect that your dog's hearing is beginning to fail, it's a good idea to get it used to the sound of a handclap. That way, once it ceases to pick up your familiar whistle or call, it will still be able to locate you.

▼ *Use a piece of clean gauze to wipe away accumulated wax from the top of the ear canals.*

Q A …

● **How should I care for my spaniel's ears?**

Don't let the hair on the earflaps become too long and matted; groom them regularly and dry the ears well after swimming. From time to time, when your dog is asleep, flip the earflap over so that the ear canal is exposed to the air.

● **My dog, Gopher, needs to have his ear canals surgically removed. Why is this necessary?**

Chronic inflammation of the ear canals can cause the lining to thicken. If this isn't controlled, the canals will eventually become completely blocked, causing the dog further complications and discomfort throughout its life. Surgical removal of the diseased tissues will prevent this happening. The canals may also be removed if there are cancerous growths.

Eye Problems

DOGS' EYES ARE VULNERABLE TO DAMAGE AND disease. It is important that you pay particular attention to your dog's eyes, noting any gradual or sudden changes in appearance. Clean them regularly with damp cotton balls or veterinary eyewipes. Several eye diseases are hereditary in certain breeds. To make sure they are not passed on, you should have your dog's eyes checked by a veterinary ophthalmologist before it is used for breeding. Screening programs are run in conjunction with veterinary associations and kennel clubs in many countries. Ask your veterinarian for information.

Disease or damage to the eye can give rise to a wide range of symptoms, from reddening of the eyelids to cloudiness and opacity of the lens (see box). The veterinarian will first check the eyelids and cornea (the sensitive surface of the eye) for superficial damage. Sometimes a stain is applied to show if there is corneal damage. Examination of the eye's interior is carried out with an ophthalmoscope, a powerful source of light. Drops may be given to dilate the pupil so that the back of the eye can be viewed. The pressure inside the eye may be measured to test for glaucoma, a hereditary disease in some breeds that affects the optic disk and causes loss of vision.

A very large number of eye problems are correctable by surgery. In extreme cases, the veterinarian may have to recommend removal of the eyeball (enucleation) rather than allow the dog to continue in chronic pain.

Some Common Problems

The eyelids are a frequent source of problems. Sometimes they turn in—a condition known as entropion—so that the lashes brush across the cornea and damage it. Selective breeding to alter the shape of the eye has increased its incidence in some breeds, such as Chows. Ectropion is the opposite: the lower lid hangs open and catches dust, as in Bloodhounds.

Conjunctivitis, inflammation of the membrane that lines the inner surfaces of the eyelid and the exposed part of the eye, is usually the result of infection, accidental injury such as a scratch or blow, or a trapped foreign body. There may be reddening of the eyes, increased tear production, heavy blinking, and a discharge. Failure to produce tears or spread them across the the surface of the eye damages the cornea. Dry eyes appear dull and sticky and are painful. If the cornea itself is diseased or injured, it lets in water from tears and turns cloudy or whitish-blue. Corneal damage and ulcers are most common in breeds with bulging eyes, such as Pekingese.

Cataracts, opacity of the lenses that can cause blindness, are hereditary in some breeds but may occur in all dogs. They are often a symptom of diabetes mellitus. Diseases of the retina, such as progressive retinal atrophy (PRA), and the optic nerve can sometimes cause blindness, though the eye itself looks completely normal. Dogs are able

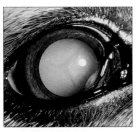

Cataracts

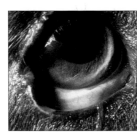

Ectropion

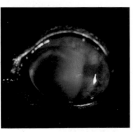

Corneal inflammation

Conjunctivitis

▲ *All the working parts of the eye are vulnerable to disease and injury. Take note of any changes in color and appearance, and have your veterinarian examine your dog's eyes as soon as you suspect a problem.*

ANATOMY OF THE EYE

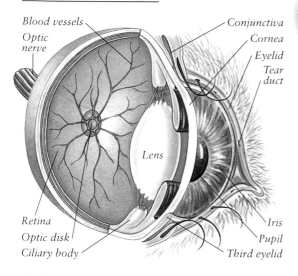

Blood vessels
Optic nerve
Conjunctiva
Cornea
Eyelid
Tear duct
Lens
Retina
Optic disk
Ciliary body
Iris
Pupil
Third eyelid

▲ *The cornea covers the exposed part of the eye and admits light through the pupil and the lens on to the retina, the sensory membrane that transmits visual nerve impulses, via the optic disk and nerve, to the brain.*

to cope with blindness remarkably well, having acute hearing and a good sense of smell. A blind dog can still enjoy a high quality of life.

Caring for Damaged Eyes

The veterinarian will often prescribe eye drops or ointments. The bottle of drops should first be warmed in your hand. Place one hand firmly under the dog's chin. Hold the bottle upside down between the first finger and thumb of the other hand. Resting the other three fingers on top of the dog's head, drop the medicine into the eye. Apply ointment by squeezing a little onto a clean finger and smearing it carefully and gently along the inside of the eyelid.

Discharging eyes should be bathed with warm salty water in a solution of 1 teaspoon per pint. You should protect a dog with sore or damaged eyes from exposure to bright lights, heat sources, drafts, and wind, and keep it from swimming. An Elizabethan collar (see page 57) will stop the dog from rubbing its eyes and causing further damage. A relatively new way of protecting the eyes is to use clear contact lenses. By acting as a form of bandage, these allow the damaged eye to heal underneath.

● *Cherie, my Poodle, keeps bumping into things. Her pupils have become quite pearllike, and I'm afraid she has cataracts. Can they be operated on, as in humans, or will she go totally blind?*

As long as the rest of the eye is healthy, removal of the lens containing the cataract may indeed restore some sight, though Cherie will never see as well as she used to. Replacement lenses are not normally put in dogs' eyes as they do not require close vision as humans do for reading or sewing, and can usually manage quite well with reduced vision.

● *My Boston Terrier, Wilma, always has tears on her face. What is causing them, and what should I do?*

Dogs with short noses often have ineffective tear ducts. These drain the tears from the corner of the eye down the nose, but if they are obstructed, the tears have nowhere to go and spill over onto the face (epiphora). Have your vet examine Wilma to see there is no other cause such as conjunctivitis. Sometimes an attempt is made to flush the tear ducts, but there is often no cure for poor drainage. You should clean and bathe the eyes regularly with cotton balls soaked in cold, boiled water or with special eye wipes. Staining of the fur on the cheeks can be treated with a special lotion.

Common Eye Symptoms

Visit your vet if you notice any of these signs, individually or in combination. In many cases of eye disease, early treatment is essential if permanent visual impairment is to be avoided.

- Redness of the eyelids and conjunctiva.
- Constantly weeping eye, tears spilling down face.
- Thick, sticky discharge.
- Half-closed eye, swollen eyelid.
- Increased, rapid blinking.
- Obvious discomfort (dog scratches and paws eye or rubs face on ground).
- Dislike of bright light (dog hides in dark corners).
- Flickering of the eyes (vestibular syndrome, see pages 66–67)
- Bulging of the eye (normal in some breeds such as Pugs and Pekingese, but may indicate glaucoma).
- Cloudiness of the cornea.
- Whiteness or opacity of the pupil.

Neutering: The Male Dog

WHETHER OR NOT A MALE DOG SHOULD BE neutered, if it is not going to be used for breeding, arouses strong passions among vets, dog behaviorists, and owners. Those who are against it believe that neutering can alter a dog's personality and will make the dog fat and overly placid. Those in favor argue that it will not affect the dog's personality and activity levels, will help to reduce the incidence of some hereditary diseases, has definite health benefits for the male dog, and reduces the number of unwanted puppies born each year. As the owner of a male dog, it is up to you to reach your own decision, having discussed it fully with your vet to ensure you are aware of all the facts.

Neutering (castration) involves the surgical removal of both testicles so that the male is no longer capable of producing sperm or the male sex hormone, testosterone. The procedure is relatively simple. The operation is performed under general anesthetic, and most dogs will recover within a few hours. The scrotum may appear to be slightly swollen afterward, but there is little apparent discomfort to the dog. Most are eager to have their walk the very next day, but it is generally advisable to keep exercise to an absolute minimum for a few days until your vet has pronounced your dog fit again.

Will It Change His Behavior?

Many people decide to have their dog castrated in the belief that it will calm him down, reduce aggression, stop him from roaming, curb a tendency to mark objects with urine, and prevent problem sexual behavior (see pages 144–145). Although it is not a miracle cure, it can play a role in reducing all these problems. If carried out before the age of about 18 months, it should significantly reduce territorial aggression, but even hormonally induced patterns of behavior will become learned over a period of time; aggression in older dogs is usually rooted in fear and poor socialization. However, castration can be helpful when two dogs in the same family are competing for status (see pages 126–127). It can slow down a hyperactive dog, but you'll have to monitor his exercise and diet to prevent obesity.

Medical Castration

By puberty, both testes (testicles) should have descended into the scrotum from the groin or abdomen. Sometimes they fail to do so, a condition known as cryptorchidism. If you suspect this is the case with your puppy, have your vet examine him once he reaches puberty at about 6 months. Castration may be advised, as there is an increased probability that the retained testicles will become cancerous in later life. A dog with only one retained testicle (monorchidism) may pass the undesirable characteristic on to his male offspring so should not be used for breeding. A retained testicle in the abdomen may develop into an estrogen-secreting tumor. Neutering can prevent other medical problems from developing in the older male dog (see box).

UNDESCENDED TESTICLE

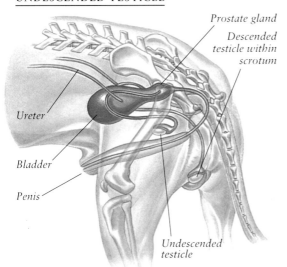

Prostate gland

Descended testicle within scrotum

Ureter

Bladder

Penis

Undescended testicle

▲ *During the first few weeks of life, the testicles normally descend into the puppy's scrotum, but sometimes one or both of them are retained within the groin or abdomen.*

▲ *If you are not planning to breed from him, you can have your male dog neutered at any age after 6 months. It will not impair his zest for life and love of a game of chase. Watch his diet to avoid overweight.*

Advantages of Male Neutering

A number of health advantages can be put forward for having your dog neutered. Castration reduces the incidence of:

- **Testicular Tumors**, relatively common in the older unneutered male dog.

- **Anal Adenomas**, tumors that appear around the anus, often causing severe irritation, bleeding, and sometimes problems with defecation.

- **Benign Prostatic Hyperplasia**, enlargement of the prostate gland due to the effect of testosterone, the male sex hormone. The prostate gland sits at the neck of the bladder and lies just below the rectum. The condition can therefore cause problems with urination and normal defecation.

● My 3-year-old Cocker Spaniel, Milton, is quite aggressive toward other dogs. Will neutering calm him down?

There may be many explanations for Milton's aggression, not all of them necessarily solvable by neutering. For example, at this age castration may not be successful in reducing territorial aggression. Discuss your concerns with your vet, who may advise giving Milton an injection that will temporarily block the effects of his male hormones. If this succeeds in calming him down, it is more than probable that castration will have the same effect.

● *Is it better to have my dog castrated when he is a puppy, or should I wait until he is a few years old?*

As regards the actual surgery, age makes no difference. However, if you do not intend to use him for breeding, early neutering can be a good idea, as he is less likely to learn hormonally induced, undesirable behavior patterns, which can be difficult to correct in an older dog.

The Female Dog

FEMALE DOGS GENERALLY HAVE THEIR FIRST season (estrus, or period of being "in heat") at around 6–9 months of age. However, there is quite a wide variation, dependent on breed. As a general rule, the larger breeds, particularly giants such as Great Danes or St. Bernards, have their first season later than the smaller breeds, sometimes not until they are 18 months old. Classically, a female comes in heat every 6 months, but again there is great variation, and some may only have one season in a year.

The season lasts around 3 weeks (see diagram on page 94). There is normally a bloody discharge from the vagina, quite profuse to start with but becoming gradually thicker and scant-ier. The female becomes attractive to male dogs, who will be able to sniff her out from a great distance. You may find stray males form a crowd outside your house unless they are restrained in some way. Toward the middle of her season, the female becomes equally desperate to find a mate and will seize any opportunity to escape. To avoid unwanted pregnancies, you should keep her on the leash for exercise, preferably well away from other dogs. For most owners, this is an inconvenience they can happily do without.

▼ *A female in heat (on the right) welcomes the attentions of a courting male. Her tail is lifted, indicating that she is ready to mate.*

Unless planning for their female to have puppies, they will choose some method of stopping the heat cycle. There is no menopause in the dog—the female will continue to come in heat once or twice a year for life.

Long-acting injections of one of the female sex hormones, usually at 5-month intervals, can be given to prevent or postpone a female from coming in heat. They disrupt the female's reproductive cycle, but once the injections are stopped, the normal seasons return. As the female's future fertility may be affected, the injections are not generally recommended for females who may be used for breeding at a later date. They may increase the risks of pyometra, diabetes, and mammary cancer. Tablets to postpone a female's season, perhaps because she is due to be shown, also have side effects and should not be used long-term. Nor should they be used during a female's first season. However, sprays are available that will help mask her odor and hopefully make her less attractive to males.

Should the female escape during her season and manage to mate accidentally, your veterinarian can stop the unwanted pregnancy developing by giving a series of injections starting within a day or two of the mating. The female will remain fertile so long as she continues to ovulate, so you should still keep her confined until her season ends.

Spaying

The most effective and most common method of canine birth control by far is to have the female spayed (neutered). Aside from the convenience factor, there are a number of good medical reasons for recommending spaying in any female that is not being used for breeding or has had all the litters her owner wishes her to have (see box). More correctly called an ovario-hysterectomy, spaying involves the removal of the uterus and both ovaries. The operation is normally carried out through an incision made in the female's abdomen around the area of the umbilicus or "belly button." Recovery is usually very rapid, and most females are back to normal within a day or two. As the ovaries have been removed, estrus ceases altogether and the female no longer comes in heat.

● **Will spaying make Brandy, my Labrador, fat?**

... Spayed females do sometimes put on weight easily, but there shouldn't be a problem if you maintain Brandy's exercise levels and cut back on her food as soon as you notice any increase in weight.

● **When Sky, my Pomeranian, ended her season, she seemed to be pregnant. She began making nests, and her breasts looked bigger. She even seemed to be producing milk. The vet said she was having a phantom or false pregnancy. Can you explain what this is?**

Most females become "broody" at the end of their season due to hormonal changes, but the effects usually pass after about 5 days. In some females, this behavior is more severe and prolonged, and they may become aggressive. It could happen to Sky in the course of every cycle, so discuss with your vet whether you should have her spayed.

● **How will I know when Melissa, my Samoyed, comes in season for the first time?**

You will probably find a few spots of watery blood around the house, especially where Melissa has been sleeping. If you examine her, you will find her vulva has become swollen.

Advantages of Spaying

● Inconvenience of half-yearly or yearly season disappears.

● Risks of mammary cancer are considerably reduced. They are negligible if spaying is carried out before the female comes into season for the first time.

● Early spaying reduces the chances of your pet developing diabetes mellitus, which is related to hormone changes in the unspayed female. A female with diabetes will have to be spayed, but is at higher risk from anesthesia.

● Pyometra (a life-threatening infection of the uterus) cannot occur in spayed females.

● Stops false pregnancies; advisable in females with a history of the condition.

● Reduces number of unwanted pregnancies.

● A spayed female will not wander to find a mate and stands less chance of being lost or injured.

Mating and Breeding

BREEDING A LITTER OF PUPPIES IS TREMENDOUSLY rewarding and exciting. However, it should not be undertaken lightly. Before you decide to breed from your dog, look at the available market for the puppies. Can you be sure of finding loving and caring homes for them all—regardless of the size of the litter? Your aim should be to produce a litter of puppies that is healthier and stronger than either parent, so look for a mate that balances out your own pet's shortcomings. For example, a small animal for the breed could be matched with a larger one. If there are known hereditary health problems such as hip dysplasia, eye diseases, or deafness within the breed, arrange for your animal to have all the screening tests available (ask your veterinarian for details). Do not agree to a mating if the owners of the other dog cannot produce certification to show that their animal has been cleared for breeding.

THE REPRODUCTIVE CYCLE

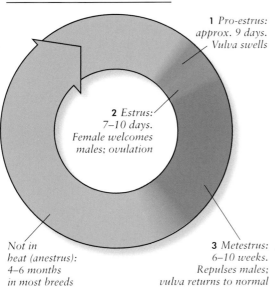

1 Pro-estrus: approx. 9 days. Vulva swells

2 Estrus: 7–10 days. Female welcomes males; ovulation

Not in heat (anestrus): 4–6 months in most breeds

3 Metestrus: 6–10 weeks. Repulses males; vulva returns to normal

▲ In most breeds the season occurs twice yearly, but some females, especially the larger breeds, may have only one cycle a year. Conception takes place during the estrus (standing heat), when ovulation occurs.

When To Mate

A female should have had one, preferably more, seasons before being mated for the first time. The season usually lasts about three weeks, although individual animals vary. During the first phase (pro-estrus), the ovaries produce hormones that stimulate the lining of the uterus in readiness for pregnancy, and the female becomes more attractive to males. Next comes the estrus stage, lasting about 7–10 days, when the eggs are released and the female is ready to mate. She is normally considered at the height of her fertility on day 12 of the season, but there is great variation in the estrus cycle, and some females ovulate as early as day 4, others as late as day 30. The behavior of the female will often show that she is ready to mate. She shows great interest in males, lifts her tail to reveal her vulva, and there may be a straw-colored vulval discharge.

For purposes of mating, the female is often taken to the stud male. This is because males sometimes show reluctance to mate in another dog's territory. Mating can last quite a long time. After the male has mounted the female, the "tie" usually occurs—the male's penis swells within the female's vagina, making it impossible to separate the two animals. During this time the male normally dismounts the female and turns, so that the two are tail-to-tail, and the pair may remain locked in this position for up to half an hour before separating. The reasons for the tie are not fully understood, and mating can take place successfully without it. Some females will conceive even though the mating appeared very brief and no tie was achieved.

At the end of her estrus, the female begins to come off heat (metestrus). She will not stand for a male to allow mating to take place, and after a few days ceases to attract male attention. If the mating has been successful, pregnancy will have started. About two weeks after the mating took place, the female's nipples may begin to enlarge. The veterinarian may be able to palpate (feel) the

◄ *A Collie male and female in a mating tie. They usually remain locked together for about 30 minutes, though longer matings than this have been recorded.*

fetuses in the uterus. A blood test can be carried out around this time to confirm pregnancy. The gestation period in the dog generally takes between 63 and 65 days.

From week 6 onward, begin to increase the amount of food you give your pregnant female so that she is receiving about half the amount again that you normally feed her. She needs to have a nutritionally complete and balanced diet, so ask your vet's advice about feeding. If your female is carrying a large litter, you may notice her abdomen beginning to swell as the pregnancy advances, but some females may not look obviously pregnant until only about a week before giving birth. Females with very large litters tend to give birth early. First-time mothers are also liable to give birth earlier than those who have already had one or more litters.

Q&A

● **Can the puppies in a single litter have different fathers?**

... Yes. An egg is fertilized only once, but many eggs are shed in each season, so it is possible for several eggs to become fertilized by different males if multiple matings occur. After a desired mating has taken place, you must continue to isolate the female for as long as she continues to welcome male advances in order to prevent a subsequent accidental mating.

● *On her last two seasons, I have mated Portia, my Shar Pei, on day 12 of her season, but she has failed to conceive. The stud male has already mated successfully with other females, so I know there is nothing wrong with him. Do you think Portia is unable to have puppies?*

Don't give up yet. Have Portia examined by your vet to see she is in good health. It is possible that she has an unusual estrus cycle and that the best time for mating her is not on day 12. A vaginal cytology test and blood test to measure progesterone levels can be carried out to show when she is at her most fertile.

● *Trudi, my 1-year-old German Shepherd, is very nervous. A friend has suggested that having a litter would calm her down. Is this true?*

Some excitable dogs do become more placid with motherhood, but it is equally possible that a nervous female will produce nervous puppies. She is far more likely to panic during labor and may even eat her own puppies in her distress and confusion. Only breed from your dog if you want to produce puppies, not to correct any behavioral problems.

THE WHELPING BOX

Siderails prevent mother from lying on the pups

Blanket lining should be covered with sheets of newspaper

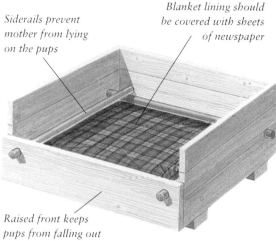

Raised front keeps pups from falling out

▲ *The female gives birth and raises her pups in a whelping box. Introduce this two weeks before the birth date to give her time to get used to it.*

Giving Birth

About a week before the end of the pregnancy, the female may start to slow down. A day or two before whelping (giving birth) she can become restless and unsettled. Most females are capable of giving birth without assistance, though it is best if someone is on hand to act quickly if a problem should arise. Avoid having too many people around, however. As labor begins, she will start to pant excessively. The unaccustomed sensations sometimes cause panic at this stage, but most females soon settle down as their natural instincts take over.

Each pup is contained within a bag of membranes. The head and legs usually appear first, though a tail-first delivery is not exceptional. Some litters are born very rapidly, with only a few minutes between each birth, but some may be born at intervals of up to three hours. As long as the female is relaxed and comfortable, there is no need to panic, but consult your vet if you are concerned. The female may eat the placenta (afterbirth) delivered after each puppy. In the wild the female did this to keep predators from knowing of the presence of newborn young.

If any of the puppies do not appear to be breathing, clear the membranes from around the mouth. Holding the puppy in both hands, swing

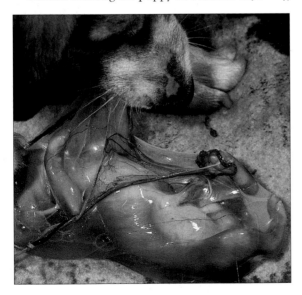

▲ *The mother uses her tongue to remove the bag of membranes surrounding each newborn puppy. The vigorous licking action helps to stimulate breathing.*

When to Call the Vet

Most pregnancies and births take their natural course, and there is no need for human intervention. However, you should call the vet if any of the following occurs:

- The pregnancy runs for more than 65 days.
- No puppy has emerged 2 hours after the start of contractions, or has not been delivered within 30 minutes of first becoming visible.
- More than 3 hours pass between the delivery of the puppies, especially if the female is straining hard and appears unsettled.
- The female appears lethargic and her contractions are not strong enough to expel the puppies, or she seems exhausted.

● *Laura, my Weimaraner, is going to litter for the first time. How will I know when the birth is imminent?*

She will probably start to refuse food about 24 hours before delivery, and will become restless and show signs of nesting. This may take the form of tearing up bits of paper and rummaging in her bedding. You may be able to squeeze a few drops of milk from her nipples. As the contractions start, she may start to look at her flanks, paw at the ground, and walk restlessly around. As it is a first-time birth, she will want lots of reassurance at this stage.

● *How do I care for the newborn pups?*

Their most important need is warmth. As each one is delivered, place it in the draft-free whelping box on a heating pad or well-wrapped hot-water bottle (make sure the temperature remains below 85°F/30°C). Between deliveries put the pups onto the female's nipples. At this stage, her breasts will produce colostrum, which contains antibodies that will protect them from disease.

● *When will it be safe to start handling the puppies?*

Most females will allow their puppies to be handled immediately, though this should be done for short periods, by someone familiar to her. Stop if the mother appears unhappy or defensive. By the time the eyes are open, at 10–14 days, the pups should be used to daily gentle handling. By 4 weeks they should be spending much of the day away from their mother and should have begun to take solid food.

it down toward your feet to clear the mouth and lungs of mucus. Rub the puppy with a rough towel to mimic the mother's licking and stimulate breathing. If this fails, blow gently into the puppy's mouth and nose until the chest starts to lift (don't carry on for more than 15 minutes).

You may want to have your vet examine the female within 12 hours of the birth. A retained puppy, embryo, or placenta could lead to a life-threatening infection. Other potential post-natal problems are mastitis (inflammation or infection of the breasts) and eclampsia (milk fever). With

▲ *Nine-day-old pups. For the first few days of life they are blind, deaf, and totally dependent on their mother. The eyes usually open about day 10–14.*

the latter condition, the dog breathes rapidly, is abnormally hungry and thirsty, and has muscular spasms. Seek immediate medical help.

Give a nursing mother as much food as she will take—up to four times her normal amount. By week 4 the puppies should be receiving additional food, and by week 8 they should be fully weaned and ready to go to new homes.

First Aid and Emergencies

WHEN A DOG SUFFERS A SERIOUS INJURY OR THE sudden onset of illness, your first priority is to keep calm (panic will only waste valuable time) and contact a local veterinary practice without delay for advice and assistance. You can take the following action if unable to reach help immediately, but do not attempt first aid if you are at all uncertain of what you are doing.

- Make sure that the dog can breathe by removing debris from its mouth and gently pulling the tongue forward.

- Place the dog in a recovery position, with its left side uppermost, and keep it warm.

- Check for a heartbeat by placing the heel of your hand on the left side of the dog's chest just behind the elbow. Give cardiac massage if you are unable to feel a heartbeat.

- Stop any bleeding.

- Take the dog as quickly as possible to the nearest veterinary practice.

The First-Aid Kit

It is a wise precaution to carry a first-aid kit for your dog in the house or car in case of an accident or emergency. Many veterinary centers supply special first-aid kits, but you can make your own by including the following items:

✓ Bandages of different widths, including a self-adhesive bandage.

✓ A gauze pad and sterile dressings.

✓ Antiseptic cream.

✓ Cotton balls.

✓ A length of cord or tape to make an emergency muzzle or tourniquet.

✓ Scissors and tweezers.

✓ A foil blanket in case of collapse.

✓ Disposable gloves.

Moving an Injured Dog

An injured dog is likely to bite, so if the animal is conscious, improvise an emergency muzzle (see page 100). Two or more people will be needed to carry a heavy dog. Use a blanket to lift the dog or, if severe spinal injuries are suspected, carry it carefully on a board or door to avoid sudden movements.

Bleeding

Unchecked bleeding can quickly lead to shock and death.

Surface wounds
1. Apply pressure at the bleeding point with your thumb, or place a wad of cotton balls or a gauze pad against the wound and bandage it tightly. If the bleeding continues, you may have to apply another dressing on top of the first.
2. Use a tourniquet on a profusely bleeding leg or tail. Tie a narrow piece of cloth (not string or elastic) between the wound and the dog's heart. Insert a pencil or stick into the knot and twist it to stop the bleeding. Do not apply the tourniquet for more than 15 minutes at a time.

Internal bleeding
Suspect internal bleeding if a dog has been in a road accident, had a serious fall, or suddenly becomes pale and lethargic.
1. Keep the dog quiet and warm.
2. Minimize movement and seek immediate medical attention.

Artificial Respiration

Blood, vomit, or water inhaled by the dog after an accident or drowning may stop it from breathing. Send someone for help and attempt to resuscitate the dog:
1. Pull the tongue forward and clear away any obstructions from the mouth. In the case of

drowning, drain the water from the lungs by turning the dog upside down.

2. Lay the dog on its right side and extend the head and neck forward to give a free airway.

3. Cup your hands around the dog's nose and breathe through them into its nostrils for about three seconds to inflate the lungs. Pause for two seconds, then repeat. Carry on until the dog starts to breathe on its own.

Cardiac Massage

If the dog's heart has stopped, give cardiac massage at once.

1. Place the heel of your hand on the left side of the dog's chest just behind the elbow. Place your other hand on top, then press both hands firmly down and forward toward the head.

2. Rapidly and firmly pump the chest three times in succession, then blow into the dog's nostrils: pump, pump, pump, breathe, allowing less than a second for each pumping action.

3. Repeat this sequence about 15–20 times a minute until you feel a heartbeat, then cease pumping. Continue with mouth-to-nose resuscitation while someone helps you rush the dog to a vet. Do not abandon your efforts as long as you continue to feel a faint heartbeat.

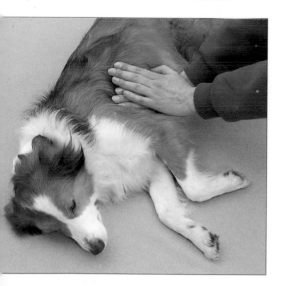

▲ *To restart a dog's heart, place both hands on the left side of the dog's chest just behind the elbow and press firmly and rhythmically.*

Burns and Scalds

A quick response is needed to limit the extent of skin damage.

Boiling water or oil

1. Cool the burned area of skin by sponging at once with cold water. Do not apply ointment.

2. Cover the area with a wet cloth or apply an icepack, and take the dog to a vet at once.

Chemical burns

1. Muzzle the dog to stop it from ingesting any of the contaminant.

2. Sponge the area gently with water to remove all of the chemical and consult a vet at once.

Electrocution

Major shock

1. Switch off the current before attempting to move the dog or use a nonconducting object, such as a wooden (not metal) broom to move the dog away.

2. Contact a vet at once. Keep the dog warm and check its heartbeat and breathing. Resuscitate if necessary (see above).

Minor shock

The only sign the owner may see of a minor shock (after the dog chews an electric cord, for example) is difficulty in breathing shortly afterward. Check the inside of the mouth and lips for burns, and apply cold water.

Insect Stings and Bites

An allergic reaction to insect stings or bites shows up as hives (swellings all over the face and body). The dog may have difficulty breathing. Consult a vet at once. Treat with antihistamines.

Wasp stings: The venom is alkaline, so treat by washing the area with a diluted acid such as vinegar.

Bee stings: Try to remove the stinger with tweezers—it looks like a dark, short hair. Bee stings are acid, so the swelling should be bathed with an alkaline such as bicarbonate of soda.

Snake Bite

If, on a walk in snake country, your dog begins
to drool and tremble, and its pupils dilate, suspect a snake bite. The site of bite is usually on
the head or legs. There will be rapid swelling.
1. If possible, apply an icepack or cold water
to the wound to slow down the flow of blood.
2. Contact an animal emergency center at once
to make arrangements for an antivenom to be
ready for your arrival.
3. If the bite is on the paw, a tourniquet
between the bite and heart may delay the
spread of the venom. Do not let the dog exert
itself in any way, as this will raise its heart rate
and spread the venom more rapidly around the
body. Carry it to and from the car.

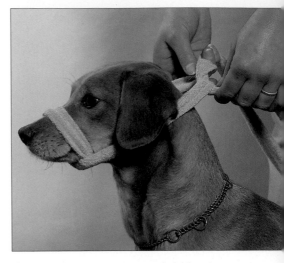

▲ *An emergency restraint is made by looping a tape
around the dog's muzzle. Knot it under the jaw, pass
either side of the neck, and tie it at the back of the head.*

Accidental Poisoning

This occurs most commonly when the dog eats
a toxic substance such as prescribed drugs or
garden pesticides, but some poisons can also be
inhaled or absorbed through the skin.
1. Call a vet for advice. If swallowed, induce
vomiting *only* if the substance ingested was not
corrosive or irritating, the poison was swallowed within the last hour, and the dog is conscious and alert. To induce vomiting, give
hydrogen peroxide in the following amounts:

  2 teaspoons for a toy breed,
  1½ tablespoons for a medium-size breed,
  2–4 tablespoons for a large breed.
Alternatively, place a large crystal of washing
soda (sodium carbonate) on the back of the
dog's tongue.
2. Waste no time in getting the dog to a vet. If
you know what has been swallowed, take a
sample of the substance, if possible with the
packet label listing the ingredients.

Common Poisons and Their Effects on Your Dog

SUBSTANCE	SIGNS OF POISONING	ACTION
Corrosive fluid: From car battery acid, paint stripper, oven cleaner. Dog walks in spilled fluid	Inflamed skin, vomiting, diarrhea	Do not induce vomiting, wash skin and coat, contact vet immediately
Slug and snail bait: Dogs like the taste	Tremors, convulsions, coma. Can be fatal	Induce vomiting, contact vet immediately
Rat poison: Dog eats poisoned rat	Bleeding gums, bruising to skin. Can be fatal	Induce vomiting, contact vet immediately
Antifreeze: Leaks from car. Dogs like the taste	Convulsions, vomiting, collapse, coma	Induce vomiting, contact vet immediately
Sedatives and antidepressants: Owner's packet lying around	Depression, staggering, coma	Induce vomiting, contact vet immediately
Lead: Dog ingests from old paint, lead fishing weights, discarded batteries	Vomiting and diarrhea, followed by collapse and paralysis	Induce vomiting, contact vet immediately

Objects in the Mouth and Throat

Sticks and bones: Sometimes splinter and become wedged between the teeth or at the back of the throat. Attempt to remove the object yourself only as a last resort. Extreme care must be taken in case the dog bites. Get someone to restrain the dog firmly.
1. Keep the dog's mouth open by placing a wooden object (such as a kitchen utensil) between the upper and lower jaw.
2. Reach over and carefully remove the object with tweezers or kitchen tongs.

Small balls: If trapped at the back of the throat, they can quickly cause asphyxiation.
1. Grab the dog around its waist and squeeze, elevating the abdomen. This should force the ball out over the back of the tongue (the Heimlich maneuver).
2. Alternatively, press on the throat from the outside, and try to push the ball up and out over the back of the tongue.

Fish Hooks

Fish hooks can imbed themselves, especially in the lips. Don't pull one out by the end as the barb will cause further damage. Be careful.
1. With wire cutters or pliers, cut the hook in two, then push the barb through to the outside. Clean the wound with antiseptic.
2. If you cannot remove the hook, take the dog to the vet. Do not pull on or cut a fishing line trailing from the mouth. This will make it more difficult for the vet to remove the hook.

Fight Injuries

Bites: Fighting dogs most frequently bite their opponent's face, ears, neck, or chest. Even though the surface wound may seem clean, it is best to have any laceration looked at.

Ears: Frequently torn in fights and will often bleed profusely.
1. Clean the wound and apply a pressure pad to the site to stop bleeding.

2. Tape the ear upward onto the top of the head by winding the bandage over and round the head under the chin. Leave the other ear outside the bandage so that it helps to keep it in place. Bandaging will prevent the ear from bleeding when the dog shakes its head.

Prolapsed eye: Sometimes results from a fight, most usually in short-nosed breeds such as Pekingese and Pugs. Speed is vital if the eye is to be saved.
1. Keep the eyeball covered with a moist cloth.
2. Take the dog to the vet immediately.

Heatstroke

Heatstroke occurs rapidly in dogs, often proving fatal in minutes. The first signs are rapid, heavy breathing. The dog becomes distressed, salivates, gasps for breath, and collapses.
1. Take the dog out of the heat.
2. Cool the dog by pouring water over it. Use tepid water at first, then gradually reduce the temperature as the dog cools. Cover the dog with damp towels.
3. Offer water to drink.
4. Take the dog to a vet if it has failed to recover after a few minutes.

▼ *An effective way of treating a dog with heatstroke is to cover its body with damp towels. Continue to pour water over the towels to maintain a cool temperature.*

TRAINING AND BEHAVIOR PROBLEMS

THIS SECTION DEALS WITH COMMON BEHAVIOR problems of dogs. It is easy to forget that your family pet is descended from wolves. An understanding of pack behavior and of the way dogs communicate with each other will go a long way toward helping you establish a good relationship with your dog. You should take steps to introduce your puppy to as many new experiences as possible if it is not to grow up fearful and shy.

The programs outlined here for dealing with problem behavior require patience and persistence. It cannot be emphasized too strongly that the best treatment is to prevent problem behavior developing in the first place, through early training, preferably in an obedience class. The case studies help illustrate the origins and complexity of behavior problems. They are based on real-life situations, and the suggested treatments should not be taken to apply in all circumstances. The reader with a problem dog is strongly urged to seek professional advice through his or her veterinarian, particularly in cases involving aggression or children.

Pack Behavior

DOGS ARE DESCENDED FROM WOLVES. THOUGH thousands of years of selective breeding have changed their behavior as well as their appearance, many aspects of our relationships with our dogs can be best understood if we think of them as playful wolves.

Wolves live naturally in packs of at least two, and usually more, animals of all ages. There are separate, strictly defined hierarchies of males and females. Social interaction involves complex signals that express dominance or submission. The dominant (alpha) male and female are physically superior to their subordinates. This gives them rights and privileges: the right to reproduce, to eat first, to choose where they sleep, to initiate contact or grooming with others. They also defend the pack and always precede lower-ranking pack members through narrow openings. Alpha dogs do not need to maintain their rank by squabbling with the pack. Lower-ranking dogs treat them with respect, while competing with each other for resources.

The Family Pack

For your dog, your family is the pack. From the moment a new puppy or dog enters your home, it is picking up signals about where it stands and who is in charge. Establishing the proper hierarchy takes time. The first 18 months of a puppy's life are the most critical. The dog must learn that it is subordinate to everyone else, including the smallest child. This is not cruel or uncaring, but simple common sense. If the dog thinks it ranks high in the family, it will try to take charge. You do not want a dog that growls when told to get off the furniture or snarls if its favorite toy is taken away: such behavior easily leads to aggression. Once your dog has learned its position, you may decide to allow it certain privileges, such as sitting on a particular chair. But remember that pack hierarchy is not static and if circumstances change in a household, an ambitious puppy or dog will be quick to take advantage.

Case Study

Christy: a 3-year-old female Cocker Spaniel

Circumstances: Has lived with the Mendoza family from 9 weeks.

Problem: Normally a friendly dog, Christy has started to act aggressively and is overly possessive of her toys. She steals possessions such as shoes, particularly from the Mendozas' daughter, Linda.

Explanation: Christy is challenging her position in the family by opportunistic displays of dominance. The aim is to reduce Christy's status so that she no longer shows aggression.

Recommended treatment:

▶ For a week, the family should ignore Christy, except to feed and exercise her. She should be given more exercise than usual, walked in a different place, and fed after the family has eaten. Christy should not be allowed to join the family circle in the evening. Her toys should be removed, and she should be kept on a long leash in the house to discourage stealing. The object at this stage is to avoid confrontation, and the family must not grasp Christy by the collar or the scruff of her neck.

▶ Next, Christy can be allowed into the family room on condition she lies quietly in her basket. She may play noncompetitive retrieving games, but not with Linda.

▶ After this, the adults can start to give Christy more open affection, but on their own terms. Linda can now begin to join in the games, but should limit her affection.

▶ Daily grooming sessions should be initiated. Linda should play a prominent role in these.

▶ Christy's aggression should have diminished. To maintain this, her retrieving instinct should be encouraged throughout her life, but the game should be stopped and the toy taken away if she shows *any* sign of aggression.

Ground Rules in the Family Pack

A few simple rules will establish the dog's place in the family and serve as the basis for an affectionate, balanced relationship.

1. Feed your dog when it suits *you*, not when the dog demands it.

2. Don't feed it tidbits from your plate or share your snacks with it.

3. Don't let your dog sit on the furniture or sleep on your bed, except by invitation.

4. Occasionally sit in *its* bed (even if you feel very silly doing it).

5. Ignore your dog if it is being demanding, but give plenty of love and affection at other times.

6. Play with it frequently, but do not let it win all games of strength, speed, and possession.

7. Have regular grooming sessions when the dog stands and allows itself to be handled all over. Reward it for cooperating.

8. Teach your dog to wait while you pass first through doorways and narrow entrances.

9. Never let your dog assume a position above you by jumping onto a chair or table and staring down at you, or by standing with its paws on your shoulders.

10. Never use physical force to control your dog. Always make sure your instructions are clear, and reward the dog when it obeys them.

● *Would my dog be happier if it were allowed to think of itself as the alpha member of the family?*

Your dog might be happier, but do you really want your household to be ruled by a dog you cannot control? An owner who knows how to behave like the pack leader will feel more confident in maintaining authority throughout the dog's life. Then you can break the rules—on your own terms.

● *Is there such thing as an alpha puppy in a litter, and should I avoid choosing it?*

Yes, on both counts. A puppy that seems considerably bolder than the others in the litter should be avoided except by an experienced, highly confident owner.

● *What makes some dogs more willful than others?*

Individual character depends on the mother and father, but also on food supply, birth weight (bigger pups have an advantage), and especially the owner's influence. A weak-willed owner with a strong-willed dog may find that the dog is disrespectful and difficult to control.

▼ *The social hierarchy within the wolf pack aids its survival. It encourages cooperation and prevents continuous life-and-death fighting, which would reduce pack numbers and weaken it overall.*

How Dogs Communicate

DOMESTIC DOGS HAVE INHERITED THE SYSTEM of signals used by their wolf ancestors within the pack. Information is exchanged in three ways: by sight, sound, and smell. They use the same signals to communicate with us. Misunderstandings arise when we fail to recognize what our dogs are clearly telling us.

Visual signals are very important. This is why dogs are so sensitive to their owners' body language. Different postures of the eyes, mouth, ears, tail, and the whole body itself, convey different messages (see box). Eye contact is used to establish dominance: submissive dogs avoid eye contact, whereas assertive individuals will stare in order to show superiority. Selective breeding has reduced the effectiveness of visual signaling in many breeds, particularly those with drooping ears or long facial hair. Cropping ears or tails also impairs a dog's ability to communicate.

Vocal signals are useful over distances and in dense vegetation. Barking in different tones can convey alarm, warning, greeting, or the desire for play or attention. Grunts indicate greeting or contentment; growls, threats or defensive warnings; whines, pain, defense, submission, or attention seeking. Howling is used to assemble the pack for hunting, but is also the call of a lone wolf seeking contact with other pack members. A dog left on its own may howl mournfully to summon its family back.

A dog uses its acute sense of smell to recognize other individuals. Unique body odors are produced by skin glands around the head and tail. Wolves will urinate to mark the boundaries of their pack territory with scent, and frequent urinating for scent-marking purposes can be a common habit of unneutered male dogs. A female's urine when she is in heat contains scent signals that show she is ready for mating. They can be detected by males over long distances.

● *My English Bull Terrier, Spuds, wants to be friends with everyone. He rushes up to other dogs with his tail up, but they often respond aggressively. Why is this?*

Spuds may not be as friendly as you think in his advances to other dogs. The raised tail position can be part of the show of strength in a dominant individual. Furthermore, the facial expressions of the bull breeds are sometimes misread by other breeds because their eyes face forward, hence appear to be staring. This may be perceived as a threat by the other dog, who then decides to attack.

● *When he sees another dog, JR, my young Jack Russell, will drop down in a crouch with his rear in the air, his ears back, and his front legs stretched in front of him. What does this posture mean?*

JR is signaling to the other dog that he's friendly and ready for a game. Sometimes the dog will bark as well to draw attention to itself and heighten the excitement.

Ears erect

ASSERTIVE AGGRESSION

Hackles raised on back

Ears down

Pupils dilated

FEARFUL AGGRESSION

Dogs' Body Language

EYES	Wide-eyed stare; dilated pupils	Fear
	Prolonged stare	Threat: never stare at a dog unless deliberately challenging it
MOUTH	Bared teeth	Aggression (usually)
	Lolling tongue	Relaxation
EARS	Laid back	Submission/fear
	Erect and forward	Alertness
TAIL	Wagging	Intention to interact (not always friendly: could be threatening)
	Raised, motionless	Dominance
	Low, not drooping	Relaxation
	Hanging, curled around a leg or between the legs	Submission/fear

▲ *Facial expressions, used in combination with one another and with posture and sound, make up a wide vocabulary. Assertive aggression is shown when the dog raises its ears, tail, and hackles (the hairs on the back of its neck). It may quickly decide to attack. Fearful aggression is indicated by ears and tail down, lips curled, and dilated pupils. The dog may growl, bark, or bite if pushed too far.*

◀ *This German Shepherd female has adopted a classic submission posture, rolling on to her back, raising her right hindleg, and allowing her owner to rub her vulnerable underparts.*

▶ *A puppy, startled by a sudden noise, takes avoiding action. Its ears are laid back and its tail down between its legs—clear signs that it is feeling apprehensive.*

Educating Your Puppy

IT IS VERY MUCH EASIER TO PREVENT BEHAVIOR problems at the outset than to correct them later on, so the systematic education of your new puppy should begin from the moment you bring it home, ideally at about 8 to 9 weeks. It will make your task simpler if your puppy comes from a breeder who has taken care to select parents of sound, calm temperament. The personality of the mother in particular will help to shape her litter's behavior toward people, other dogs, and the world at large. If she happens to show nervousness or aggression toward strangers, the puppies are likely to copy this behavior from her. If she is placid and friendly to everyone, it will have a beneficial effect on their behavior.

As a pup grows older, it should become used to meeting dogs, people, and other animals without fear and anxiety. This process is called socialization. It learns to cope with unfamiliar environments and situations through a process known as habituation. By the time the puppy is 4–8 weeks old, it should start to meet children and people of both sexes and other pets (if possible), and become used to external noises and stimuli such as radios, vacuum cleaners, and dishwashing machines. It is important to find a breeder who is aware of the benefits of handling the puppies and introducing them to a wide variety of experiences long before they leave their mother. The most confident puppies are usually those raised amid the noise and activity of family life.

After the age of 14 weeks, a puppy becomes increasingly suspicious and fearful of unfamiliar

▶ *A snowfall gives these puppies something strange and new to taste, smell, and explore.*

● *My 10-week-old Shetland Sheepdog puppy, Casey, was the only one of the litter. I have been taking her to puppy classes, but she seems very timid and hides under my chair. Should I make her mix?*

Single pups often have difficulty communicating with other dogs, probably because they have had no early experience of playing with litter mates. If you force Casey to mix, she may grow more fearful and possibly become aggressive. Let her observe events from the safety of your lap until she feels more confident.

● *There is a horse in a paddock close to where I live. I am worried that he will frighten Jimbo, my 9-week-old puppy, when we start going for walks. What can I do to prevent this?*

Carry Jimbo to greet the horse from the other side of the fence. Stroke the horse. If Jimbo stays calm, praise him and give him a reward. Repeat this many times. Whenever he sees a horse later on, the association will be a pleasant one and he should have no problem.

situations. In the wild this would have been the age at which they began to wander away from protective adults, so their caution would have promoted survival. It is of vital importance for the puppy's adult behavior that it is as fully socialized as possible before entering this critical phase of its development. The owners of young puppies neglect early training at their peril; it is the most important stage in a dog's life. Under-socialized puppies grow up shy, fearful, difficult to train, and often show aggression.

What You Can Do

Once the puppy has settled, encourage friends and neighbors to visit you so that the puppy has the chance to meet as many new people as possible. Carry the puppy outside and introduce it to other animals. Familiarize it with traffic noise. Take it for short journeys in the car.

Reward good behavior right away, as this will make the puppy more likely to behave the same way next time. If your puppy has a bad experience (for example, being frightened by a car passing too close the first time it is out in traffic), do not overreact. If you seem anxious or angry, or show too much sympathy, you may end up by making matters worse. Just keep calm and adopt a confident tone of voice. Next time you are out, keep at a greater distance from the traffic and distract the puppy's attention from the passing cars until its confidence grows.

▲ *Until it has had all its shots, your puppy cannot be taken for walks. Take the puppy to meet the outside world by carrying it about in your arms.*

If you can, enroll your puppy in socialization classes before it is 14 weeks old. Classes teach it to play with puppies of the same age; it will find out how dogs communicate with each other, learn sociability with strangers in an unfamiliar environment, and acquire some basic training. A good class leader will encourage timid pups to mix without frightening or forcing them and show you how to control boisterous pups without resorting to physical punishment.

Case Study

Jessie: a 6-month-old German Shepherd

....

Circumstances: Has lived with the Perkins from 8 weeks. After falling off a chair and breaking her elbow at 18 weeks, was isolated at home for 6 weeks.

Problem: Formerly friendly with other dogs, but since resuming contact after her accident, Jessie has started barking and growling at strange dogs.

Explanation: Jessie was well socialized during the most sensitive phase of her development, but the enforced period of isolation reduced her confidence and made her fearful and aggressive.

Recommended treatment:

▶ The vet should be asked to reexamine Jessie to make sure there is no residual pain in the fracture site, as this could be the cause of her defensive behavior.

▶ Jessie should be walked outside on a leash. The Perkins should attempt to rebuild her confidence by introducing her to calm, unreactive dogs who will take no notice when she barks.

▶ If possible, they should arrange for her to share walks with a calm dog so that she learns from its example not to be aggressive.

▶ Jessie should be verbally praised and given a tidbit whenever she walks past a strange dog without barking.

Establishing Control

AIM AT ACHIEVING A HEALTHY RELATIONSHIP with your puppy as soon as possible. This means one in which humans are always in control but in which physical force is never used to enforce behavior. Treat your dog firmly and consistently but always with kindness. It will be much happier than if it is unsure of who is in charge. You need to make it clear from the start that you are top dog. Lay down the ground rules by telling your puppy where it will sleep. Provide a fixed routine for feeding. Groom the puppy regularly —this is a very important element in building your relationship with it.

Nuisance Behavior

Establishing control from the start of your relationship means you will be able to prevent habits that are only a slight nuisance, and even quite amusing, in your puppy from becoming major

▼ *This playful young puppy will think he is top dog if his young owner continues to appear to submit to him. This could lead to confusion about hierarchy later on.*

● *Bracken, my 14-week-old Springer Spaniel, growls and bites the brush when I groom him. What should I do?*

Are you doing anything to hurt Bracken—is the brush too hard, or are you tugging on his hair? If there is no physical reason for his resentment, it could be a warning signal that he is going to resent discipline in general. Take charge of the situation. Get someone to hold Bracken for you, steadying his head and neck with one hand and placing the other arm under his belly. Keep the grooming sessions to 5 minutes and reward him with a tidbit when finished.

● *Our 6-month-old Chihuahua, Salsa, steals our shoes and growls when we try to take them back. She can be very fierce. How do we cope with this?*

Give Salsa plenty of opportunity to play games like hide-and-seek with you. Make sure you don't spoil her—don't let her on the furniture or give her food on demand. Keep your shoes safely out of reach and teach her to retrieve a ball or other object outdoors. Though this will take lots of patience, praise, and tidbits, in time she should learn to give up any article when you take it from her, including your shoes.

Case Study

Tizzie: a 14-week-old Dalmatian

• • • • • • • • • • • • • • • • •

Circumstances: Lives with the Martin family, who have 3 children between 8 and 15.

Problem: Is always under the family's feet, demanding games and attention, and chewing the children's clothes and toys.

Diagnosis: This is fairly normal behavior for a young Dalmatian puppy, but the family needs guidance in how to control her before matters deteriorate further.

• •

Recommended treatment:

▶ When Tizzie is particularly active and playful, channel her energy by taking her for a short walk (20 minutes is enough at this age), or let her have a good play session outside.

▶ Make sure she has time on her own when she can relax and does not demand attention. Put her for short periods in a separate room or use a puppy crate. Place her bed inside. Reward Tizzie with a tidbit every time she goes in on her own until she is used to it.

▶ Tizzie should have her own toys reserved for her to play with. They shouldn't be left lying around the house but should be given to her at required times.

▶ The children should be encouraged to keep their own toys and clothes tidy and safely out of her reach.

▲ *A puppy crate placed in a corner of the family living room is an excellent way of giving a puppy time alone. Place its bed and toys inside.*

behavioral problems in the adult dog. These include such things as boisterous greeting behavior. Many puppies become overexcited when visitors arrive and will rush to jump up at them. Most owners want to have a friendly dog, but it must not be led to think it is in charge of those who enter the home. Arrange for your puppy to meet visitors frequently so that they are not a great novelty. Ask your visitors not to greet and fuss the puppy until it has gotten over the initial excitement of their arrival and has all four feet firmly on the ground—and remember to do the same when you come home yourself, difficult though it is to resist an enthusiastic welcome.

Play biting is another common form of nuisance behavior that should be discouraged from the start. Puppies play physical games with adult dogs and litter mates as they are growing up. When a puppy bites, even in play, its sharp little milk teeth inflict pain. If it bites too hard or persistently, another dog will respond by yelping or growling at it. An adult dog will often growl and walk away from an overexcited pup, then ignore it altogether for some time. React in just the same way when your puppy becomes overexcited and bites your clothes or arms. Take control of the situation—yelp or growl and walk away; the worst punishment for a pup is to be ignored. Give it time on its own for 5–10 minutes until it has calmed down. If it continues in an excitable mood, give it an alternative object, such as a chew, to bite on.

Time Alone

You should accustom your puppy to being on its own for short periods each day. This will stop it from becoming overly dependent on you and help to prevent separation problems developing later on (see pages 132–135). Take things slowly at the beginning—allow the puppy to see you but not be with you (a baby gate between rooms is useful for this), then close the door between you. Little by little, increase the time you leave the puppy alone from 10 minutes to an hour or so. Don't make a ceremony of your departure and do not return to offer comfort if the puppy starts whining. Wait until it has quietened and then come back. Praise its good behavior, but avoid making a great fuss of it.

Training Your Dog

THE OBJECT OF TRAINING IS TO TEACH YOUR dog to understand and respond to simple commands. This will make everyday life more harmonious and enjoyable for you both. Training is much easier if your pet is confident, happy, and eager to please. That will depend on the relationship you have established with your pet and how well it has been socialized.

Starting with the Basics

Two of the most important skills for a dog are to walk at heel on a leash and to come to its owner when called. If your dog cannot be relied on to do these, you are likely to have problems whenever you take it out in public. You are at risk of allowing the dog to become a nuisance or even a menace to others. You cannot assume everyone it meets will be a dog lover.

Before teaching your puppy to walk on the leash, get it used to wearing a collar. Then, in the house or yard, persuade the puppy to follow you by concealing a tidbit in your hand.

Reward it when it does so. Now attach the leash and get the dog to follow you. Don't put any tension on the leash. Go for a walk, using the tidbit and praising the dog as it walks beside you. Tell the dog to "walk" or "heel" if its attention wanders. If all else fails, produce a squeaky toy from your pocket. Do not make the lessons too long and keep them enjoyable. Stop as soon as the puppy tires or becomes obviously bored.

To teach the puppy to come when called, get one person to hold it while you move away. Then call it to you by name. Do not reach out to grab the collar before the puppy reaches you. Praise it lavishly when it comes and reward it with a tidbit. Call the puppy to you every chance you have. Keep the puppy on a long leash and practice calling it several times during a walk. Once the puppy comes regularly to you, you can begin to let it off the leash for short distances.

Use the same system of reward to teach your puppy basic instructions such as "sit" (it should always do this at the curbside before crossing the

"SIT"

"DOWN"

▲ 1. Kneel down in front of the puppy. 2. Make sure it sees the food reward in your hand. 3. Hold the reward in front of the puppy. As it follows it with its nose, raise your hand, forcing it to bend its hindlegs. 4. As it does so, say "sit." Repeat the exercise over and over.

▲ 1. As before, show the puppy you have a food reward. 2. Move your hand down toward the ground in front of the puppy. It should follow it with its nose. 3. The puppy should begin to lie down to get closer to the reward. 4. As it does so, keep repeating the command "down."

Q & A...

● *How can I stop my adult Collie, Peggy, from begging food from us when we are at table?*

Try feeding Peggy just before you sit down to eat. If she still comes to the table and you cannot keep your family or visitors from feeding her, then tie her up at the other side of the room or put her in another room while you are eating. Save table scraps to put in her dish if you want to, and feed them to her when you have finished.

● *Wink, my crossbred puppy, has taken a step backward in his toilet training. After putting him outside, I stand in the doorway to watch him "perform," then reward him as he comes back into the house. Now he has started messing in the house even after a trip outside. What I am doing wrong?*

Your mistake has been to reward Wink when he comes back inside, so he thinks you will be pleased if he relieves himself when he comes indoors instead of out in the yard. Go outside with him and reward him with a tidbit or lots of praise immediately after he has finished.

● *Our 2-year-old Pointer, Roscoe, pulls really hard on the leash. My daughter has real difficulty controlling him. How do we get him to hold back?*

Try using a head collar; they are usually excellent for increasing control. You might also try playing a vigorous game before you go out for a walk. This will allow Roscoe to let off steam first.

street), "down," and "stay" (see below). Never use similar sounding command words for two different actions—you will confuse the puppy, who will not know what you want. Teach it a release word such as "OK" or "finish" so that it knows when to stop the exercise. Never shout at or strike a puppy who is slow to respond.

Training Classes

First-time owners will find their task made easier if they attend a course of training classes. They are also effective in dealing with a strong-willed dog that has proved to have bad habits. Even more experienced owners will often find that classes improve their training methods and help them understand their dog's behavior. Personal recommendation is the best way of finding a good trainer in your area. Arrange a visit without your dog being present to observe the class and see if you like the methods being used. Do not enroll for classes if the trainer relies on punishment rather than reward or encourages the use of choke chains or prong collars. Young puppies should not usually start classes until they are 14 weeks old. Make sure the class is small (6 to 12 puppies only) and that it is for puppies only. Your puppy will not benefit from being with adult dogs, especially if it is timid or excitable.

"STAY"

▲ **1.** *With its leash on, make the puppy sit. Reward it as usual. Stand beside the puppy and say "stay." If it remains sitting, reward it again.* **2.** *Gradually increase the duration of the "sit" and "stay."* **3.** *Tell the puppy to move by using a release word such as* "OK."

"HEEL"

▲ **1.** *Have the puppy stand next to you on a short leash of about 3 feet (1 m). Reward it.* **2.** *Slacken the leash and move forward, saying "heel."* **3.** *If the puppy does not cooperate, stop walking. Recall it to your side.* **4.** *Start again. Praise it when it walks beside you.*

The Importance of Play

DOGS ARE NATURALLY PLAYFUL. IT IS THROUGH playing together that members of the litter discover their siblings' strengths and weaknesses, improve their own fitness and coordination, and learn hunting skills. Domesticated dogs carry on playing games into adulthood. Dogs with strong predatory instincts will be less likely to develop behavior problems if they allowed regular play sessions that give an outlet for their instinctive desire to stalk and chase. Many working breeds are bred to be mentally and physically active at all times. Unless their owners are able to provide a range of stimulating games, they easily become bored. This quickly leads to destructive behavior, inappropriate chasing, and aggression.

Wrestling matches and play fights take place frequently between puppies and between adult dogs that know each other. When dogs play in this way, they use their whole bodies, including

▲ Playing games with your dog helps to develop a bond of closeness between you. In addition, play provides strenuous physical exercise and mental stimulation.

their mouths. Hard biting is not tolerated; puppies develop a soft or inhibited bite so that they do not hurt each other. However, when people join in this sort of game, dogs become overexcited and will mouth or even bite arms, hands, and clothing. Don't allow this, especially if young children are involved.

Toys For Your Dog

You can buy many toys for your dog to play with, either with you or on its own. Keep one or two in reserve for use only when you are there. This will make both you and the toys more interesting to the dog. Don't leave your dog on its own with a destructible rubber or plastic toy; its sharp teeth will make short work of it, and it may end up in small pieces in its stomach, requiring emergency treatment.

Terriers and other dogs bred to hunt small animals enjoy playing "shake and kill" games with squeaky toys. For obvious reasons, this type of play should never be encouraged if there are babies or very small children in the family.

Playing With Your Dog

Active dogs love to play games of chase, tag, and hide-and-seek. This is great exercise for dogs and owners alike. Do not always do the chasing; let your dog chase you, too, and romp with it as foolishly as you like (children are often far better at this than adults, as they are less inhibited). If your dog becomes overexcited and starts leaping up or biting at your clothes, stop playing right away and ignore it for a while.

Games of fetch are popular with herding and retrieving dogs. The advantage for you is that it allows you to be lazy, provided you have taught your dog to bring back the object you throw for it. It should be trained to give the toy up on request at the end of the game, not try to retain possession of it. Don't throw your dog branches of wood to retrieve—they may splinter and the sharp points stick in the dog's throat. Small balls are also a danger, as they can lodge in the throat and asphyxiate your dog in minutes. A solid rubber ball on a strong rope is a good retrieving toy.

Most dogs enjoy tugging on a thick rope or strong pull toy. With certain breeds, such as Bull Terriers or Rottweilers, these games can easily become trials of strength, so don't let the dog win every time. Stop playing if there is any growling. Always take the toy away at the end.

● My children love playing with our 14-week-old Flat-coated Retriever, Sarah, but the sessions always seems to end in tears when she gets so excited that she starts biting at them. I'm concerned that Sarah will really hurt them one day. What do you think?

If Sarah's play biting is not discouraged now, it could develop into adult aggression. Get your children to react to Sarah as they would if they were another dog—yelp, growl at her, and walk away. If she does not get the message, then a "time-out" period is called for until she calms down. It sounds as if more adult supervision would be advisable.

● My Lhaso Apso puppy, Kayla, shows little interest in her toys and rarely plays with them. Does this matter?

Some breeds of dog are less playful than others, and the Lhaso Apso is one of these. You may find she responds better to interactive games than object play. Try playing chase games or hide-and-seek with her instead, but don't worry too much so long as Kayla seems happy and healthy.

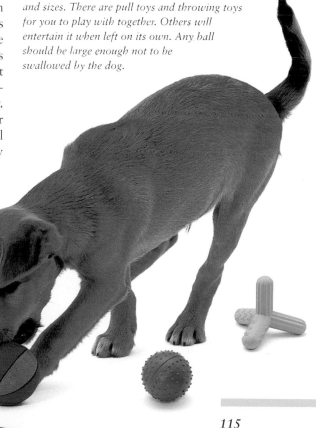

▼ *Toys for your dog come in all shapes, colors, and sizes. There are pull toys and throwing toys for you to play with together. Others will entertain it when left on its own. Any ball should be large enough not to be swallowed by the dog.*

Adopted Dogs and Their Problems

BEFORE GIVING A NEW HOME TO AN ADULT dog, try to find out all you can about its previous home, what daily routine it is used to, and if it has any behavior problems. If it comes from an animal shelter, you may not be able to discover answers to all these questions. Some adopted animals have had a bad start in life, and will need particularly sensitive care and handling.

From the moment your new dog arrives home, it will learn what is expected of it through the signals you give out. If it has been allowed to "run the show" in its previous home, you must very quickly show it who is in charge. But very often an adult dog who has been ignored and neglected all its life and has never had any fun becomes introverted or fearful. If this is the case with your new pet, you will need to draw it out of its shell with kindness and confident handling, encouraging it to become more relaxed.

Do not force too much activity on a nervous or subdued dog. Give it a quiet place to retreat to, especially if yours is a noisy family home and the dog is used to quieter surroundings. Don't introduce it to too many strangers at once. Warn your friends and family that it'll need gentle handling and quiet, friendly encouragement until it has settled down.

If you have another dog, introduce them outside in the yard or garden or on neutral territory, preferably both off the leash. Don't make any move to interfere while they sniff around each other. Be sure to make a fuss of the original dog as well as the new one so that it doesn't fear that the newcomer is going to take over.

▼ *An adopted dog will need time to get used to you. Don't force it out if it retreats under the furniture, but let it observe things quietly.*

Case Study

Gulliver: *an 18-month-old male Shih Tzu*

••••••••••••••••••

Circumstances: Adopted by new owner, Emily Chung, a month ago. Before that Gulliver lived with an elderly couple who kept five other Shih Tzus. Had never left the house and the large, fenced yard.

Problem: Gulliver has settled down well, and is friendly and intelligent at home. However, he barks hysterically at dogs and children when taken for walks.

Explanation: Gulliver had a very protected upbringing and is poorly socialized. He fails to recognize other breeds as part of the dog family, or children as small humans. It didn't matter in his old home, but Gulliver may become more aggressive and needs help to increase his confidence.

Recommended treatment:

▶ Emily should work to build up her relationship with Gulliver through games, grooming, praise, and enjoyable obedience exercises.

▶ Gulliver should be kept on the leash when out walking. If any dogs or children are encountered, Gulliver should be walked past them briskly. Praise him lavishly if he does not bark.

▶ Introduce Gulliver to a calm dog in closely supervised circumstances. Emily should ask the child of a friend or neighbor to accompany them on walks, provided Gulliver is well-behaved and not allowed too close to the child.

▶ Joining a small, well-organized training group should help build Gulliver's confidence further. Though he should learn to walk past strange dogs and children without undue anxiety, he will probably never be as accepting of them as if he had been brought up in less protected circumstances.

Establishing a Routine

It is important to establish a fixed feeding routine as quickly as possible. Don't change the dog's diet for at least the first week, to avoid digestive upsets. Make sure that the dog knows where it is expected to sleep. Show it where you wish it to relieve itself, but be patient if it doesn't get it right every time. Reward your dog when it does things correctly.

There is a real danger of adopted dogs becoming overattached. Restrain your natural desire to shower it with love 24 hours of the day—this may cause the dog to develop separation anxiety (see pages 132–135). Ensure that the dog spends short periods every day alone, gradually building up from 5 minutes to 3 or 4 hours if necessary. "Time-out" sessions, in an indoor pen or another room where it cannot do any harm, are a particularly helpful way of calming a boisterous dog, but make sure it has plenty of toys and chews to prevent it from becoming bored. Give it two 30-minute walks a day and spend time playing with it outdoors to use up some of its exuberant energy. Use an extendible leash and do not let the dog off it for the first few weeks. Although it seems obedient indoors, you may find its concentration sadly lacking when there are distractions such as people, other dogs, cats, joggers, and bicyclers about.

● *We recently rescued a Border Terrier, Candy, from a shelter. She is very reserved with us. How can we make her more outgoing?*

It's possible that Candy's previous owners ignored or mistreated her. You will need to gain her trust and give her time to settle. Many rescued dogs have never been taught to play. Try stimulating Candy with a squeaky toy (throw it, roll it, or pull it on a string toward her). If that doesn't work, wrap a ball in something smelly like a pair of dirty socks for her to investigate. Once she gets the idea of play, she should soon begin to relax.

● *We have just adopted an adult Newfoundland female, Saskia. She is usually friendly but growls fiercely when she is eating and can be quite menacing. She is always hungry and very thin, but the vet can find nothing physically wrong. How can we stop her mealtime aggression?*

Give Saskia several small meals a day of a good-quality complete dry diet. Don't use the same bowl or feed her in the same place every time and never take her bowl away from her. Avoid hovering too close to her when she is eating. After a while try dropping small pieces of food such as cheese close to her bowl at the end of a meal. As she learns to expect them, she will begin to look forward to them arriving. She should stop warning you off coming near her bowl, her condition should improve, and her food guarding should cease.

Young Children and Dogs

A FAMILY DOG CAN BRING ENORMOUS PLEASURE, fun, and interest. Children learn responsibility by taking an active role in caring for a pet. The experience can help nurture their confidence and self-esteem, and they will benefit from a dog's ability to give unconditional, nonjudgmental love—a dog can make an excellent listener for childish woes and unhappiness.

However, the experience is not always a happy one. A child brought up with a badly trained or unfriendly dog may always have a fear and dislike of them. Equally, a single meeting with an unkind, thoughtless, or indisciplined child can make a dog suspicious of all children for life.

Before acquiring a puppy, discuss the decision thoroughly with the whole family. Find a breeder who is raising puppies in the home and avoid choosing a nervous, easily startled puppy (see pages 16–17). Don't adopt a dog or puppy from a rescue center unless you are completely satisfied that it is reliable with young children.

During its first few days at home, keep the children from fussing or crowding round the new arrival. Give it somewhere it can retreat on its own. Involve older children in feeding and caring for the puppy, but make sure a responsible adult is in charge. If children are given total responsibility for its care, they may inadvertently teach it bad habits such as chasing, jumping up, and nipping. A puppy in a busy family is at risk of growing up unruly because everyone is too occupied to pay enough attention to its education. On the other hand, a puppy raised with children will be well-socialized and used to all kinds of noises and unexpected events.

When There are Children

Do

- ✓ Provide a playpen or indoor kennel for the puppy to retreat to.
- ✓ Make sure the children understand and use the basic training commands you teach the puppy. Teach by example.
- ✓ Closely supervise children, especially toddlers, when playing with the puppy.
- ✓ Encourage a responsible and caring attitude to the puppy.

Don't

- ✗ Leave a puppy alone with a toddler.
- ✗ Give the children total care—they may teach the puppy rough behavior.
- ✗ Let your children treat the puppy like a toy.
- ✗ Allow children to tease or torment a dog.
- ✗ Let the puppy become aggressive in play with the children. Stop games immediately if they are getting out of control.

▲ Though this Labrador puppy seems a little apprehensive, he is sitting calmly to receive the children's attention. They are not crowding too close. Children should be taught to use gentle movements and quiet, reassuring tones when playing with a puppy.

▲ *What greater pleasure can there be than to share a companionable walk with a well-loved canine friend? The childhood memories will last a lifetime.*

● *I'm expecting a baby shortly. I love the idea of pushing the baby in its stroller with a dog walking beside. Would you advise me to get a puppy?*

No, because the demands of looking after a baby mean that you will be unlikely to have sufficient time to give to the education and care of a young puppy. A growing puppy may also prove boisterous around a small baby. I'd advise putting off having a puppy until your family has finished with the toddler stage.

● *We want to get a dog now, but haven't ruled out the idea of starting a family in two or three years time. What advice to you have?*

Choose a breed that mixes well with small children, such as a Cavalier King Charles Spaniel, Shetland Sheepdog, or English Setter, and find a puppy that has been well socialized with children. A great deal depends on how it is brought up—you should work hard to establish a healthy and stable relationship with your puppy, ensuring that you are fully in control. Wait until the dog is at least 18 months old before starting your family.

When Baby Arrives

When there's a dog already in the household, the arrival of a baby must be handled with extreme care and sensitivity. In the last weeks before the baby is due, cool your relationship with your dog. If it is used to sleeping in the bedroom, now is the time to break this habit—not after the baby is born. Ignore the dog more than usual and don't give it all its usual treats. It'll be tough going, but when the baby arrives, you should restore affection and privileges so that the dog comes to associate the baby's presence with its own improved status. If your dog is dominant, enlist the help of a behavior counselor early on in the pregnancy to bring about a better relationship. Sadly, in extreme circumstances you may have to find the dog an alternative home.

Never leave a dog on its own with the baby, even for a second. Minimize any feelings of jealousy or resentment by making a point of giving the dog a tidbit every time you feed the baby or change a diaper. Encourage visitors to make a fuss of the dog and play with it (not too close to the infant) when you are occupied with the baby. Hand the baby to someone else, and have a short game with the dog yourself.

Dogs and Other Pets

WITH PATIENCE AND CARE, YOU CAN KEEP A dog successfully with other pets, especially cats. However, dogs are natural predators, and their instinct is to hunt any moving prey. It is always easier to introduce a puppy than an adult dog to other family pets, as its hunting instincts will not yet be strongly developed. To achieve a state of coexistence, you need to understand what is going on in both animals' minds.

Freeze, Then Fight or Flee

On seeing a strange cat, a dog may threaten it. The cat will freeze and then chose whether to fight or flee. In the freeze mode, it crouches with ears flattened and pupils dilated, waiting to see what the dog will do next. If the two square up for a fight, the cat will draw itself up to its full height and begin to hiss or spit with its mouth open. It takes a brave dog to attack it. An angry cat normally strikes at an opponent's face and is able to inflict serious eye injuries. Puncture wounds from a cat's teeth or claws are deep and painful, and easily become infected. If the cat decides to flee, the dog will instinctively chase it. Although a healthy cat can usually outrun most dogs, sometimes a dog will catch and injure, even kill, a cat. Once a dog has become used to living on the same territory as a cat, they will learn to tolerate or even like each other.

Your chances of persuading a dog to cohabit with smaller family pets such as rabbits, rodents, and birds are also higher if you acquire the dog as a puppy and train it carefully. Dogs such as terriers were bred to hunt small animals in the wild. Squeaks, rustles, and rapid, minute movements arouse their inborn "ratting" instincts, so handle small pets very carefully outside their cages or enclosures.

● *Our Bull Terrier, Skipper, chases any cat he sees outside. He gets on fine with Millie, our family cat. They even cuddle up together in the same bed. But if Skipper sees Millie outside, he will often chase her in a half-hearted way. Can you explain his behavior?*

Skipper's predatory instinct is activated by movement. When he glimpses Millie at a distance outside, he may think she is a strange cat, and he knows that strange cats normally take flight. This excites his instinct to chase but when he gets close to her, he recognizes her and the chase ceases. With a strange cat there is no suppression of the chasing response.

● *Moss, our Collie, tends to be hyperactive and nervous. Recently we've noticed his behavior deteriorating. Not long ago we inherited my mother's African Gray parrot, Charlie. He is an excellent speaker and often calls out to Moss, imitating our voices. Could this be upsetting Moss?*

It's quite likely that Moss is finding Charlie's instructions disturbing and stressful. Can you organize things so that they are kept apart most of the time? As a last resort, put a blanket over the bird's cage when Moss is in the room.

● *Our rabbit, Roger, has the run of the house. We'd like a small dog, too, but are worried they may not get on. Have you any advice?*

Choose a calm, nonpredatory breed like a Cavalier King Charles Spaniel, rather than a terrier. Introduce the puppy and rabbit gradually, following the advice given on this page (see right), but don't let Roger run around at first. Later put both animals on a leash and harness until they are used to each other.

◄ *This female crossbreed has been accustomed from an early age to sharing her home with the family cats. She is ready to protect these kittens as if they were her own puppies.*

▶ *A dog and rabbit make unusual companions. This degree of intimacy is possible only if a puppy is introduced early to other family pets.*

How to Avoid Problems

If you acquire your dog as a puppy, you can train it to accept the other pets in your home. At this age it will be much more interested in playing with another animal than chasing it. An older cat constantly pestered by an exuberant puppy may turn suddenly on the unsuspecting youngster, and a more timid cat may run away, teaching the pup to follow in hot pursuit. If your cat is very nervous and highly strung, you will need to protect it from the unwanted attentions of the puppy. Bar the puppy from some areas of the house where the cat is free to go.

Before introducing the puppy to the family cat for the first time, make sure it has been exercised, fed, and is calm. Keep the puppy on your lap, and let the cat observe events from its basket or from a safe refuge in another part of the room. Praise the puppy and give it a reward when it sits quietly while the other pet is in the room. After several encounters, the cat should begin to gain confidence and the puppy learn to accept its presence without fuss.

You will need extreme patience with an older dog, especially one not used to other pets. The training principles are similar, but you will probably have to continue with them longer. You will need the help of a professional to change the habits of a hardened hunter and chaser.

Aggression in the Home

DOGS DO NOT BITE PEOPLE WITHOUT REASON. If a dog shows aggression to its human family, growling or even biting them when they come too close, there is an underlying problem in the relationship. This may result from a failure in communication, a mismatch in personality of dog and owner, or bad training. Dogs have individual personalities, and some are more assertive than others. A strong-willed dog in the hands of a weak owner is likely to cause problems. Rottweilers, Doberman Pinschers, Bulldogs, German Shepherds, and some terriers such as Yorkshires and Jack Russells usually need firmer handling than other breeds and for this reason are best avoided by first-time owners. If you have any worries about your ability to handle your dog, seek expert advice from an animal behaviorist or professional dog trainer before any harm is done to yourself or others. Sometimes, however, there may be no other choice than to give up your pet, especially if there are children in the family.

Why Problems Arise

A dog who threatens or bites its owner is probably confused about who is in charge. You may have inadvertently led it to believe that it is the highest-ranking member of the family pack, and so it is prepared to challenge other members in situations when a resource appears to be at stake—for example, if someone comes too close to its food bowl, attempts to take a toy away, or tries to groom it. Such dogs constantly demand attention but become aggressive when the owner initiates contact without an invitation. It is essential that the dog regards all humans as taking precedence over it, but this is particularly important in a family with small children. You should also reinforce obedience training. Neutering can help in a young male.

If your dog is challenging you for position, you must immediately reduce its status by reinforcing the ground rules on pages 104–105. Cool your relationship with your dog and do not let it

● *The other day Sammy, my Shih Tzu, started barking hysterically at an approaching Great Dane. When I grabbed his collar to restrain him, he bit me. I was very upset. Why did he do this?*

Sammy was exhibiting redirected aggression. He was all worked up to bite the Great Dane when you stopped him, so he went for the nearest object, which happened to be your hand. Unless Sammy has been aggressive to you at other times, I'd say his problem is aggression to other dogs, not you, and should be tackled from this direction (see pages 126–127).

● *One night in the dark my husband tripped over our Beagle, André, and hurt his paw. Since then André growls whenever my husband comes near him. Should my husband stay away from André for a while to let him get over it?*

No, your husband needs to regain André's trust as soon as possible. Let him do all the feeding and exercising, while you stand back for a while. He should take care to speak gently to André, and to move slowly and smoothly with him until his nervousness ceases.

▲ *Attempts to remove a favorite ball have brought a show of anger. This Poodle is probably confused about its position in the family pack.*

◀ *It is very upsetting when your beloved family pet turns on you. Fear or pain can be the cause, but sometimes a failure in communications is to blame.*

If Your Dog Threatens

Do

✓ Avoid direct eye contact. If you lock eyes with it, it will challenge you even more.

✓ Approach and handle it with extreme care if it is frightened or in pain.

✓ Put it in a separate room and give it time on its own until it has calmed down.

✓ Seek professional help.

Don't

✗ Be tempted to strike the dog: you may injure it or provoke it to attack you.

✗ Push it down if it has jumped up on you, but turn away and let it "fall off."

on your lap or furniture. Ignore its demands for attention and give it time on its own. Avoid all situations that might lead to aggression.

A puppy that is removed too early from the litter (or a single pup) will have grown up without litter mates and won't have learned to inhibit its play biting. Such puppies often grow up to pull roughly on clothes or arms. This type of unruly behavior is always a nuisance and can be downright dangerous, particularly if there are small children or elderly people in the family. Play biting can be difficult to eradicate in an adult dog, so it is essential to teach good manners to your puppy. You should never engage in "play fights" with your dog; stop a game as soon as it shows any sign at all of becoming rough or starts to bite your arms.

Always supervise small children when playing with a dog, as they can easily hurt or frighten it inadvertently, and the dog will become threatening in its attitude to that child. An injured or frightened animal will often growl and bare its teeth, even if it knows and likes the person approaching it. This is less likely to happen if the dog has been handled regularly to develop a bond of trust, which is one reason why regular grooming is so important in building a relationship between dog and owner. Owners are commonly bitten when they attempt to intervene in a fight between dogs, or stop the dog from chasing and barking at an intruder or visitor such as the mailman. It is better not to restrain the dog by the neck or collar directly in such situations. Use a leash instead.

Aggression Toward Strangers

A DOG THAT GROWLS OR BARKS AT strangers is an embarrassment to its owner and can be dangerous. You are responsible for your dog's behavior and may have to face legal sanctions if it is out of control in a public place or causes injury to anyone. Usually the problem arises from fear of the unknown and unfamiliar. Most dogs that are suspicious of strangers are extremely affectionate with people they know, though occasionally a dominant animal who is already bullying its owner may resent the attentions of visitors to the house. When this happens, the problem is not fear but a lack of respect for people. It should be dealt with by reducing the dog's status (see basic ground rules on pages 104–105) and reinforcing obedience training. Early neutering can help in the male dog.

The Roots of Fear

A common cause of fearful aggression is lack of socialization in the young puppy. Puppies who are isolated during the first few months of life often become fearful and aggressive later, and these animals may also be socially inadequate with other dogs. Break down a timid puppy's suspicion of strangers before it builds into something stronger and never try to force it into situations it cannot handle.

Ask visitors to the house to ignore the puppy until it is bold enough to make its own approach and comes cautiously to investigate. Then the visitor can offer back of a hand for the puppy to sniff. If they have come supplied with some tasty tidbits, these can be scattered for the puppy to pick up. The owner should remain close at hand to give verbal praise. Once the dog learns to regard strangers as a source of treats or fun, its anxieties should soon disappear.

Some puppies, however, may have their natural timidity reinforced by a painful encounter with a stranger. Unhappy experiences acquired during puberty can also have long-lasting effects. Distrust learned early on in a dog's life can be difficult to eradicate and may lead to extreme displays of aggression. It takes a lot of patient work to build up a nervous dog's confidence and remove the roots of its fear. Seek professional advice if you have a troubled dog.

Dogs that Want to Bite the Mailman

This is a problem that many owners want help in dealing with. Like most social animals, dogs are territorial to some extent and quick to defend their home territory. Encouraging your dog to bark if the doorbell rings or if it hears intruders reinforces this behavior. Problems start when the dog carries on barking or keeps visitors away. Fear, isolation, poor socialization, and confusion about hierarchy all help bring it about. Biting the mailman is an extreme form of this behavior.

The dog sees that the mailman wears a uniform that singles him out from other visitors. Because he does not come into the house, the dog concludes he is an unwanted visitor. He advances only as far as the mailbox and then retreats again, and the dog may come to believe it is his barking that drives the cowardly mailman away. Try to persuade your dog he is no threat. Introduce him to the mailman away from the mailbox, demonstrating relaxed and friendly behavior as you would with any other visitor. You may have to do this many times.

◄ *The roots of territorial aggression lie in fear of the unknown. Some owners encourage barking and guarding, but at best it is a nuisance and at worst endangers the safety of visitors such as the mailman.*

● *Is there any circumstance in which you would advise the use of a choke or electric collar to control an aggressive dog?*

Quite definitely not. It is an unfortunate fact that many restraint devices are available for dog owners to buy and use. They all work on the punishment principle, through the infliction of pain. This only increases fear and excitement in an aggressive dog, and its behavior is likely to worsen as a consequence. Electric collars and prong collars are particularly harsh in their effects and, if wrongly or inappropriately used, can impose real cruelty.

● *Fonzie, our crossbred dog, is friendly with absolutely everyone—except the veterinarian. He has to be dragged into the consulting room, and last time he even tried to bite the veterinarian when he was examining him. Is there anything we can do to stop him, apart from putting a muzzle on him, which Fonzie simply hates?*

Many dogs fear a visit to the animal hospital. Take Fonzie to the hospital, but ask if you can just sit quietly with him in the waiting room. Give him some tasty treats. Go back several times, and ask the veterinary nurses and receptionists to give him a tidbit and make a fuss of him. The vet should come out and make a fuss of him, too. Next time, take Fonzie into the consulting room, but don't place him on the table or get the vet to examine him. Reward him if he stays calm. Once his fears have subsided, Fonzie should be fine when the time comes for a real examination.

Case Study

Subject: *Rufus, a 13-month-old male Bloodhound*

Circumstances: Has lived with the Jackson family since a puppy, and has always had free run of the house and yard. The Jacksons' older Basset hound, Mac, barks at strangers but is too fearful to attack them.

Problem: Rufus is aggressive to strangers and has recently attacked visitors to the house.

Explanation: Rufus probably learned defensive and territorial aggression from Mac as a puppy, and now that he is mature, is bold enough to take action on his own. Rufus is a large dog, and could cause serious injury if the problem is allowed to continue.

Recommended treatment:

▶ Walk Rufus without Mac and keep him on a leash with a head collar so that he is fully under control. He should never be let off the leash, except in the yard which is escape-proof.

▶ Neutering should reduce the intensity of his reactions and curb his territorial tendencies.

▶ His owners must exert more control over Rufus by obedience training to carry out simple commands such as "sit" and "stay."

▶ When visitors arrive, keep Rufus and Mac in another room. Allow time to settle, then let Rufus in, under close supervision, on a leash and head collar. The visitors should be told to ignore him, but the Jacksons should reward him if he remains quiet and calm. In due course he will come to realize that he is not required to defend the house and that calm behavior brings rewards.

Aggression Toward Other Dogs

Many dogs are perfectly well behaved with people but not with other dogs. Aggression toward strange dogs is usually caused by fear or anxiety of a perceived threat. It is sometimes seen in extremely dominant (usually unneutered male) dogs who regard other dogs as potential challengers. These dogs tend to play rough and try to throw their weight around. However, in common with other forms of behavior, aggression toward strange dogs can also be learned, especially by puppies who imitate their parents or another adult dog. Fearful aggression of this kind is often shown by a dog that was poorly socialized when young or had bad experiences with other dogs in the first two years of life. Such behavior can be difficult to eradicate, so prevention is the best course. If you allow your puppy to mix with others of the same age at socialization classes and puppy parties, your pet will be more likely to develop good patterns of play and learn to interpret body language appropriately.

If you can, give the puppy contact with an adult dog that is not too rough in its behavior and will teach it some manners.

It is rare, but impossible, for dogs to fight to the death. Owners should not intervene physically in a dog fight, as the risk of getting bitten is very high. Get them to stop by turning a garden hose on them or making a loud, unpleasant noise by banging two metal objects together. Special alarms, marketed as "dogstops," are available. However, training your dog to respond to your call when off the leash and faced with a growling rival is the best strategy of all.

Dogs in the Same Household

Family dogs may behave aggressively toward one another if they are of the same breed (or size) and gender, if the owner lacks control over them, or if there is competition between them for food, space, toys, or attention. This type of aggression is a contest for status. The problem often escalates in male dogs between the ages of 9 months

Case Study

Subject: *Ben, an 18-month-old Staffordshire Bull Terrier*

Circumstances: Lived since puppyhood with the Rossi family. Most attached to Tony, the 20-year-old son.

Problem: Ben is a friendly dog at home, but on walks he growls at other approaching dogs and sometimes attacks them. This behavior is worse when Tony is walking him.

Explanation: Ben was insufficiently socialized at an early age not to react to other dogs. He probably feels protective toward Tony and is seeking to defend him from other dogs.

Recommended treatment:

▶ Ben should always be walked on a leash with a head collar. Tony should cease to walk him for the time being, and the task should be shared among other members of the family.

▶ The Rossis must practice obedience exercises with Ben, such as heel work and responding to simple commands. He should be rewarded with praise, play, or tidbits to encourage him to pay attention.

▶ The help of a calm, nonreactive dog should be enlisted. If Ben growls and shows aggression when he is walked past it, he should be severely reprimanded and immediately praised if he ignores it. Repeat until Ben ignores the other dog every time. Repeat for several more days, and then try the exercise with other quiet dogs.

▶ Ben should eventually become calmer around strange dogs but should still be kept at a distance from excited animals. It will probably be necessary to enlist the help of a professional trainer or behavior counselor before Ben can be trusted off the leash.

Q & A ● *Will two females in the same household always fight?*

… Some females get along fine together, but if they are closely matched in temperament and physical features, they may become strongly competitive. This can lead to fighting, particularly if they are mother and daughter or sisters. Aggression flares up when one of them is in season, and females have been known to fight to the death. This type of aggression is difficult to eradicate. Spaying the lower-ranking female, or both, can help.

● *I have agreed to look after my sister's 1-year-old Whippet, Pippa, when she goes into the hospital for a few days. Bilko, my own West Highland, is quite territorial. How can I keep the peace between them?*

Let the dogs play freely together outside, but respect Bilko's feelings indoors and treat him as the favorite. Feed the dogs separately to avoid competition at mealtimes and don't leave bones or special toys lying around for them to fight over. Once Bilko has become used to having Pippa around, he will cease to feel threatened by her.

▼ *Displays of aggression between sibling puppies can sometimes develop into real fighting in later life, arising out of competition for food and attention.*

and 3 years and is exacerbated by situations that cause excitement, such as feeding time or the arrival of visitors. To deal with it, you need to reinforce both dogs' instinct to respect the pack hierarchy. If the two dogs are quite close in age, neutering of the lower-ranking dog (the one that submits the most readily), or both dogs, should be considered. If a younger dog is challenging an older one that is beginning to lose his physical and mental abilities, you may have to decide to emphasize the status of the younger one, by feeding the higher-ranking dog first, letting it go out of doorways or enter the car ahead of the other dog, and giving it the preferential sleeping position next to the heater or radiator.

You can further reduce the potential for conflict by allowing the dogs time apart from each other. Feed them separately to avoid competition over food and allow them their own toys. Do not always walk them together. If a fight is about to start, intervene immediately to stop it, if necessary by squirting the dogs with a water pistol or making a loud, unpleasant noise. Reprimand and remove the lower-ranking dog from the scene first. It is important that every member of the family understand the situation and be consistent in their attitude toward both dogs.

Unpredictable Aggression

NOT ALL AGGRESSION IS CAUSED BY THE LACK of socialization, inadequate training, or a failure of control. There are a number of behavioral and medical conditions that can make a normally calm, well-behaved dog show sudden, unexpected aggression toward its owner, other people, or dogs. Some females occasionally snap, growl, or bite during a false pregnancy or after giving birth. Usually the mother's instinct to protect her puppies passes when her hormone levels return to normal, but in some circumstances a female constantly worried by intruders may turn on her own puppies. A female with this problem should be left undisturbed. Sometimes the breeder may decide to remove her puppies to hand rear them. It would be inadvisable to allow the female to breed again.

A dog that has rage syndrome will suddenly become vicious without any apparent provocation. It may give no warning other than a sudden glazed expression and perhaps a growl before turning on any dog or human within reach. The episode may last only a few seconds, and the dog may be completely normal afterward—until the

Q&A...

● *Can tranquilizers ever be helpful in treating aggression?*

To a limited extent, yes, but only certain types of aggression, mainly those that are related to epilepsy. Tranquilizers are inappropriate in treating most other forms of aggression because they blunt both normal and abnormal behavior patterns and allow the aggressive behavior to become more pronounced.

● *We were watching TV last night when Cally, our 2-year-old female Golden Retriever, suddenly began to growl and viciously attacked our Jack Russell for no reason at all—they are normally the best of friends. She looked glazed and confused while this was happening, but recovered quickly after a few minutes and was soon back to normal. What made her behave like this? We are very concerned.*

Quite rightly so. You must take Cally to the vet for a full clinical examination as soon as possible. One explanation for her behavior is that Cally is suffering from a form of epilepsy. This can be controlled with anticonvulsive drugs, but an EEG is needed to confirm the diagnosis. Much more seriously, however, Cally could be developing rage syndrome. She needs professional assessment to decide how treatable her condition is—and quickly.

Case Study

Ruby, a 2-year-old female Toy Poodle
....

Circumstances: Unspayed. Has not been mated. Was in heat 8 weeks ago.

Problem: Ruby is normally good-tempered but has recently become jealous of her toys and bed. She is often irritable with her owners, and has become snappish. She has started to produce a little milk from her mammary glands.

Explanation: Ruby is having a false pregnancy. Her irritability is caused by rising levels of prolactin in her bloodstream. This hormone stimulates milk production in pregnancy, and makes the female defensive on behalf of her puppies.

Recommended treatment:

▶ Her owners should make sure that Ruby is given plenty of exercise.

▶ She should be put on to a diet that is not too rich in protein. It should be supplemented with extra fiber, such as vegetables or bran.

▶ The symptoms of false pregnancy require medical treatment, so the vet should examine Ruby immediately. It is particularly important to prevent mastitis (mammary inflammation).

▶ As Ruby has had one severe false pregnancy, it is very likely she will have another one next time she comes in heat. Unless her owners are very eager for her to breed, they would be advised to have her spayed once she returns to normal, usually about 3 months after the end of her season.

next time. The condition is not well understood, but may be associated with extreme dominance aggression and have a hereditary component. Unpredictable aggression is very risky in a pet, especially if there are children in the family. Behavioral therapy can occasionally help, but in many cases an owner may have no other course than to euthanize the dog.

Old age is frequently accompanied by behavior changes. A formerly good-tempered dog may turn grouchy as it begins to age. It will snap if it is touched or picked up suddenly, woken up from sleep, or pestered by children. Handle an elderly dog gently—its muscles and joints are not as supple as they used to be.

Medical Causes of Aggression

It is important that you have your veterinarian examine your elderly dog regularly to make sure that there isn't an underlying illness that is responsible for its increased tendency to snappishness. There are a number of chronic medical conditions that may cause irritability in a dog at any age, including pain, failing vision, canine cognitive disorders, heart, kidney, and liver disorders. Dogs suffering from hypothyroidism, in which the thyroid gland is less active than normal, may turn also aggressive. Other signs to look for are lethargy and skin alterations (see pages 56–57). Blood tests will diagnose the problem. Medical treatment is usually successful.

An unpredictable outburst of aggression is sometimes occasioned by a form of epilepsy. In such cases, the affected animals do not actually have seizures or convulsions (see pages 64–65), but their expression becomes glazed, they may appear unable to recognize their owner or companion dogs, and will snap and growl. As with rage syndrome, their behavior returns to normal after a few minutes, and it will seem as though nothing has happened. The attacks may be triggered by an intense stimulus such as loud noises or bright, flickering lights. They often occur after the dog has been resting or has just woken from sleep. If you notice your dog behaving like this, you should lose no time in consulting your vet.

▲ *Rage syndrome appears to be hereditary in certain breeds and color of dog. The golden-haired English Cocker Spaniel, on the left, is at higher risk than its brown and white companion.*

▼ *If you are unsure of your dog's behavior, you may decide to muzzle it in public. A plastic, basket-type muzzle is perhaps the most suitable one to choose.*

Destructive Behavior in Puppies

PUPPIES ARE KNOWN FOR THEIR DESTRUCTIVE behavior. Many owners accept it as the price of having a cute pet of their own, but when the dog is older, the cuteness tends to wear thin, particularly if the damage is more than the occasional chewed-up shoe. It is possible for a bored dog, left on its own for long, to chew up carpets and drapes, bite large chunks out of solid items of furniture, and even strip wallpaper off the walls. For some owners it is only a matter of time before the expense and the stress leads them to decide the dog must go. Animal shelters are full of dogs who have been rejected for this reason.

Puppies chew when they are teething (from about 3 to 7 months of age) in order to relieve their gums as they lose their baby teeth and the adult teeth are erupting. Although their jaws are not very powerful at this age, the baby teeth are extremely sharp and will leave marks. Provide plenty of hard, safe chews such as rawhide bones and rubber toys for the puppy to gnaw on. Praise it when it settles down to chew one of these and then leave it in peace. Avoid giving it old slippers, as this may convey the wrong message about what it is allowed to chew.

Q&A...

● **How long should a puppy or immature dog be left on its own?**

This varies a great deal according to the age and type of dog, but all young animals find it hard to cope with long periods of isolation. Even a mature dog should not be left for more than 4–5 hours.

● **My puppy is always chewing the leg of a particular chair in the living room. Have you any suggestions for stopping him?**

A well-aimed squirt from a water pistol to startle the puppy can be an effective deterrent. Try not to let him see that you are operating the pistol. Hide behind the chair—he will think the jet of water came from there and won't want to approach it again. Immediately offer him something else to chew. Tossing a can full of pebbles near (not on) the puppy has the same effect.

▼ *"See what I can do!" Should this puppy have its way, an innocent game will quickly spell destruction for a well-loved pair of shoes.*

Case Study

Polly, a 10-month-old Collie/Husky cross

....

Circumstances: Ryan and Ellie Sullivan have had Polly since she was 6 weeks old. Confident and outgoing, she has no socialization problems. Polly is seldom left more than 2 hours on her own; her walks are short and infrequent. She is independent, and not overattached to the Sullivans.

Problem: Polly is increasingly destructive when left at home by herself. She is obsessive with her toys when owners are present and is generally difficult to discipline, though not aggressive. Has begun to pull hard on the leash when walked and does not return to command when off the leash.

Explanation: A dog of Polly's type needs a lot of physical exercise and mental stimulation. She is not getting either, and is bored. It is vital that the Sullivans work hard to give her time and attention at this critical phase of her development. If they can manage it, they should have a very rewarding relationship with Polly.

••

Recommended treatment:

▶ Polly should be given at least half an hour's exercise in the morning, then allowed 10–15 minutes to settle and eat her breakfast before the Sullivans leave the house.

▶ She should be left in a room where she can do no damage, and given a special toy and some chewy items. A puzzle feeder or a hollow toy stuffed with dog biscuits or bits of cheese will challenge her mentally, burn off some energy, and keep her entertained, too.

▶ When Ellie returns mid-morning, she should take Polly outside for an energetic play session. Ellie should always initiate and terminate the play sessions and keep charge of Polly's toys when they are not being used.

▶ Polly should have a good long walk in the afternoon. She should be taken to different locations so that she encounters new smells and dogs. Ellie and Ryan must work hard to develop her training with progressive exercises that challenge and stimulate her mentally. She should receive frequent praise and be given a food or play reward when she cooperates.

Use a baby gate to close off forbidden areas of of the house and remember to keep bedroom doors closed. If you do catch the puppy gnawing on the furniture or other banned object, reprimand it immediately and direct its attention to a legitimate substitute.

Many puppies go through a second, even more destructive phase of chewing between 8 and 12 months. Hunting and retrieving dogs are notorious for this as they have an instinctive urge to use their mouths. Give your dog plenty of novel items to chew, such as cardboard boxes and old newspapers, as well as strong rubber chews.

Preventing Boredom

Adolescent dogs are particularly prone to boredom. They need exercise, mental stimulation, and a variety of outlets for their energy in the form of games and exposure to different environments and challenges. Lacking them, they will find their own amusements—chewing up the furniture or digging their way under the garden fence. Mental stimulation is every bit as valuable as physical exercise. Hide objects for the dog to find. Give it puzzle toys to play with.

A dog left alone for long periods in the day quickly becomes bored and will turn to destructive activities. A dog is not the right pet for an owner who works full-time, unless alternative arrangements can be made to look after it while the owner is absent.

▲ *Left unsupervised, a bored dog can cause havoc in the back yard or garden, digging up plants, knocking over pots, and chewing the heads off flowers.*

Anxiety Problems

A WIDE VARIETY OF BEHAVIOR PROBLEMS IN THE adult dog are the result of anxiety. It shows itself in numerous ways—destructive chewing, house-soiling, whining and barking, growling or fearful aggression, and hyperactivity—and can be rooted in a wide variety of situations. For example, an overbearing owner, especially one who scolds the dog frequently, is liable to make a dog apprehensive in certain circumstances. When the owner returns home, a fearful dog like this may show extreme submissive behavior and even urinate. On receiving a reprimand from its owner, the dog is liable to become still more anxious, and the behavior is reinforced.

The uncertainty and disruption of routine surrounding the arrival of a new baby, a sudden illness in the family, an event like Thanksgiving or Christmas, with the flurry of visitors and opening of gifts, can make a dog anxious and insecure. At times like this, your dog needs plenty of reassurance. Make sure you or another member of the family knows where the dog is at any time. Try and keep it away from all the activity so that it doesn't get under people's feet and shouted at. Give it its own space and plenty of toys and chews to keep it occupied. Don't allow the disturbances in the house to disrupt its regular feeding, exercise, and play routines. Make sure it has its normal pattern of rest and sleep if possible. This is particularly important for older dogs.

Separation Anxiety

A dog that exhibits one of a variety of forms of behavior, such as barking, howling, destructive activity, house soiling, or obsessive behavior (see pages 142–143), only when it is left on its own, may be suffering from separation anxiety. It is important that the dog be thoroughly examined to make sure there is no other underlying cause, such as physical illness. If the problem behavior also occurs when the owner is present, as well as away from the house, then another cause should be looked for.

▲ *It's heartwarming to have a friend look out for you, but keep the excitement low when you return. Then your dog will find it easier to cope while you're away.*

Dogs with separation anxiety are usually over-attached to their owners and unable to cope with isolation. They may well be obedient and affectionate but will follow their owner all over the house, even into the bathroom. Typically, they become distressed when their owner gets ready to go out and show elation on his or her return. Their aberrant behavior generally begins shortly after the owner's departure but does not necessarily continue for the whole time that he or she remains absent from the house.

Certain factors seem to predispose dogs to separation anxiety. Puppies that spend every hour of the day and night with their owner and are then suddenly left alone will not be able to cope well with the unexpected long period of isolation. It is important to leave a puppy on its own for short periods of 10 minutes or so to begin with, gradually working up to longer absences. Puppies that have been hand reared, raised in kennels, or sold through pet stores are particularly vulnerable to separation anxiety. It is also common in dogs adopted from rescue shelters.

● *My two dogs were constant companions. Troy, a 1-year-old Cocker Spaniel, always snuggled up at night to Lizzie, an older Labrador. Sadly, Lizzie had to be put to sleep recently. Since then Troy's behavior has deteriorated and he has begun chewing the carpet when left on his own. Why is he doing this?*

Troy has never known a time without Lizzie, and his behavior is due to his sudden separation from her. Overattachment often develops between companion dogs. It can be avoided by giving them some time apart during the day and taking them for separate walks from time to time. Troy needs lots of love and attention to help him through this period. Maintain a regular, steady routine, but vary it with some new walks to stimulate his interest. The presence of another dog, or even a cat, can help—can you find a friendly dog to keep Troy company from time to time?

● *I have heard that certain breeds are particularly prone to separation anxiety. Is this true?*

Studies of separation problems show that rescue dogs, many of which are crossbreeds, are most prone to this syndrome. One survey found that Labradors, German Shepherds, and English Cocker Spaniels were more highly represented than other pure breeds.

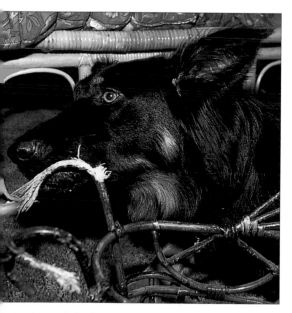

▲ *Most of the destructive damage carried out by a dog left on its own begins in the first 30 minutes after the owner leaves the house.*

Case Study

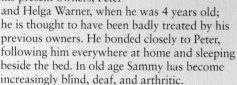

Sammy, an 11-year-old Old English Sheepdog

Circumstances:
Sammy was adopted by his present owners, Peter and Helga Warner, when he was 4 years old; he is thought to have been badly treated by his previous owners. He bonded closely to Peter, following him everywhere at home and sleeping beside the bed. In old age Sammy has become increasingly blind, deaf, and arthritic.

Problem: In the last 5 months Sammy has been messing in the house whenever he is left alone. He is not incontinent at other times, and a veterinary checkup revealed no urinary or digestive problems. He compulsively licks his forepaws and left front leg.

Explanation: As there is no medical cause, Sammy's incontinence can be attributed to separation anxiety caused by his increasing dependence on his owners, particularly Peter, as he becomes increasingly deaf and blind, and contact is mainly by touch and scent. Sammy is particularly distressed by his growing isolation because of his history of mistreatment by his previous owners.

Recommended treatment:

▶ Sammy should be given plenty of attention and physical contact by the Warners when they are home.

▶ He should be fed 2–3 small meals daily so that his stomach is always full and his digestion improves.

▶ Sammy needs to have exercise and food before being left, and he should be given an opportunity to relieve himself. He should be left in the living room, where he spends most time with Peter and Helga when they are at home, rather than be shut up in the kitchen, as is the practice at the moment.

▶ Sammy should have a warm, comfortable, draft-free bed. If he is provided with an old coat of Peter's to sleep on, this will give additional comfort and act as an emotional bridge during the Warners' absences. Peter should wear the coat for a few minutes from time to time to renew the smell, or leave it with a pile of his worn clothes for a while.

▲ *Professional dog walkers are one solution if you are at work for a part of the day. You should, of course, make sure the dog walker is able to control all the dogs.*

Dogs often undergo a second period of sensitivity between the ages of 6 and 12 months. This is the time in the wild when they would be finding a mate, and at this age they may become overattached to their owners. A young dog that is left alone for excessively long periods may also develop an anxiety about isolation.

It may sometimes happen that separation anxiety develops quite suddenly in a normally well-adjusted dog that has become accustomed to having its owner around all day—for example, if the owner is home on sick leave for a few months but then goes back to work. Elderly dogs may also become subject to separation anxiety as their loss of physical well-being makes them feel less secure and deepens their dependency. This is especially likely to happen if the dog becomes blind or deaf. In such cases, it may be necessary to find a dog sitter to stay with the dog during the times you are out.

Dealing with Anxiety

Behavior problems arising from separation anxiety can be difficult to eradicate, and it is quite likely that you will need help from a behavior counselor to deal with them successfully. The most important requirement is not to punish the dog for any damage it may have caused in your absence. Many owners say that their dogs look guilty after destroying the furniture or making a mess in the house. In fact, the dog is behaving submissively in anticipation of your anger—it has either learned to read your body language accurately, or else it associates your return with a scolding or punishment. Confronting the dog with its crime and reprimanding it in a loud voice will only make it more anxious. It does not understand why you are punishing it, as it does not associate what it did some hours earlier with the punishment you are giving now.

If your absences from home are unavoidable, perhaps you can arrange for a friend or neighbor to look after the dog while you are out, at least on a temporary basis while the dog is being treated. Many people who are out at work all day, or

● *I'm worried that Conan, our 3-year-old German Pointer, is developing separation anxiety. He barks furiously when we leave the house. When we return, he has often caused a major disturbance like scattering the contents of the garbage bin. He is disobedient at other times. For example, he will refuse to get out of my husband's chair when he wants to sit down and always wants attention. How do we deal with him?*

Conan's destructive behavior is triggered by pack hierarchy confusion rather than separation anxiety. He is used to having attention and resents it when the other members of the "pack" go off and leave him. You and your husband need to establish some ground rules in your relationship with Conan so that he knows that you are in charge. You would benefit from help from a behavior counselor.

● *I have a part-time job. Recently I have had a long spell off due to sickness, but am returning to work in 3 weeks. Oscar, my 10-month-old Golden Retriever, has obviously gotten used to having me around all day. How can I prevent him becoming anxious when I go back?*

You are wise to be thinking about this problem now. Prepare Oscar for the change by leaving him on his own for short periods during the day and slowly build up the time you are away. You should soon be able to leave the house for several hours with confidence.

● *Joey, my Dalmatian, is 9 months old. I'm thinking of having a long vacation abroad and putting Joey into a kennel. Would this be a good time to go?*

From Joey's point of view, it would be much better if you could hold off for 6 months or so. Adolescent dogs go through a sensitive period between ages 6 and 12 months, when they form attachments. A prolonged absence from you at this critical time might make Joey particularly anxious.

those who have to make frequent trips away, make use of professional dog sitters, who will spend time with the dog during the day and take it for walks. Meanwhile, try to accustom your dog to brief periods of being on its own while you are at home. Leave it in one room while you get on with a task in another. When the dog seems happy with that, slip out of the house for five minutes or so. Don't make a fuss about leaving or coming back. Stay away a little longer each time you leave the dog on its own. Some vets may prescribe antianxiety medicines.

Cushioning Your Absence

There are a number of things you can do to help make your absences more bearable for your dog. Establish a good exercise and feeding routine in the mornings before you leave for work. If the dog has had a walk (even a short one helps) and has some food in its stomach, it will find it much easier to settle after you leave. Avoid elaborate good-byes—this will only build up the dog's anxieties about your departure. Keep it casual, and do the same when you return—no big "I'm home!" ceremony.

If the dog is deeply attached to you, give it an old garment of yours to lie on. It will smell of you and compensate for your absence. Leave the radio or TV on, turned down low. At night it may help to leave a lamp burning. Giving the dog a new rawhide bone, a toy stuffed with biscuits, or a chew or two will distract it from the most anxious moment of all—your departure.

▶ *Leaving a dog with an old garment of yours provides an "emotional bridge" while you're away.*

Fears and Phobias

FEAR IS PART OF A DOG'S SURVIVAL STRATEGY when threatened. When facing an object it does not recognize or one that behaves inexplicably, its natural reaction is to back away or—if it cannot escape—growl, bark, or snap in a show of defensive aggression. Dogs have sensitive hearing and are startled by loud, sudden noises, yet we expect them to share our lack of concern for the washing machines, vacuum cleaners, doorbells, telephones, and other background noises that fill our lives. Early education is essential to prevent a dog reacting fearfully to such stimuli.

Excessive fearfulness in a dog often results from a combination of genetic and environmental factors. Fearful parents are likely to pass on the trait to their offspring, which is why it is so important to breed only from animals of equable temperament. A puppy will imitate and learn timidity from its mother or any other adult dog that belongs to the household. Obviously, bad handling and cruelty will instill fear into any animal and reinforce a tendency to timidity in one that is already fearful by nature. Nervous owners can contrive to make their dogs nervous—by communicating feelings of fear during a thunderstorm, for instance.

Extreme Fearfulness

A fearful dog is not a happy dog. Its lack of confidence will inhibit learning, make training difficult, and may lead to aggression. Fear can also induce phobias—an extreme reaction to particularly intense stimuli such as firecrackers, emergency alarms, or electrical storms. Phobias can be extremely debilitating. The dog may shake uncontrollably, salivate, whine, urinate, crawl under the bed, or try to to dig a hole in which to hide. It is natural for a concerned owner to want to pet and fuss over the dog, but this will only increase its anxiety. Use a firm, confident tone of voice instead to show that you are fully in control of events. Reward the dog with praise or a tidbit if it begins to calm down (avoid physical contact as you may inadvertently pass your own anxiety on to the animal). If the stimulus comes from outside, close all windows and doors, play music, or turn on the TV to mask the sounds. Encourage the dog to stay in a secure place, such as a favorite chair or its own bed.

Associated Phobias

Sometimes it is the association of one stimulus with another that initiates a phobic reaction. For example, a dog may cower at the sound of rain as it hits the window because it associates the noise with thunder, even though the rain is gentle and there isn't a storm raging. A fear of loud bangs may extend itself to fear of any door or window being closed or a chair being pushed back from the table. If the source of the fear is linked to a particular place such as the backyard or car, the dog may become unwilling to go there. Agoraphobia can develop: the dog has to be dragged out for walks and runs home in blind panic if it is allowed off the leash. You should consult your veterinarian who may prescribe anxiety-reducing medication and refer you to a behavior counselor. Problems like this normally have complex origins. Professional help is needed to unravel the causes and formulate a suitable program of treatment.

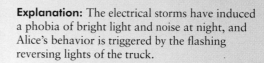

Case Study

Alice, a 3-year-old Standard Poodle

••••••••••••••••••••••

Circumstances:
Alice lives with the Brewer family and sleeps in the kitchen at night. The window overlooks a well-lit street. Living next door is a truck driver who frequently returns home between 4 and 6 am. The truck is noisy, and its lights flash when it is backed up off the street.

Problem: Since a series of severe electrical storms last August, Alice has begun waking up at night and rushing around the house, panting, barking, and whining. She jumps on and off the bed, urinates on the floor, and will not settle until daylight, by which time both she and the Brewers are exhausted.

Explanation: The electrical storms have induced a phobia of bright light and noise at night, and Alice's behavior is triggered by the flashing reversing lights of the truck.

••

Recommended treatment:

▶ Alice should be prescribed medication to calm her anxiety.

▶ At night she should sleep at the back of the house away from the street.

▶ If she wakes and panics, the Brewers should assume a "no-nonsense" approach, using a confident tone of voice to convince her there is nothing to fear.

▶ Comfort items such as an article of her owner's clothing placed in her bed, or a radio left playing quietly, may help.

● My dog, Biggles, has an extreme fear of loud noises such as firecrackers. My vet thinks that medication might help him. Will he get hooked on the drugs?

The common antianxiety drugs given to animals do not cause dependency, but the use of all drugs should be carefully monitored for side effects. Your vet will certainly do this, and will not prescribe them unless Biggles is 100 percent healthy—a blood test can check this. The drugs alone do not effect a cure, just help the behavior modification to work.

● Liesl, my Weimaraner, was riding in the back of my car when someone broadsided us. Two months later Liesl is still terrified of going in the car. What should I do?

Dispel Liesl's fears of the car by feeding her outside, choosing a spot from where she can see the car but is not too close to it. Tell her to sit and then place the bowl in front of her. Add a tasty morsel, such as a piece of chicken, to increase her enthusiasm and try to feed her small amounts several times a day. Let her eat only if she is calm. Gradually work your way closer to the car until she will feed beside or in it. When she's used to that, feed her with the engine running (reduce the amount of food you give her at this stage). Take Liesl on short journeys and give her a walk or game at the end to reinforce the association of the car with pleasant things. It will take time and constant repetition at every stage, but Liesl should slowly lose her fear.

◀ *This dog shows combined fear and predatory behavior toward the vacuum cleaner. Careful exposure to domestic appliances during the first three months of life should teach a puppy to ignore them.*

Why Does My Dog Chase?

THIS IS A PROBLEM THAT LIES ROOTED IN THE dog's instinct to hunt small animals. Wolves hunt by observing, stalking, chasing, grabbing, and killing. The instinct to chase remains very strong in the domestic dog, and certain breeds have been selectively bred for their skills in pursuit. What triggers the chasing instinct in the wild is the movement of the stalked prey as it panics and takes flight. A domestic dog with a tendency to chase may react in exactly the same way to any moving form that comes into view, be it another dog, cat, squirrel, or other small animal, poultry or livestock or a car or train.

Out walking, your dog may return obediently to heel most of the time, but if a bicycler or jogger appears on the horizon, its predatory instinct is triggered and the pursuit begins. The dog chases after the bike or the unfortunate jogger, perhaps snapping and biting, too, and it can be almost impossible to distract it. Chasing can have more serious consequences. An uncontrolled dog in the country that harasses sheep, cows, and horses may cause substantial injury, even death, if the animals panic or the dog attacks. The law in many countries allows farmers to shoot on sight any dog that is running loose among livestock. The predatory instinct puts cats and other small animals at risk, and endangers the life of the dog as well when it chases close to traffic. It may cause a dog to turn on a baby or small child because they act in a manner similar to wounded prey, moving abruptly and in an uncoordinated fashion and make high-pitched noises.

How to Prevent Chasing

As with most behavior problems, the key to stopping your dog from chasing lies in good socialization and obedience training as a puppy. Active dogs need to have their energy used up through long, enjoyable walks and challenging games so that they don't become bored and seek excitement by chasing. Do not allow your dog to

wander too far from you when out on a walk. Give it the opportunity to explore strange smells and places, but call it back at frequent intervals and reward it as soon as it returns so that it is always ready to abandon what it is doing to come to you.

If your puppy shows a tendency to chase joggers, keep it on a long leash for the time being and try diverting its attention by throwing a ball or toy in the opposite direction to the path the jogger is taking. Reward it every time it passes the jogger without fuss. After a while, the puppy will find the jogger far less interesting than you.

▼ *A Collie drops low to observe and stalk a flock of geese. The moment one of them moves, she will dash forward in pursuit. In herding breeds such as Collies, the natural instinct to herd and chase stampeding animals has been developed to human advantage.*

Case Study

Tess: a 2-year-old German Shepherd
•••••••••••••••

Circumstances: Tess's owners, the Franklins, both go out to work, leaving Tess in the small back yard. She has a 30-minute walk a day.

Problem: On walks, Tess has started to chase bicyclers, snapping at their wheels.

Explanation: Tess has the strong observe-stalk-chase instinct of a herding dog. She lacks stimulation and is bored.

••

Recommended treatment:

▶ Tess should have two sessions of strenuous daily exercise on a long line (9ft/3m).

▶ The Franklins should give her obedience and agility training to challenge her mentally and provide an additional physical outlet. They should play retrieving games and give her toys such as puzzle feeders when she's alone.

▶ They should teach her the "leave" command by slowly propelling a toy across the floor, and rewarding her when she comes straight to them rather than pursuing the toy.

▶ When a bicycler appears, Tess should be given the command to "leave." A ball should be thrown in the opposite direction for her to chase, and she should be rewarded every time she obeys.

▶ If the Franklins cannot find extra time to look after Tess and keep her stimulated, they should consider parting with her.

Q & A...

● As a puppy, Rushmore, my Beagle, chased everything in sight. He's stopped now, after obedience training, but cannot resist going after the ducks he meets on the riverside path close by the house. They always get away. Should I be concerned by this?

In a dog with a history of chasing, the answer is yes. Keep working on his training, using exactly the same principles you used to stop him chasing other things. If you can't dissuade him, you'll have to walk him elsewhere or keep him on a long leash when walking by the river.

● My terrier, Milo, wants to play chasing games with every dog he sees. As soon as he spots one, he's away before I've time to get his leash on, and he ignores my shouts and whistles. Not all owners and dogs welcome his attentions. What can I do?

This suggests incomplete training and control, and could lead to trouble if Milo meets an aggressive dog. Ideally, you should never allow your dog to approach a strange one until you have established with the owner that he is friendly, reliable, and willing to play. You need to teach Milo to hold back until you give the command "play." I think both you and Milo would benefit from training classes.

Nuisance Barking

FEW PEOPLE LIVE HAPPILY NEXT TO A NOISY DOG. Barking, howling, and whining are all part of the normal means of canine communication (the Basenji is the only totally silent breed). All too often, however, a dog's noisy outbursts can reach unacceptable levels. Dogs that bark frantically whenever anyone passes the gate, howl all day, or endlessly whine for attention are animals with behavior problems.

Some dogs with high levels of excitability, such as certain terriers and other small dogs, are particularly inclined to bark, whine, and yelp when aroused—for example, when visitors come to the house, food is imminent, or when playing with another dog. Dogs are quick to learn by imitation, and a dog sometimes picks up the habit of noisy vocalization from others. You may find that during a stay in kennels your normally quiet dog is encouraged to bark by other noisy dogs nearby. Early education is the key to

● *Our German Shepherd, Freya, always barks noisily at us from the house as we approach the front door. Why does she do this?*

Freya is barking to show she's excited to see you. Don't be tempted to shout at her to make her stop—this will only increase Freya's excitement levels and worsen the problem. Wait until she has quieted down and then greet her calmly.

● *Our neighbor says Katy, our 3-year-old Skye Terrier, barks constantly while we are out. Would a citronella antibark collar be an effective deterrent?*

Citronella collars are certainly a more humane alternative than electric antibark collars, which should never be used. They release citronella whenever the dog barks—dogs hate the smell, so if they learn to associate it with barking, they will stop. The collars are most effective for excitable barking. If Katy barks only when you are out, she is probably anxious, so your best course is to treat the underlying cause. If you simply silence her, she may show her anxiety in other ways, such as destructive activity.

Case Study

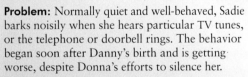

Sadie: a 5-year-old Miniature Schnauzer

. . . .

Circumstances: Lives with Donna Stone and her toddler, Danny.

Problem: Normally quiet and well-behaved, Sadie barks noisily when she hears particular TV tunes, or the telephone or doorbell rings. The behavior began soon after Danny's birth and is getting worse, despite Donna's efforts to silence her.

Explanation: This is territorial/defensive behavior. Sadie is protecting Donna and Danny, and perceives the TV tunes and other noises as unwanted intrusions. When Donna shouts to silence her, Sadie thinks she is "joining in," confirming the rightness of her action. The noise then stops (the theme tune ends, the phone or doorbell is answered), and Sadie believes she has fended off the threat.

Recommended treatment:

▶ Donna should cool her relationship with Sadie, ignore her demands for attention, and make Sadie work for treats and praise.

▶ She should teach Sadie to lie in her bed when told, using the command "quiet," in return for a reward.

▶ The doorbell should be disconnected, and the telephone alarm made inaudible. The TV tunes should be taped and played back on low volume. When Sadie becomes excited, she should be given the "quiet" command and rewarded when she obeys and goes to her bed.

▶ This exercise should be repeated many times, gradually increasing the volume of the music. Eventually, the command "quiet" should be given on its own and the food rewards replaced with praise.

▶ Once Sadie has learned to ignore the TV, she should be desensitized by the same methods to the doorbell and telephone in turn.

prevention. A dog that rushes to bark at visitors may not have been properly socialized. Its lack of confidence with strange people or dogs causes it to say "Keep away from me, I don't like the look of you!"—classic territorial behavior. The territorial/defensive urge is one reason why dogs bark noisily in the car, to warn off passersby. Stress and excitement can also lead to noisy behavior in the car. Once again, early familiarization may stop the problem from developing.

Whining or barking as an attention-seeking device usually begins during puppyhood because the owner gives in too readily to the puppy's demands. While it can be amusing to have your

▼ *In the wild a dog barks to convey many different messages to the pack—warning, greeting, pain, or aggression. A dog that barks excessively is trying to tell you something—look for the underlying meaning.*

10-week-old puppy yelp and bark when it sees you get out the leash for a walk, this behavior is a nuisance in an adult dog and encourages barking at other times of excitement. Put the leash back on the shelf or hook, tell the puppy to sit, reward it, and wait for it to become quiet. If the barking begins again, ignore the puppy and walk away. Postpone the walk until the puppy is calm.

"Where Are You?"

A dog that howls, whines, or barks incessantly when left on its own is suffering from separation anxiety (see pages 132–135). Pack dogs such as Huskies and Beagles hate being left on their own, and you can often alleviate the problem by acquiring another dog as company. Extreme cases of separation anxiety almost certainly need treating by a behavior counselor. To deal successfully with the problem, you have to reduce the dog's dependence on you. Punishing the dog will only increase its anxiety. Don't simply try to silence it—methods such as debarking (removal of the vocal cords) or the use of electric antibarking devices are very cruel and inflict further suffering on the dog. They will not eliminate the underlying motivation for the barking.

Obsessive Behavior and Other Problems

ANY REPETITIVE AND APPARENTLY MEANINGLESS behavior in your dog, such as circling, pacing, compulsive barking, excessive grooming, fixed staring, and self-mutilation, should always be thoroughly checked out by your veterinarian as there may very often be an underlying health problem. If no medical cause is discovered, the dog may be reacting to stress or boredom. Dogs from shelters and rescue centers are especially prone to obsessive disorders because their environment frequently fails to provide stimulation and a varied routine. However, dogs from comfortable and loving homes may also exhibit these traits. Sometimes there is an obvious cause of stress, such as the arrival of a new baby, but in other cases the problem is due to lack of interest, stimulation, and exercise. You may be able to eliminate the behavior by giving the dog extra time and attention and providing it with stimulating toys, but if it persists, your veterinarian may prescribe psychoactive medication.

Some breeds are genetically predisposed to obsessive behavior. For example, Bull Terriers quite often chase their tails; Dobermans sometimes lick and suck their flanks. If a dog of working descent, such as a Border Collie, is given no outlet for its normal, instinctive herding activities, its boredom and frustration may give rise to a variety of behavior problems such as aggression, inappropriate chasing, nipping heels, pacing, and chasing lights and shadows.

Nuisance Digging

A type of behavior that frequently causes owners difficulties is excessive digging. Many kinds of dog, especially terriers, are instinctive diggers. Some northern breeds like Huskies and Malamutes will excavate cooling holes for themselves in hot weather. A dog that feels the heat should be provided with a shelter to lie under on sunny days. Many dogs appear to enjoy digging just for the sake of it—perhaps because their ancestors dug hollows to lie in or for hiding food. If you

● *Our timid little crossbreed, Spritzer, constantly licks us when we get home in the evening. Is this obsessive behavior?*

It could become so, but Spritzer is probably seeking to appease you. Timid or submissive dogs will often attempt to lick their owners, especially under the chin. This is a gesture used by young puppies to appease adults in the pack; it also stimulates the adult to regurgitate food. When you greet Spritzer, avoid leaning over him or stroking the top of his head; get down to his level and stroke his flanks or the sides of his face. More assertive dogs sometimes lick their owner as a dominant gesture, and it can also be a form of attention-seeking.

● *When my Papillon, Schubert, was ill, he stopped eating, and I had to feed him by hand because he was getting so thin. Although he's completely recovered now, he still expects me to do this for him, and refuses to eat from his bowl. What can I do?*

Schubert has an acquired dependancy—he has learned to enjoy your exclusive attention. Give him palatable foods such as chicken, turkey, or fish, or try adding a little cheese to his diet. Serve it warm or with a little gravy, and feed your dog twice a day. Ignore him at mealtimes and pick his bowl up after 20 minutes if he hasn't eaten. If all else fails, appetite stimulants such as multivitamins and anabolic steroids may help—ask your veterinarian.

● *How can I stop Kelpie, my Jack Russell, from eating horse droppings when we are out walking?*

Aversion tactics often work. Keep Kelpie on a long leash wherever you know there are likely to have been horses about. Have something noisy like a small container filled with pebbles in your pocket. If Kelpie sees a heap of manure, allow her to sniff it, but the moment she tries to eat it, throw the container near her to startle her. She will then come to you for comfort. It is important that she should associate the sudden noise with the heap of manure, not you, so make sure she doesn't observe you. You may have to repeat the operation many times before Kelpie loses all interest in horse manure.

▲ *"I know you're down there somewhere." It can be hard to deter a terrier-type dog with a strong ratting instinct from excavating holes outdoors.*

own a compulsive digger, try to direct the activity to a designated part of the garden by burying a bone there and then encouraging the dog to dig it up. Repeat this several times and hide other tasty morsels under the soil in this particular area until digging here becomes a habit. If your dog digs obsessively in the house or garden, it may be reacting to anxiety and fear by trying to create an escape route for itself. If this is the case, you should obtain professional help.

Eating Disorders

A significant number of behavioral problems are centered on food. Dogs are notoriously greedy, but one that suddenly begins to gorge itself may be reacting to stress or boredom. Rule out any medical problem (see pages 72–73), then look closely at the dog's lifestyle to see what may be causing the increased eating. If the dog lacks stimulation, try feeding some of its daily rations in a toy such as a plastic cube that has to be picked up, tossed, or shaken to release the food. The meal takes much longer to eat this way.

Dogs sometimes lose their enthusiasm for food when stressed—for instance, after the death of an owner or a canine companion—but it is usually short-lived. Give a grieving dog plenty of attention and coax it to eat with tasty treats such as chicken or fish.

Sometimes a dog will eat its own or other animals' feces (copraphagia). This habit usually begins in the young, growing dog and is relatively harmless, but it disgusts the owner and may lead to the dog's being rejected. If your dog is obsessively copraphagic, have your vet examine it to ensure there are no health problems. Check that the diet is sufficient in quality and quantity. It often helps to increase the number of meals to three or four a day while maintaining the same daily intake of food. A few pieces of acidic food such as pineapple or zucchini added to the dog's food can help make its own feces less palatable.

Case Study

Judy: *a 2-year-old neutered female Labrador*

....

Circumstances: Lives with Tracy Lang in a small house that has no outside access. Has only one 15-minute walk a day and never has a chance to meet other dogs.

Problem: Constantly paces, barks, and scratches the carpet. Tracy responds to this behavior by feeding or petting Judy.

Explanation: Deprived of all outlets for her mental and physical energy, Judy is slowly going crazy. Her hyperexcitable behavior earns her attention from Tracy, thereby reinforcing it.

Recommended treatment:

▶ Judy needs three half-hour walks a day, with plenty of strenuous play sessions and retrieving games. She should also be fed twice daily.

▶ If possible, a dog should be found with whom Judy can share walks and outdoor play, providing a necessary outlet for her energy.

▶ At home, whenever she begins to look restless or overexcited, Judy should be told to lie on her bed. She should be praised when she does so, but without any extravagant fuss.

▶ Tracy should withdraw all attention when Judy becomes noisy or overexcited, if necessary leaving the room and closing the door.

▶ If Tracy cannot manage this program, she should find Judy another home.

Problem Sexual Behavior

ONE OF THE MOST FREQUENT COMPLAINTS OF dog owners is that their pet has an unacceptable habit of mounting inappropriate objects such as cushions, stuffed animals, or people's legs. This behavior is more typical of males. All the same, some degree of "practice" mounting does occur in female puppies and can be a sign of dominance in an adult female—or simply gender confusion if she grew up with a predominantly male litter.

Inappropriate mounting in the male usually ceases after the dog reaches full sexual maturity, between 6 and 12 months of age. Sometimes, however, it may become persistent. Neutering will usually cure it (see pages 90–91). An injection that temporarily blocks the activity of the male hormone testosterone will show if it is likely to be effective—if the mounting stops, then castration should deal satisfactorily with the problem. The earlier that neutering is carried out, the more successful it is likely to be. If the dog is just entering puberty and the mounting has only recently started, the hormone injection on its own may be enough to end it, especially if adequate steps are taken to increase the dog's mental stimulation and daily exercise.

Mounting is not always associated with hypersexuality, however. In some cases it is related to problems of rank—the dog will mount another dog or its owner's leg to show superiority. To deal with this, ignore the behavior and take steps to reduce the dog's rank (see pages 104–105). A dog,

▶ *Puppies and young dogs often indulge in "practice" mounting. The behavior usually passes, but consult a vet if it continues.*

especially an intelligent one, that is bored and frustrated and has no other outlet for its energy will sometimes mount at times of excitement, for example when visitors arrive. Such behavior can indicate considerable disturbance. It is particularly worrying if the dog exhibits other forms of obsessive behavior or aggression, and calls for prompt diagnosis and treatment by a behavior therapist. However unpleasant you may find the behavior, you should never attempt to punish a dog that is mounting, as this may simply provoke the dog to aggression.

Urine Marking

It is normal for males to scent mark their territory by urinating on bushes and posts outdoors. Occasionally, however, unneutered males will urinate on the furniture indoors. These dogs may be exhibiting overdeveloped territorial behavior. They are often pushy and confident and may show aggression toward other dogs. Indoor urine marking may also occur if something happens to make a dog feel insecure, such as the

arrival of a new baby or a new dog in the household. Behavior therapy combined with antimale hormone injections or neutering will often end indoor marking, but treatment is usually more successful in an adolescent than an older male in whom the habit is deeply ingrained.

Sexual Behavior in Females

The hormones present in the female's bloodstream fluctuate according to the stage of her estrus cycle (see page 94) and can have considerable effect on her behavior patterns. Her mood changes when she comes into heat, and she often shows irritability toward other females. When two or more females are living in the same household, aggression often occurs when one of the lower-ranking females is in season. This is because the genetic programing of the "alpha" (dominant) female directs her to drive the lower-ranking female out and stop her mating, even though no male dog is present. The remedy is to spay (neuter) the lower-ranking female, or both, or to give regular hormone injections to prevent them from coming into heat. Even then, fighting females can be extremely difficult to deal with.

◄ *An eager male will cross all obstacles to reach a female when her scent is calling. It is up to you to keep him secure at home.*

● *Dusty, my 2-year-old male Whippet, shows a strong determination to wander. I'm worried that next time it happens we'll lose him. Will neutering help?*

If the sex drive is causing Dusty's wanderlust, neutering should probably help to keep him home. However, some dogs roam simply because they are bored at home; an overattached dog left on his own may escape to look for his owner. Your first objective must be to strengthen all your fences.

● *Our 8-month-old male Border Terrier, Benjie, mounts everything in sight, including visitors' legs. It can be very embarrassing. How do we stop him?*

The most effective way of breaking this habit is to interrupt Benjie immediately with a sharp "no" or a deep growl. Then put Benjie into another room for ten minutes or so to teach him that this behavior is

unacceptable. Puppies who develop this behavior are quite likely to be overassertive, so you must take care not to allow Benjie the upper hand. If the mounting behavior persists, talk the problem over with your veterinarian, who may suggest injections or neutering, or refer you to a behavior counselor for treatment.

● *Ricardo, my Dalmatian, has begun urine marking on the furniture. Have you any advice?*

Clean the area thoroughly with hot water, then apply a biological odor eliminator. This will have the effect of removing all traces of odor from the site so Ricardo will not be drawn to spray in that spot again. A solution of one-part vinegar to one-part water is also effective, but avoid ammonia-based household products as they smell like urine. Have your veterinarian examine Ricardo to rule out any underlying medical problem such as cystitis.

DOG BREEDS

THE DELIBERATE SELECTION OF PARTICULAR TRAITS for breeding purposes has resulted in the hundreds of literally man-made pedigree breeds of dog we see today. The 25 breeds described in the following pages have been chosen on the basis of their worldwide popularity. They all make suitable family pets, though some are not advised for first-time owners or families with children, and some need the open spaces of the country rather than a cramped city apartment to enjoy life fully.

There are drawbacks to selective breeding. As many pedigree breeds have started from only one or two bloodlines, the smallness of the gene pool means that inherited defects can quickly become established. The Breed Profiles summarize the principal health problems of each breed. To prevent such problems from arising, all animals should be rigorously screened before being used for breeding. The crossbreed has fewer health problems and makes a robust, loyal, and affectionate companion.

Pedigree Problems

THE RELATIONSHIP BETWEEN DOGS AND HUMANS started several millennia ago when prehistoric hunter–gatherers discovered that the wolf dogs that scavenged around their campsites could be trained for hunting. They selected for breeding those animals with the physical and temperamental attributes for chasing and killing prey, (long legs, strong jaws, and muscular body) or for digging small animals out of burrows (a quick eye, squat body). As humans settled down to farming, dogs were chosen for their skill at herding and guarding livestock.

Humans also bred certain characteristics into dogs merely because they liked them. Lap dogs have been in existence for thousands of years, and flat-faced breeds such as Pekingese and Pugs were developed for their appealing appearance. In the middle of the last century, the enthusiasm for breeding pedigree dogs for show purposes led to the development of standards that lay down precise rules for the appearance and temperament of individual breeds. Breeders emphasize those aspects of the breed that help win placings at dog shows, such as the Yorkshire Terrier's long, silky coat.

Inherited Defects in Pedigree Dogs

While this genetic fine tuning ensures that fit, elegant, and well-behaved specimens of the breed are produced, it increases the likelihood of particular inherited defects becoming established in individual family lines within pedigree breeds. For example, the inherited hip condition, hip dysplasia, is found in several of the larger breeds that were originally bred for strength but almost never occurs in Greyhounds, bred for speed and agility. In some flat-faced breeds, the respiratory passages have become foreshortened, and they are prone to breathing difficulties. Temperament has been overlooked in some breeding lines, giving rise to unpredictable behavior. Occasionally, demand for a particular breed outstrips supply, and ill-advised breeding takes place using sub-

Points to Consider

✓ Remember that some breeds are more likely to be troublefree than others.

✓ If you have decided on a breed, ask your vet if it has any inherited problems and what can be done to avoid them.

✓ Reduce the chances of your puppy having a disease by asking the right questions about his ancestry.

✓ Check that both parents were screened for defects before breeding, where appropriate. In breeds with a known tendency to hip dysplasia, ask to see copies of both parents' OFA certificate (in the US).

✓ Do not neglect temperament. You can lower the risk of picking a pup with behavioral problems if you observe both parents closely. Avoid choosing any puppy that appears overly timid (see page 16).

standard dogs. This has affected, for example, German Shepherds, Cocker Spaniels, Cavalier King Charles Spaniels, and the smaller poodles.

The inherited defects associated with most of the breeds are well known. But it is not always easy to tell which dogs are affected. Some types of inherited blindness, for example, do not appear until after the dog is past breeding age, when it may already have produced affected offspring. It is even more difficult to know which dogs are the symptomless carriers of genetic conditions or suffer from behavioral problems.

Known carriers of inherited defects should never be used for breeding. Early tests can establish the presence of some inherited conditions and amateur breeders should always arrange for their veterinarian to carry out such checks. In the US, the OFA (Orthopedic Foundation for Animals) evaluates hip conformation in breeds with a tendency to hip dysplasia and issues certificates that indicate the likelihood of individual dogs passing on the defect.

▲ *Left to right, a Wirehaired Fox Terrier, Shetland Sheepdog, Cairn Terrier, Golden Retriever. These are all healthy, but always check out the parents' health record before buying a pedigree pup.*

Q&A

● **I like flat-faced dogs like Pekes. Do they have problems?**

... Unfortunately, yes. Their prominent eyes are prone to damage and disease. The foreshortened nose can cause breathing difficulties and restrict tear drainage, and the infolding of skin on the nose can lead to painful ulcers.

● **What is a good choice of family dog?**

All the Retriever breeds—the Labrador, Golden, and Flat-Coated—have excellent temperaments. They love children and family life, and are particularly easy to train. The breed does have a number of inherited diseases, but if you choose a puppy from healthy parents who have been genetically screened for problems of the hip and eye, your Retriever is likely to give you and your children years of happy, healthy, and troublefree companionship.

English and Irish Setters

Neck weakness, caused by bone malformation, can be a problem in both breeds

Coats of both breeds are long and silky. The Irish Setter's is of one color only, a distinctive rich red

ENGLISH SETTER

IRISH SETTER

Deep chest can sometimes lead to digestive problems

THE SETTER FAMILY COMBINES STYLISH LOOKS with stamina and a friendly disposition. They have been bred as hunting dogs since at least the 17th century: the name "setter" comes from the half-sitting position adopted by the dogs to show the hunters where the birds have fallen. Setters were trained to wait patiently, not touching the game, until the hunters arrived to claim the kill. The Irish Setter, the larger of the two, is very independent but loyal. Its reputation as a scatter-brain is possibly unfair, as the breed reaches maturity relatively late in life. The English Setter, though generally calmer and more stoic, is also capable of exuberance. Both breeds need firm training and vigorous outdoor exercise if their energy is not to turn to hyperactivity.

Both breeds are glamorous in looks, though the Irish Setter, which has been selectively bred for its pure, rich red coat, is the most striking

▲ *Off the leash the Setter exercises with exuberant energy, giving infinite pleasure to its owner as it leaps, twists, and turns with an athlete's grace and elegance.*

of the two. (Its close relative, the original red-and-white Irish Setter, is unacknowledged by some kennel clubs and is still bred as a working dog in Ireland.) The coat of the English Setter is quite different, being mostly white, with a generous flecking of black, lemon, or liver. Sometimes the black or liver is mixed with tan to produce a tricolor coat. In both breeds the hair is semilong and wavy, and is surprisingly easy to groom. The ears, which are fairly long, are set low and hang down to the cheeks. The muzzle is long and pointed, and the dogs have a look of alert, lean intelligence. The elegant, medium-length tail is well feathered underneath. Lively in action, it is carried level with the back.

● *Jonah, my 4-year-old English Setter, has an ear infection, and the vet thinks he may need an operation to cure it. Why is this?*

The English Setter has long, heavy ears that fold down over the cheeks. This weight can kink the ear canal so that air cannot enter to ventilate the canal, and wax cannot escape. In severe cases an operation is needed to expose the ear canal, allowing unrestricted ventilation and drainage.

● *We have a 9-week-old Irish Setter puppy, Sukey. She is lovely in every way, but she seems nervous when strangers come to the house, and backs away and barks. Would it be advisable to keep visitors away until she is a bit older?*

No—it is Sukey's lack of knowledge of strangers that is causing her nervousness. It should be corrected now. If you wait till she is more than 16 weeks old, the problem may never be eradicated. Arrange to have a friend come by. Ask her to bring some tasty tidbits for Sukey, but tell her to ignore the puppy at first. As curiosity gets the better of Sukey and she approaches to where you are sitting, suggest that your friend drop some of the tidbits on the floor. Arrange for other friends (different ones each time) to visit and do the same. Sukey will gradually lose her fear of strangers.

● *My vet has warned me that my Irish Setter, Timber, may be prone to a condition called gastric torsion. Can you explain what this is?*

Gastric torsion is a serious, life-threatening condition that occurs when the stomach fills up with gas and then rotates. The torsion prevents the gas from escaping, and if it is left untreated, the dog may die. Deep-chested breeds such as Setters are particularly vulnerable as their stomachs are more likely to turn in this way. Gulping down food quickly, eating fermentable foods such as raw vegetables or milk products, and eating immediately before or after exercise increase the risk. If your dog's abdomen appears bloated, seek immediate veterinary help.

Breed Profile

Life expectancy:	11 years

Adult height at withers

Irish:	male 25–27in (63.5–69cm)
	female 23–25in (59–63.5cm)
English:	male 23–25in (59–63.5cm)
	female 22–24in (56–61cm)

Adult weight

Irish:	55–70lbs (25–32kg)
English:	55–66lbs (25–30kg)

Temperament: Friendly and enthusiastic; the English Setter is somewhat calmer. Good family dogs, but need outdoor space and plenty of exercise. Not suitable for beginners as they need firm training.

KNOWN HEALTH PROBLEMS

Hip Dysplasia, an inherited abnormality in one or both hip joints, may not be detectable until the dog is a young adult or later. Stiffness on getting up, a bunny-hopping gait or lameness are the usual signs. Reduce the chances of your dog being affected by checking the hip status of the puppy's parents before purchase, and by keeping exercise to a gentle level until your dog is at least 6 months old.

Hemophilia A is a failure of blood-clotting mechanisms leading to uncontrollable hemorrhaging. Although uncommon, it is seen in both breeds.

Von Willebrand's Disease, an inherited disease of the blood platelets, leads to unexpected and unexplained bleeding. It occurs in both breeds.

Progressive Retinal Atrophy (PRA) is a progressive degeneration of the retina of the eye that may lead to total blindness. It occurs in the Irish Setter, but is declining due to testing to detect the faulty gene. Known carriers should never be used for breeding.

Cervical Spondylosis is a type of degenerative bone disease of the neck. Abnormal new bone forms and can fuse the neck vertebrae together.

Gluten Enteropathy is an inability to digest food containing gluten (a carbohydrate). Affected dogs suffer recurrent diarrhea and remain underweight. Several gluten-free commercial diets are available.

Megaesophagus is a condition in which the dog's esophagus does not have enough muscle tone to send food down to the stomach, but regurgitates it instead. There is no treatment. Affected dogs must be given a special fluid diet. They are fed often, and in small amounts, from a raised feeder so that their head is higher than their esophagus.

Epilepsy is an inherited problem in Irish Setters. The dog has sudden convulsions that last for a few minutes. Treatment with anticonvulsant tablets is usually successful.

Atopy, an allergic skin disease caused by inhaled allergens such as pollen, house dust, or house-dust mites, is quite common in English Setters. It results in recurrent or continuous severely itchy skin. Intradermal skin tests can ascertain the precise cause.

Rottweiler

THE ROTTWEILER IS A LARGE, IMPOSING, AND handsome dog. Descended from the mastiff, it is believed to have accompanied the Roman army north across the Alps. The modern breed comes from the town of Rottweil in southern Germany, where it was originally bred to drive and guard cattle. Its popularity spread in the early 20th century, and today the breed is used worldwide for police and security work. Careless breeding from animals of poor temperament has encouraged an aggressive trait, which breeders are attempting to reduce. In the right hands the Rottweiler is a tranquil and affectionate companion. Unfortunately, its reputation has suffered from irresponsible owners who seek to enhance the "macho" image of these fearless, powerful dogs and fail to control them properly. Newspaper and TV stories of dangerous dogs only feed public fears.

Though the Rottweiler is not naturally vicious, it is an instinctive guarding dog, with a commendable desire to protect its home and family. It is very responsive to training but its strength and potential for aggression make it an unsuitable pet for a first-time owner. Avoid it, too, if you have small children, as their unpredictable behavior may provoke the dog, no matter how well trained. A Rottweiler easily becomes bored if left too much on its own. It needs plenty of living and running space and should be avoided by people who are too busy (or too lazy) to take it out for regular vigorous exercise.

▼ *Used for driving cattle to market since the Middle Ages, the Rottweiler nearly became extinct as railroads arrived in the 19th century. Modern breeders are attempting to reduce the dog's potential for aggression.*

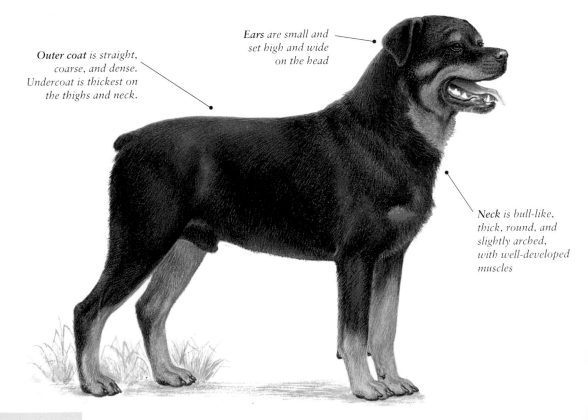

Ears are small and set high and wide on the head

Outer coat is straight, coarse, and dense. Undercoat is thickest on the thighs and neck.

Neck is bull-like, thick, round, and slightly arched, with well-developed muscles

Breed Profile

Life expectancy:	10 years
Adult height at withers:	male 25–27in (63.5–68.5cm) female 23–25in (58–63.5cm)
Adult weight:	male 110lbs (50kg) female 85lbs (38.5kg)

Temperament: Self-confident and fearless, a classic guard breed that can easily become territorial with strangers. Needs time, space, plenty of hard exercise, and strict control. Not suitable for the first-time owner or young family.

KNOWN HEALTH PROBLEMS

Hip Dysplasia, abnormality of one or both hip joints, is fairly common. It develops during the puppy phase of growth but may not be detectable until the dog is a young adult or even older. The usual signs are stiffness on getting up, a characteristic bunny-hopping gait, or lameness in one or both back legs. Reduce the chances of your puppy developing hip dysplasia by checking the hip status of both parents before purchase, by restricting exercise until the pup is at least 6 months, and by always feeding your dog the correct amount and type of food to prevent obesity.

Von Willebrand's Disease, an inherited disease of the blood platelets, causes unexpected and uncontrolled bleeding.

Congenital Deafness is occasionally suffered by Rottweilers. There is no cure.

Retinal Dysplasia, a congenital eye defect, causes folding of the retina. Its effects can vary from very slight loss of sight to total blindness.

Dark and Powerfully Built

Well-muscled, compact, and sturdy in build, the Rottweiler has a large head, powerful neck, and broad chest. The male frame is considerably heavier than the female. Short and glossy, the black coat has clearly defined rust or mahogany markings above the eyes, on the cheeks, around the mouth, and on the chest and legs. The head is broad, with a well-developed stop before the muzzle, and powerful jaws. In proportion to the head, the ears are quite small and fold over flat against the cheeks. Dark brown is the preferred color for the eyes, which normally have a friendly expression. The tail is carried horizontally. It is naturally long and tapering, but traditionally it has been docked close to the body.

▲ *The Rottweiler is by nature a guard dog. It does not fully deserve its reputation for violence but needs firm control. It responds very well to training.*

● A year ago I became the proud owner of a male Rottweiler puppy, Walter, who is now huge, boisterous, and very friendly. It really upsets me when people cross the street to avoid getting too close. How can I convince them that Walter will not harm them?

The macho image sought by some Rottweiler owners has given them a reputation for violence, and it is difficult to overcome this. If you have not already done so, enroll Walter in a dog-training class to ensure he is always totally under your control. But though your friends and neighbors will come to love him, strangers will probably always treat him with suspicion.

● We have a 2-year-old female Rottweiler, Roseanne. She is very gentle but a little bit territorial. I am expecting my first child in a month and am worried about how Roseanne will react to the baby's arrival. What should I be doing to prepare her?

Begin to cool your relationship with Roseanne now. Ignore her, stroke her only to reward her, and put her in a separate room for some time each day. Then, when the baby is born, start treating her as one of the family again. Roseanne will think the baby is the reason why you are suddenly showing affection for her again and won't feel displaced by the new arrival. No dog should ever be left alone with a baby, even for a second. You may wish to consider finding a new, loving home for Roseanne if you think the risks are too great.

Doberman Pinscher

LIKE THE GERMAN SHEPHERD AND THE ROTT-weiler, the Doberman Pinscher has a poor reputation. However, people who know the breed well champion it for its loyal, reliable character as well as its elegant appearance and evident intelligence. The Doberman is alert and responsive, making it a highly suitable breed for police and guard, obedience, or agility work. Properly trained, "Dobies" make excellent family pets and can be trusted more than most breeds. They love traveling in cars and curling up—or stretching out—on armchairs and sofas.

Recent bad breeding practices have produced some dogs of nervous temperament, and it is these dogs that are prone to bite when threatened. If you are offered a dog that seems shy or defensive, it is best to refuse it. A Doberman with a sound temperament should be bold and confident but nonaggressive.

A Natural Athlete

Though powerful and muscular in appearance, Dobermans are medium-sized dogs and are very fast and athletic. A bounding Doberman can knock passers-by right off their feet, so care is needed to control them. The smooth, short coat is thick and close-lying. The usual color is black and tan, but can be brown, blue, or fawn with tan (more accurately, rust-red) markings. These markings are above each eye, on the muzzle, throat and forechest, legs and feet, and below the tail. Dobies have long heads and pointed muzzles, with deepset, almond-shaped brown eyes. The nose is usually black but can be gray in blue-colored dogs and brown in brown and fawn dogs. The small ears are normally folded over but can be held erect. The jaws are the same length and should form a neat scissor bite. Compact and neat, the feet have a strong arch. The dew claws are usually removed. The tail, when left undocked, is long, elegant, and finely tapered. It curves down gently over the rump and extends horizontally to the tip.

Breed Profile

Life expectancy:	10–12 years
Adult height at withers:	male 27in (69cm) female 25½in (65cm)
Adult weight:	male 77–88lbs (35–40kg) female 66–77lbs (30–35kg)

Temperament: Loyal, easily trained. Good with children; enjoy family life. Need firm handling, early training, and plenty of exercise.

KNOWN HEALTH PROBLEMS

Wobbler Syndrome is a condition found quite often in Dobermans. It occurs when cervical vertebrae in the neck are unstable and tilt, which has the effect of narrowing the spinal canal and putting pressure on the spinal cord where this happens. The dog becomes weak and wobbly; in severe cases paralysis may occur. Surgery is needed to stabilize the affected bones.

Folliculitis (inflammation and infection of the hair follicles) is common in Dobermans. It is extremely itchy and causes patchy skin with numerous small spots all over the body. The condition can be treated with antibiotics and special bacteriostatic shampoos.

Hormonal Alopecia (baldness) is quite common. The hair on both flanks begins to thin, usually in symmetrical shapes. There is no itchiness. The condition is usually due to a hormone imbalance, typically a thyroid hormone deficiency. A blood test will be needed to identify the exact cause before treatment can be given.

Von Willebrand's Disease, an inherited disease of the platelets in the blood, is known to occur in the Doberman. It leads to unexpected and unexplained bleeding.

Cardiomyopathy (weakness of the heart muscle) is seen more commonly in the Doberman than in many other breeds. As the muscle weakens, the heart enlarges to compensate. The most obvious symptoms are breathing difficulties, coughing bouts, and sometimes fainting, usually after exercise. Congestive heart failure often follows. The condition can be diagnosed by X-rays and an EKG, and drugs may be prescribed to control the symptoms.

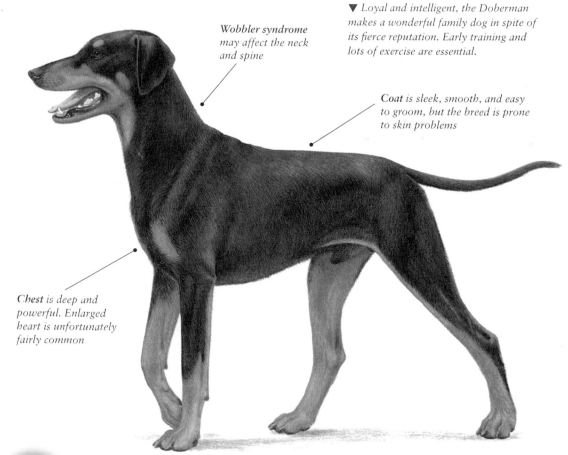

Wobbler syndrome may affect the neck and spine

▼ *Loyal and intelligent, the Doberman makes a wonderful family dog in spite of its fierce reputation. Early training and lots of exercise are essential.*

Coat is sleek, smooth, and easy to groom, but the breed is prone to skin problems

Chest is deep and powerful. Enlarged heart is unfortunately fairly common

Q&A...

● *Tanya, my 2-year-old Doberman, always has a lot of grayish-colored sleep matter in the corner of her eyes. I have to wipe it away at least twice a day. Is it serious?*

The Doberman has very deepset eyes, and the tears do not immediately drain down into the tear duct but accumulate in the gap between the lower lid and the eyeball. What you are seeing are partly evaporated tears in the corners of her eyes. There is no need to worry about this, but you should keep wiping or bathing Tanya's eyes whenever you see the discharge.

● *Spock, our 6-month-old Doberman, constantly wants to bite the tip of his tail. He was docked as a puppy, but the end is very hard and sore. What can we do to help him?*

It sounds as if the skin where the tail was amputated has shrunk back (a bit like a sock slipping down) so that the bone left underneath is now pressing on the very tight skin. It has caused a callus, which is hurting

him. It occurs quite commonly in Dobermans that have been docked. You cannot leave things as they are, so have your veterinarian examine Spock. He will almost certainly have to have the tail redocked under general anesthetic, and some of the bone and callus will be removed. All should then be well.

● *We are thinking of adopting a 3-year-old male Doberman that formerly belonged to a security company. Can a young guard dog make a successful transition to family life? We have three children, ages from 10 to 15, and no other dog. Our previous Dobie died two years ago.*

In your particular circumstances, I would advise against this dog. He will have been trained to be very obedient to his handler and to no one else, and will have been taught to respond to strangers on command. An experienced single owner, or a couple without children, might make a good job of taking him on as a pet but it is not worth risking the safety of your young family.

German Shepherd

THERE ARE PROBABLY MORE GERMAN SHEPHERD dogs, or Alsatians, than any other breed in the world. It is not hard to understand the reasons for their great popularity. German Shepherds are intelligent, handsome, and very adaptable. They make excellent "Seeing Eye" dogs for the blind and excel in obedience training. For this reason, they are used as guard and search dogs by military and police forces all over the world.

Unfortunately, indiscriminate breeding in the past has given rise to a number of behavioral traits, such as nervousness and aggression, which breeders are now trying to eliminate. When carefully bred, German Shepherds are calm, quiet, and reliable dogs. They are not recommended for the novice owner, however—typically, the dog is so smart and confident that it easily becomes the dominant one in the partnership. Puppies need firm early handling and training, but given these, they will make loyal and tireless companions. A well-trained German Shepherd never strays far from its owner on a walk, and will keep glancing back and returning to check that all is well.

Breed Profile

Life expectancy:	10–12 years
Adult height at withers:	male 24½in (56–61cm) female 22½in (51–56cm)
Adult weight:	male 75lbs (34kg) female 65lbs (29.5kg)

Temperament: A classic guard dog that can easily become very territorial. Easy to train. If properly socialized, is good with children and enjoys family life. Needs open spaces and plenty of exercise.

KNOWN HEALTH PROBLEMS

Hip Dysplasia is easily the most common inherited disease. Abnormal development of one or both hip joints during puppy growth may not be detectable until the dog is a young adult, or older. Stiffness on getting up, a characteristic bunny-hopping gait, or lameness in one or both back legs are the usual signs. Check the parents' hip status before buying a puppy, and keep exercise at a gentle level until it is at least 6 months old.

Ununited Anconeus Process in the elbow is another common developmental problem. A small piece of bone fails to join correctly to the rest of the elbow, and a painful lameness develops. Surgical removal is usually necessary.

Chronic Degenerative Radiculo Myelopathy (CDRM) is a gradual paralysis of the hind legs that usually begins in late middle age. The cause is unknown. As most dogs are past breeding age when they begin to show symptoms, it is difficult to avoid buying the puppy of an affected parent.

Exocrine Pancreatic Insufficiency (EPI) is quite common in German Shepherds. A dog affected by this condition will be thin and hungry, and have an excessive appetite. Food cannot be properly digested; consequently the feces are bulky and often fatty in appearance, with a particularly obnoxious smell (see Increased Appetite, pages 72–73.)

Small Intestinal Bacterial Overgrowth (SIBO) is often seen in association with EPI. It is caused by excessive amounts of bacteria in the small intestine. Symptoms are diarrhea and a failure to gain weight.

Epilepsy is seen more often in German Shepherds than many other breeds. The dog is subject to sudden convulsive fits. Recovery is usually quick, although the dog may be quiet and confused for a few hours afterward. The condition can usually be controlled with anticonvulsant drugs.

Anal Furunculosis is a deep penetrating infection around the anus and scent glands (anal sacs). It is thought to have a high incidence in the German Shepherd because of the way the bushy tail is carried low, preventing adequate ventilation of the anal area.

Hemophilia A is a failure of certain clotting mechanisms in the blood. It leads to virtually uncontrollable bleeding. Although the condition is not commonly found, it occurs more often in the German Shepherd than it does in most other breeds.

Q & A...

● *My German Shepherd, Jet, is 18 months old and has started a very heavy molt. His hair stands out in tufts, especially on the outside of his hind legs, and if I pull the tufts, a huge clump comes out. Is there cause for concern?*

No. This is a normal heavy molt. Pluck these tufts of hair gently, grooming Jet thoroughly at the same time. You may find it easier if you shampoo him first; this seems to loosen the dead hair and improve the coat.

● *I have an 8-week-old German Shepherd puppy, Sherri. I'm told that I must be firm with her in training, but I don't want to break her spirit.*

An adult German Shepherd is large and must be under control if she is to fit in well at home and not cause problems out in public. She must learn to obey you even at this age. Early training, like the more intensive training given to older dogs, is carried out with kindness and reward —it is merely teaching her how to behave in public. Ask your vet to recommend a local puppy training class if you are worried about how to go about schooling her yourself.

A Wolfish Appearance

German Shepherds have long bodies and backs that slope down gently from the shoulders. This characteristic can be exaggerated to the extent that the dog looks as though it is crouching. The strong head and muzzle are reminiscent of a wolf. The nose is black, the eyes are almond-shaped and dark brown, and the ears are of medium size, set high on the head and carried erect, which gives the dog an alert, intelligent expression. There is a thick double coat, usually shorthaired. Though there is also a long-haired variety, this is not recognized for show purposes in many parts of the world. Most German Shepherds are black and tan, though some dogs are solid black, cream, or sable (gray with lighter or brown markings). The tail is bushy at the base and is carried at rest in a gentle saber-like curve.

Ears have a large number of glands that secrete wax. They require regular cleaning

Hindquarters are broad and have a slight slope. The strong muscles help propel the dog forward. Limping or hopping may indicate hip dysplasia

Double coat is thick, straight, and usually short. Some may be all black or even all white

Elbows may be affected by abnormal development

◀ *A German Shepherd is a large, clever, handsome dog that was meant to work. Firm training brings out its best traits and ensures that its power and intelligence are not turned to mischief or aggression.*

Boxer

Thighs are broad, long, and very powerful, giving the Boxer its elegant stride

Gums can grow over the teeth, causing pain in eating. Surgery can help

Heart disease is a particular problem of Boxers

ONE OF THE MOST EXTROVERTED OF BREEDS, robust in appearance and in personality, Boxers were originally bred for bull baiting in Germany in the middle of the 19th century. Since then they have been developed to serve as guard, working, and companion dogs. They are intelligent, loyal, reliable, and easy to train but their strong personality means that they need a firm hand. They are neither timid, nor usually overly aggressive, but may be suspicious of strangers and are not easily intimidated. They make good guard dogs, but enjoy family life and are affectionate with children. They enjoy plentiful exercise and long walks, and are on the go from morning to night, often creating unintentional havoc. If you own a Boxer, you'll need lots of energy and time to try to wear it out—no easy task.

A Noble Dog

The Boxer's confident and alert appearance is often described as noble. Medium-sized and squarely built, they are strongly muscled, with an impressive deep chest. The short coat is easy to

▲ *The Boxer is a powerful, well-muscled dog. Its somewhat puzzled expression belies an affectionate, generous personality.*

groom and keep clean. The colors are usually fawn or brindle (brown flecked with black or gray) with white markings extending over the chest and on the legs. Ideally, the white markings should not exceed one-third of the ground color. The tail is carried high. For reasons that are now lost in the mists of time, it is traditionally docked close to the body.

The Boxer's chiseled head is unmistakable in appearance. The distinct, almost square, muzzle ends abruptly before the balanced and powerful skull. There is usually a dark-colored mask on the muzzle only, and the upper lips are large and thick. The mouth is invariably undershot, with the lower jaw longer than the upper jaw. The eyes are dark brown and look directly forward, and the ears are set wide on the top of the skull. The brow is often wrinkled, which gives the Boxer a look of intense concentration.

● *My Boxer, Pedro, is often covered in little lumps of skin that are very itchy. They are there one minute and may disappear within the hour. What are they?*

This sounds like urticaria, an allergic reaction in which plaque-like lumps form very quickly and the hairs on the lumps are raised at odd angles. It is likely to have been caused by something the dog has eaten or inhaled, or result from an allergic reaction to a wasp or bee sting. If the itching persists for more than two hours, your vet can clear it up with an antihistamine injection.

● *My 9-year-old Boxer, Lucy, fainted for no apparent reason after she had just woken up and raced to the front door to see who was there. Is this serious?*

I think you should take Lucy to see your vet. Boxers are not particularly long-lived, and 9 is quite old for the breed. Lucy may have a heart condition, which in its early stages could lead to fainting. It may not be serious at all, but your vet will be able to let you know more after an examination.

▲ *Double puppy trouble. Boxers never entirely lose their puppylike character. They are always ready for a game and the chance of a romp.*

Breed Profile

Life expectancy:	10 years
Adult height at withers:	male 22½–25in (57–63cm)
	female 21–23in (53–59cm)
Adult weight:	male 66–70½lbs (30–32kg)
	female 55–59½lbs (25–27kg)

Temperament: Good with children, enjoys family life, but needs space and time for exercise. Not suitable for apartments or city living. Needs a firm hand in training.

KNOWN HEALTH PROBLEMS

Hyperplastic Gingivitis is a condition in which the gums enlarge to envelop the teeth, causing the dog pain when it bites on the gum. Surgery is necessary to trim the gum back. The first sign may be an unpleasant smell from the mouth. Recurrence is common. Similar to it is **Epulis**, in which a single lump of gum overgrowth forms a tumor-like lesion. Surgical removal is usually straightforward.

Corneal Ulcers particularly affect Boxers. They are often treated medically, but sometimes the third eyelid is sutured to the upper lid for 2 to 3 weeks. This provides a protective cover that allows the ulcer to heal. A clear contact lens to "bandage" the eye may also help. The problem has a tendency to recur.

Spondylitis is a type of arthritis that develops in the spinal column in later life. New areas of abnormal bone form and gradually fuse the bones of the spine together. It usually occurs in the mid to low back, and the signs are pain, unwillingness to climb stairs, and restlessness. Anti-inflammatory tablets or injections often help.

Progressive Axonopathy, a degenerative disease of the nerves (not the brain and spinal cord), is inherited in the Boxer. There is no treatment.

Cardiomyopathy (heart disease) is seen more commonly in the Boxer than in many other breeds. The heart enlarges and the muscle weakens, leading to symptoms of breathlessness and an inability to enjoy exercise. Fainting will sometimes occur, often following a coughing bout. Congestive heart failure is often the end result. Diagnosis is made by veterinary examination, EKG, and X-rays. The condition is incurable, though various heart drugs are helpful in treating it.

Aortic Stenosis (narrowing of the aorta) is a deformity in one of the heart valves. It often produces no symptoms, but sudden death can occur. It is heard as a heart murmur by the vet in the course of examination with a stethoscope. X-rays or an ultrasound examination of the heart may confirm the diagnosis. Treatment is usually of limited value.

Skin Tumors of the mast cells and soft tissues are seen more often in Boxers than in other breeds.

Golden Retriever

THE GOLDEN RETRIEVER WAS ORIGINALLY BRED as a hunting dog in Great Britain, where it was used to retrieve waterfowl. Today it is one of the most popular breeds in the world. An intelligent, affectionate, adaptable, and easy-to-train dog, it is capable of performing a variety of roles. Police and security forces all over the world use it to sniff out drugs and explosives, and it makes an excellent "Seeing Eye" dog for the blind and assistant dog for the physically disabled. Active and agile, the Golden Retriever is unequaled as a fun-loving family dog. It is nonaggressive and very patient, especially with children. It rarely bites or snaps, and is not usually a fussy eater. Despite its size, it does not need a great deal of living space, but benefits from plenty of exercise. There are some breed-related health problems, and all owners should have the relevant tests for hip dysplasia and inherited eye disease (see below) carried out before breeding.

A Golden Coat

A less solid dog than its relative, the Labrador, the Golden Retriever has a similar body type, with a broad head, deep chest, and muscular loins and hindquarters. Its most distinctive feature is the golden or cream-colored coat, which is of medium length and may be either straight or wavy. There is a dense, waterproof undercoat. Although the coat is easy to keep clean, it has a tendency to molt, especially when the dog is living indoors with central heating.

The Golden Retriever has a powerful muzzle, but has been bred to have a gentle mouth for handling gamebirds. The eyes are dark brown and set well apart, with an expression often described as "kind." The ears are slightly feathered and are set level with the eyes. The thick tail, muscled at the base, is used very expressively when communicating with other dogs or people. The dog steers with it when swimming.

Breed Profile

Life expectancy:	10–12 years
Adult height at withers:	male 22–24in (56–61cm) female 20–22in (51–56cm)
Adult weight:	male 75lbs (34kg) female 65lbs (29.5kg)

Temperament: An ideal family pet. Very trainable, rarely aggressive, and gets on well with children. Requires plenty of exercise.

KNOWN HEALTH PROBLEMS

Progressive Retinal Atrophy (PRA) is a progressive degeneration of the retina of the eye that may lead to total blindness. Affected dogs of either sex must not be used for breeding.

Cataracts are a progressive opacity of the lens that affects one or both eyes. The pupil becomes gray to white in color, instead of the normal black. In advanced cases, the lens looks like a pearl and the dog may become blind. All dogs should be screened for hereditary cataracts before breeding. Cataracts in the Golden Retriever may also be caused by infection, diabetes mellitus, and trauma.

Entropion (inturning eyelid) is usually seen in puppies. The rim of an eyelid rolls in, causing the lashes to rub against the surface of the eye. The eye becomes sore and wet with tears, and is often kept closed. Surgical treatment is necessary.

Hip Dysplasia, one of the more common inherited diseases, is a developmental abnormality affecting one or both hip joints. It may not be noticed until the dog is a young adult or even older. Stiffness on getting up, a characteristic bunny-hop, or lameness are the usual signs. Reduce the chances of your dog being affected by checking the hip status of the puppy's parents before purchase, and by keeping exercise to a gentle level until your pet is at least 6 months old.

Von Willebrand's Disease, a rare, inherited disease of the blood platelets, is known in the Golden Retriever. It leads to uncontrolled bleeding.

Epilepsy occurs more often in Golden Retrievers than many other breeds. The dog has sudden convulsions that last for a few minutes. The condition can be treated with anticonvulsant drugs.

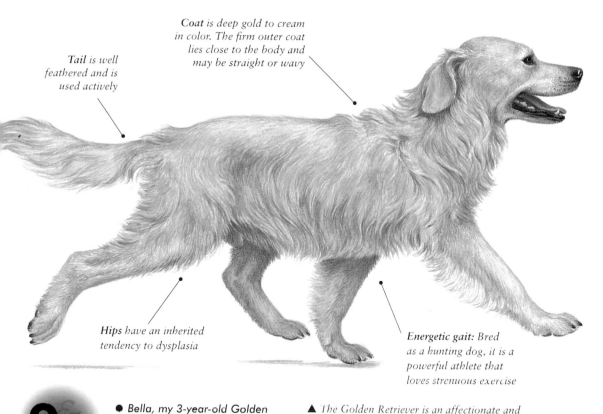

Tail *is well feathered and is used actively*

Coat *is deep gold to cream in color. The firm outer coat lies close to the body and may be straight or wavy*

Hips *have an inherited tendency to dysplasia*

Energetic gait: *Bred as a hunting dog, it is a powerful athlete that loves strenuous exercise*

● Bella, my 3-year-old Golden Retriever, often gets a painful, wet, smelly patch of skin on her cheek. The vet says it is a "hot spot." What does that mean?

A "hot spot" is a painful area of skin infection. Because the skin exudes pus, it is often called "wet eczema." The problem seems to occur more frequently in Retrievers than in any other breed, and often, though not always, affects the face. It is thought to be caused by an insect bite, often a flea, that sets up an allergic reaction at the site. The dog scratches it badly and makes it very sore, and it becomes infected. It invariably needs veterinary attention.

● The vet says my 6-year-old neutered Golden Retriever, Max, is too fat at 90lbs (40kg). I've been told to cut down on his food, but he eats only one meal a day. What more can I do?

Max is far too heavy. Most male Retrievers weigh between 70 and 77lbs (31.5 and 35kg). Neutered dogs, which tend to eat more and convert that food into fat, put on weight very easily. Retrievers (and their Labrador cousins) seem to find it particularly easy to gain weight. To slim him down, he needs fewer calories, not less food. Try giving him grated raw

▲ The Golden Retriever is an affectionate and rewarding companion for any family. Gentle by nature, it is generally very well-adjusted and extremely reliable with children. It has a great love of water and is an enthusiastic swimmer.

(or cooked) carrots instead of biscuits with his meat for the next three months. It is also important not to give him any tidbits, perhaps just some vitamin tablets, vegetables, or fruit as a reward. And it would be a good idea to increase his exercise as well.

● My 2-year-old Golden Retriever, Goldie, is very thin, despite eating well. The vet says there's nothing physically wrong. I take her for a long walk every day, but she never seems to tire and is constantly on the go. How can I get her to put on weight?

It sounds as if Goldie has the opposite problem to Max and is not getting enough calories for the amount of energy she is using up. We are so worried about our pets putting on excess weight that we sometimes forget that their dietary needs are not the same. A young, hyperactive dog like Goldie needs many more calories than an older, slower dog. Try putting her on one of the special high-energy diets for working dogs.

Dalmatian

With its distinctive spotted coat, the Dalmatian is easily recognizable. The origin of its name is a mystery; it does not come from Dalmatia in the former Yugoslavia. In the 19th century, when it was fashionable for the affluent to have a Dalmatian running alongside their carriages, the breed was given the nickname of "carriage dog." Capable of running 30 miles a day, these dogs are obviously much happier in the country than in town. In addition to the need for exercise, prospective owners should be warned that Dalmatians need a lot of control. Although friendly, they have a tendency to be excitable and disobedient. Early training and firm, experienced handling are essential requirements for a rewarding relationship between owner and dog. In the right hands, Dalmatians make faithful house dogs and wonderful companions. They are fond of playing with children and are in their element if there is a committed jogger in the family.

Deafness in one or both ears is a major problem with the breed. In the United States nearly 30 percent of Dalmatians are affected; in Britain the figure is between 15 and 20 percent. Females and those dogs with blue or partially blue eyes are more likely to be deaf, whereas those with patches rather than spots (less desirable in the show ring) are more likely to have normal hearing. This has led some experts to call for show standards for the breed to be changed, because the practice of destroying puppies with undesirable patchy markings is promoting deafness by reducing the genetic pool for breeding.

Breed Profile

Life expectancy:	10–12 years
Adult height at withers:	male 23–24in (58.5–61cm) female 22–23in (56.5–58cm)
Adult weight:	male 60lbs (27kg) female 50lbs (22.5kg)

Temperament: A very lively, active, muscular dog. Fun-loving and excitable. A good house and family dog in experienced hands. Ideally, it should live in a rural setting.

Known Health Problems

High Uric Acid Secretion in the urine is a particular characteristic of the Dalmatian (and English Bulldog) caused by a slightly unusual process in liver function. It is usually unimportant, but sometimes the concentration of uric acid is so high it crystallizes, causing stones to form in the bladder. Treatment and prevention of these stones differs slightly from that normally prescribed for bladder stones in other breeds.

Deafness is a serious inherited problem in some Dalmatians. Specialized tests known as Brainstem Auditory Evoked Responses (BAER) can be carried out in puppies from 5 weeks old to detect if the condition is present. It may occur in one or both ears, and there is no treatment. To diminish the problem, all breeding animals should be screened for deafness.

Juvenile Nephropathy (premature kidney failure) occurs in certain family lines of the Dalmatian. There is no effective treatment.

Dalmatian Bronzing Syndrome is a metabolic deficiency that causes a tan discoloration to the coat. Affected dogs are predisposed to severe skin irritation and bacterial infection.

White Pup to Spotted Dog

The Dalmatian is a muscular, symmetrical dog with a long head. Its coat is short and dense, but very sleek and glossy. The main color is pure white and the spots are dense black or (less commonly) liver in color, but never both. For show purposes the spots should be well distributed and separated from each other, not merging together. The more defined the spots, the greater the value of the dog. At birth the puppies are completely white; they develop their spots during the first weeks of life. Depending on the color of the coat, the nose may be black or brown. The eyes are round with an intelligent expression. They should also match the coat in color. The large, rounded ears are carried close to the head. The tail is long and tapered.

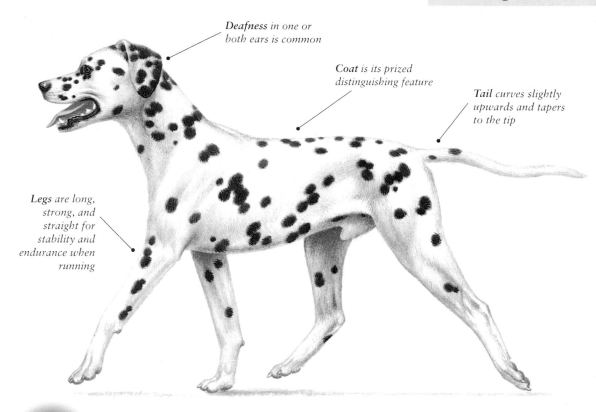

Deafness *in one or both ears is common*

Coat *is its prized distinguishing feature*

Tail *curves slightly upwards and tapers to the tip*

Legs *are long, strong, and straight for stability and endurance when running*

Q & A ...

● Our old Doberman, Caspar, has just passed away. We want another dog, but as a mark of respect for Caspar, we'd prefer a different breed. Our two children are now ages 7 and 9—is a Dalmatian a suitable choice?

As you have previously kept a large dog successfully, a Dalmatian may be just right for you, provided you attend to its early training and socialization. Dalmatians love the hustle and bustle of family life and enjoy being with children, but they need lots of attention. If you're able to spend time playing with and walking your Dalmatian pup, you'll find it will soon become an enthusiastic new member of the family.

● Ever since I saw the movie "101 Dalmatians," I have wanted to have a Dalmatian pup for myself. The problem is that, although I work only part-time, I am still out of the house for four or five hours a day. Would it be better to have two puppies from the same litter so they can be company for each other?

Unless there is someone at home all day, you shouldn't be planning to keep one Dalmatian pup, let alone two. Dalmatians hate being left alone, and having two won't improve the situation. If you don't have time to train them properly, they will become thoroughly bored

▲ With its glossy coat, well-proportioned body, and smooth gait, the Dalmatian is an elegant dog. Although the name suggests a place of origin in former Yugoslavia, the modern breed was developed in Britain as a result of crossing Pointers with Bull Terriers.

and frustrated, and are likely to express their feelings by wrecking your home. If you are really eager to have a dog and haven't just fallen for the idea of a cute Dalmatian pup, then how about an adult dog from a stray home or animal shelter? Look for one with a good temperament that can happily be left by itself for a few hours.

● We want a female Dalmatian puppy, but when we went to look at a litter, the only female had lots of irregular black patches instead of spots. The breeder strongly advised against choosing her, but we really loved her. What do you think?

At present, only spotted Dalmatians are acceptable for showing, which is why you were advised not to choose her. But your patchy female is much more likely to be free of deafness, an inherited problem in the breed, than her spotted brothers. If you don't intend to show her, you should certainly choose her. She'll probably be the pick of the litter, in health terms at any rate.

Siberian Husky

ORIGINALLY BRED BY THE NOMADIC INUIT OF the Arctic to pull sleds, the Siberian Husky was introduced to North America in the 19th century after its discovery by Russian fur traders. It is one of the most active of all dogs and particularly loves to pull. If a sled is not available, the leash will do just as well, so those taking it for exercise must be strong enough to resist being tugged right off their feet. Huskies love to run and are likely to develop instant selective deafness if you ever dare let them off the leash. Exceptionally fleet of foot, a Husky could be half a mile away before you even realize it has gone. To gain its freedom, it will leap over tall fences or even dig a way out from under them.

In compensation, the Siberian Husky is a faithful companion and loves people. Bred to run in dog teams, Huskies also need the company of at least one other dog. In general, they are easy to keep—they do not need much grooming, are not fussy eaters, and are nonaggressive toward other dogs. However, though they seldom bark, they do engage in communal howling, and those living as family pets retain this disconcerting habit.

In addition to the absolute need for frequent vigorous exercise, there is one other important requirement in owning a Husky. Since their natural environment is the Arctic, they should only live in areas of temperate to cool climate, where they will not be exposed to extreme heat.

▼ *Wolflike in appearance, the Siberian Husky is hard-working and has almost unlimited stamina. It is strictly a dog for the serious fitness enthusiast.*

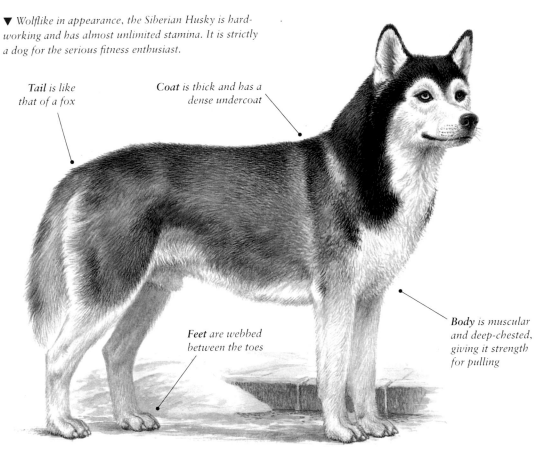

Tail *is like that of a fox*

Coat *is thick and has a dense undercoat*

Feet *are webbed between the toes*

Body *is muscular and deep-chested, giving it strength for pulling*

Breed Profile

Life expectancy:	11–13 years
Adult height at withers:	male 21–23½in (53–58cm) female 20–22in (51–56cm)
Adult weight:	male 45–60lbs (20–27kg) female 35–50lbs (16–23kg)

Temperament: Extroverted, pleasant. Needs the company of another dog as well as people. Cannot tolerate warm climates.

KNOWN HEALTH PROBLEMS

Glaucoma, an inherited disease, develops when the pressure of the fluid inside the eye increases, due to a fault in the eye's drainage mechanism. Swelling leads to pain, inflammation, and excessive tear production. Surgery is needed to provide drainage, but the eye is often permanently damaged.

Corneal Dystrophy appears as a small, faint white area, sometimes donut-shaped, in the cornea the clear part of the eye. It is caused by an accumulation of fat, and the dog can easily see through it even if both eyes are affected. Although it rarely disappears, it equally rarely enlarges to any degree.

Von Willebrand's Disease, an inherited disease of the platelets (a blood component), occasionally occurs in the Siberian Husky, causing unexpected and unexplained bleeding.

Hemophilia A is a failure of certain clotting mechanisms leading to virtually uncontrollable hemorrhaging. Although rare, it is seen occasionally in the Siberian Husky.

Ventricular Septal Defect—literally a hole in the heart, an opening in the muscle wall between the two ventricles—is a rare heart defect in the Siberian Husky. It is very serious and can lead to heart failure. A congenital defect, it can be heard as a murmur when a vet listens to the dog's heart.

Nutritional Deficiencies caused by the feeding of soybean meal, a major ingredient of many commercial dog foods, has been shown by some scientific studies to occur in Huskies.

A Small, Friendly Wolf

In general appearance the Husky resembles a small wolf, with an alert, friendly expression. These dogs are very striking to look at. Their fur comes in a variety of colors, and they are unusual in having eyes that are hazel, blue, brown, or multicolored. Sometimes the eyes may be of different colors. The head is clean cut with a well-defined stop (break) between the forehead and muzzle. The triangular ears are set high and close, and are held erect. The Husky's double coat provides maximum protection against cold and ice. There is a dense undercoat and an outer coat consisting of smooth-lying, medium-length guard hairs. The tail is also thickly furred, rather like a fox's. The feet are compact and well covered in fur, with considerable webbing between the toes to keep the dog from sinking down into snow. Though its build is medium, the chest is deep, providing space for the powerful heart and lungs needed for long-distance running.

Despite its wolflike appearance, the Husky is very docile and nonaggressive when in human company. It does not make a good guard dog for this reason. Huskies have enormous stamina and are normally robust, though there are a few breed-related health problems.

● It is almost impossible to get my 6-month-old Husky, Nannouk, back onto the leash after I let her off. What can I do?

Training a Husky to come to your call is not easy. They just love to run and run. Most Husky experts recommend that this breed is never let off the leash, so the best advice is to buy a long extender leash. One about 26 feet (8 meters) in length will give your Husky a reasonable amount of freedom.

● My neighbors all complain that Kolya, my year-old Siberian Husky, howls while I am at work. Can this be controlled in any way?

Huskies were originally bred to be part of a sled team and are temperamentally unsuited to being alone. You should consider getting another dog (not necessarily a Husky) to keep him company. If this is impossible, try and find someone to act as a "dog-sitter." If you do not provide a companion, Kolya's howling will continue.

● We want a dog that will join in with our summer outdoor activities and are considering a Husky as they are so athletic. What do you think?

Reconsider. Huskies are bred for cold weather; most sports simply aren't for them. They collapse and mope in the heat. They cannot be trusted off the leash in open, crowded places and aren't cut out to play ball games. Choose a retrieving dog instead.

Labrador Retriever

THE LABRADOR RETRIEVER IS ONE OF THE MOST popular breeds in the the world. Labradors have excellent temperaments, usually love children, and make ideal family pets, provided they are given enough space and exercise. Their instinctive desire to retrieve makes them highly suitable as hunting dogs. Their combination of muscular strength and stamina enables them to withstand long hours working outdoors in difficult terrain and in all conditions. More recently, their intelligence and high trainability have suited them for a new role as one of the most successful "Seeing Eye" (guide dog) breeds. Sadly, the great demand for these ever-popular dogs has led to a high incidence of inherited health problems, which breeders are doing their best to eradicate.

A Water-loving Dog

Labradors come originally from Newfoundland, Canada, where the local fishermen used them to help pull in their loaded nets. They love water and will seize any opportunity for a swim. They are protected by a water-resistant coat, which keeps them warm even when swimming in winter. They use their powerful otterlike tail, one of the breed's most distinctive features, as a rudder in the water. Medium in length, the tail has no feathering but is thickly covered with dense hair.

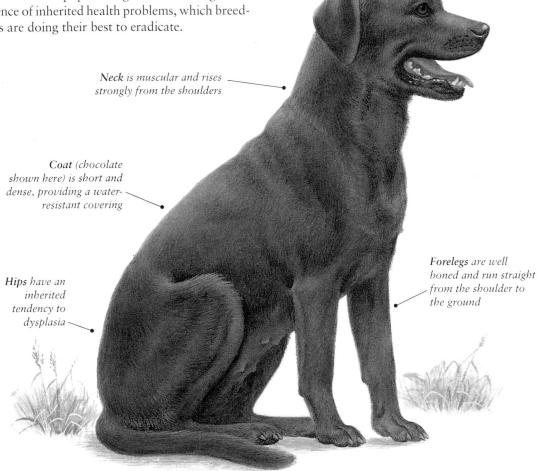

Neck is muscular and rises strongly from the shoulders

Coat (chocolate shown here) is short and dense, providing a water-resistant covering

Hips have an inherited tendency to dysplasia

Forelegs are well boned and run straight from the shoulder to the ground

The dogs use it very expressively when communicating with humans and other dogs.

Labradors are very strongly built. The chest has good depth and width, and the hindquarters are broad, muscular, and well developed. If they are insufficiently exercised, Labradors easily run to fat. The coat is short, straight, and dense and is in solid colors of black, yellow, or chocolate. The ears, legs, and tail lack feathering, and the coat feels quite hard to the hand. Labradors that spend most of their time living indoors in heated homes have a tendency to molt more or less continuously throughout the year.

The Labrador has a wide, clean-cut head with powerful jaws. The nose may be black or brown, depending on the color of the coat. The ears, which are set far back and moderately low on the skull, hang quite close to the head. The eyes are usually brown or hazel. They have a kind and friendly expression, which gives the dog its characteristic appearance of alert intelligence, gentleness, and good humor.

◀ *The Labrador Retriever possesses intelligence, good temperament, and character. It is patient, reliable, and hard-working, and makes an ideal "Seeing Eye" dog for the visually disabled.*

● *Tammy, my 6-month-old Labrador puppy, has started to limp on her left hindleg, and the vet says she may have hip dysplasia. He wants to X-ray her to confirm this, but says she will need a general anesthetic. Should I agree?*

Unless you can remember a specific accident that caused the lameness, it is very likely that Tammy has hip dysplasia. She is just at the age when symptoms usually start to show. An X-ray is absolutely necessary for diagnosis, and she will need to have an anesthetic to ensure that she lies very still on her back with legs outstretched. Modern anesthetics are very safe, and she will be up and about within hours.

● *I have a 2-year-old yellow female Labrador, Bliss, and would like her to have puppies so I can keep one. The owner of a black Labrador in my neighborhood has suggested we mate our dogs. Is this a good idea, and what color will the pups be?*

By mating a black Labrador with a yellow one, you will get some black and some yellow puppies. The temperament of both animals is very important. Do you know the other dog well? Are you happy with his reliability? You should ask your vet to X-ray Bliss for hip dysplasia before she comes in heat, and ask for an eye examination with an ophthalmoscope. Make sure your neighbor's dog has also been tested before you agree to the mating.

Breed Profile

Life expectancy:	10–12 years
Adult height at withers:	male 22in (56–57cm) female 21in (54–56cm)
Adult weight:	male 67lbs (30.6kg) female 62lbs (28.4kg)

Temperament: Gentle, affable, loyal, and dependable. Good with children. Enjoys family life, but needs space and regular exercise.

KNOWN HEALTH PROBLEMS

Entropion (inturning eyelid) is sometimes seen in growing Labrador puppies. The rim of the eyelid rolls inward, causing the lashes to rub against the surface of the eye, irritating the eyeball. The eye becomes sore and wet with tears, and is often kept closed. Surgical treatment is necessary.

Progressive Retinal Atrophy (PRA) is a progressive degeneration of the retina, which may lead to total blindness. Affected dogs of either sex must not be used for breeding.

Cataracts are a progressive opacity of the lens in one or both eyes. The pupil becomes gray or white instead of the normal black color. In advanced cases the lens looks like a pearl, and the dog may be blind. Cataracts can be inherited or have another cause, including infection, diabetes mellitus, and trauma.

Hip Dysplasia is a developmental abnormality in one or both hip joints. It may not be noticed until the dog is adult. Stiffness on getting up, a bunny-hopping gait, or lameness are the usual signs. Reduce the chances of your dog being affected by checking the hip conformation of its parents, and by keeping exercise to a gentle level until your puppy is at least six months old.

Osteochondrosis Dissicans (OCD) is a disease of the cartilage affecting one or more joints in dogs under a year old. Surgery is usually necessary.

Epilepsy occurs more often in Labradors than many other breeds. It can usually be controlled with anticonvulsant drugs.

Chow Chow

CHOWS ARE THOUGHT TO COME ORIGINALLY from China, where they were used for hunting, herding, pulling carts, and as guard dogs. Chows are reserved by nature and can appear aloof, but they are capable of forming deep attachments to humans. A "one-person dog" by nature, a Chow will readily defends its owner or territory when annoyed or threatened.

These characteristics can make Chows a bit of a handful. Without careful training, they can be difficult to control. If they are not fully socialized when young, they may become overterritorial, and their tendency to bond to one person makes them difficult with other people and other dogs. Their quietness can mean that strangers do not get the usual warning before a show of aggression—and have less time to take avoiding action. The Chow's deep-set eyes limit its peripheral vision, so it is always advisable to approach them from the front. They have a considerable tendency to eye problems.

Thick Coats for Cold Weather

The Chow has a very thick, semi-long coat, either rough or smooth, that requires thorough grooming every day. Red is the most usual color, though black, blue, and fawn also exist. The coat is not designed for hot climates, and Chows suffer more than most breeds from the heat. Washing them more often in summer may help. The tail is carried forward over the back, and this can be a disadvantage when it is warm, causing a skin irritation in the area covered by the tail. The hindlegs are very straight, leading to a stiff style of walking. The face is somewhat bear-like, with small ears carried stiffly but tilting forward. The eyes are small, dark, and almond-shaped.

The Chow's dark blue or black tongue is a unique feature of the breed. Professors of veterinary medicine have been known to trick their students by asking them to check the tongue of an anesthetized Chow. In any other breed, a blue tongue indicates heart or circulatory failure.

Breed Profile

Life expectancy:	10 years
Adult height at withers:	male 19–22in (48–56cm) female 17–20in (43–51cm)
Adult weight:	male 60lbs (27kg) female 55lbs (25kg)

Temperament: An independent, one-person dog that needs a firm owner. It is not always an ideal family dog, as it may not be tolerant of children. It requires only an average amount of exercise.

KNOWN HEALTH PROBLEMS

Entropion (inturning eyelid), the most common inherited problem of this breed, is usually noticed in the growing dog. Selective breeding for the Chow's eye shape has increased the likelihood that one or more of the eyelids will be too fleshy. The rim rolls in, causing the lashes to rub against the surface of the eye, which becomes sore and wet with tears. It is often kept closed. Surgical treatment is necessary. Make sure both the parents have been tested for the condition before purchasing a puppy.

Hip Dysplasia, fairly common in Chows, is a developmental abnormality in one or both hip joints. It may not be detected until the dog is an adult. Stiffness on getting up, a bunny-hopping gait when running, or lameness are the usual signs. Reduce the chances of buying an affected dog by checking the hip status of the puppy's parents before purchase, and by keeping exercise gentle until your pet is at least 6 months old.

Luxating Patella (dislocating kneecap) can occur due to a deformed stifle or knee joint. Usually the dislocation is to the inside of the leg, and the dog becomes severely lame. The vet will try to move the kneecap into place by pulling the foot gently to straighten the leg, at the same time pressing on the front of the knee. In recurrent cases an operation is usually necessary.

Hereditary Myotonia is a rare muscular disease. Puppies become lame in the hind legs at about 8 to 12 weeks old and often display a bunny-hopping gait; sometimes they cannot walk at all. Drugs can be helpful, and puppies often make a thorough recovery.

Eyes *are deep-set.
There is not much
peripheral vision*

Tail *is long and thick
like the coat, and curls
over onto the back*

Tongue *is blue to
black in normal, healthy
Chow Chows*

Coat *is heavy and
thick, to withstand
cold temperatures*

● My year-old Chow, Charlie, has
started to growl at passersby in the
street. I'm afraid he might bite
someone. What can I do?

Charlie is asserting himself as he approaches sexual
and social maturity. You must prevent him from
becoming too dominant and overattached to you. On
walks, as a stranger comes toward you, give Charlie a
tidbit. If the passerby seems amenable, suggest he or
she gives Charlie a tidbit too. Reinforce this with praise.
Do the same with visitors at home. Cool your relationship with Charlie—only give him attention when he has
done something to deserve praise (such as sitting to
command), not when he demands it.

● A friend thinks that my Chow's tongue is too blue
and may indicate a heart problem. He seems well
and enjoys his walks. Should I have him checked?

There is no need. All Chows have a dark blue pigment
on the gums and the tongue, so yours is quite normal.

▲ *The Chow Chow's collar resembles a lion's mane,
while its face looks like a little bear's. Its history in
China did not produce a highly domesticated breed,
but the dogs do become deeply attached to one owner.*

● I live on my own and am thinking of keeping a
dog for company. I would like a strong dog to act as
a guard dog, but also want one I can take jogging
with me. I am used to dogs and really admire
Chows. Would this be a suitable choice?

A Chow would certainly seem to fit the bill in some
respects. They are one-person dogs and have strong
guarding instincts. Though usually nonaggressive, they
will defend their home or owner if threatened.
However, a Chow is probably not a good choice if you
want it as a jogging companion. Their very thick coat,
which equips them for living in Arctic conditions, makes
them overheat rapidly if they are exercised too much,
though they do enjoy a good walk every day.

English Springer Spaniel

Eye problems occur quite frequently in the breed

Ears are long. Well covered in hair, they need careful combing and grooming

Coat is long and well feathered

THE ENGLISH SPRINGER SPANIEL WAS DEVELOPED as a hunting dog to "spring" or flush game birds from cover—a role it has fulfilled since at least the early 17th century. It is frequently portrayed in hunting scenes and paintings of domestic life dating from that period. Springer Spaniels are hard-working dogs, and love water. They will rarely refuse an opportunity for a dip in a pond or river. Loyal and eager to please, they make excellent family dogs, but need firm training to ensure that their hunting instincts are kept under control. They adapt well to city life but need plenty of exercise, and are a good choice for an active, growing family looking for an energetic companion that loves to go for walks. Springer Spaniels do require time and attention, though. Without plenty of mental and physical stimulation, they quickly become bored and destructive. Though most Springer Spaniels are usually very healthy, with plenty of stamina and go, the breed has a handful of inherited health problems.

▲ *The English Springer Spaniel is a typical sporting dog, full of energy and stamina. If asked, it will keep going all day across rough country. It makes an excellent companion for an active family.*

Built for Activity

The English Springer Spaniel is a medium-sized, compact, and sturdy dog, designed to spend all day following hunters across rough terrain. Its long, forward-driving stride carries it quickly over the ground, and its square, strong jaws are built to handle gamebirds. The straight, thick coat, with long feathering on the legs and tail, needs careful grooming, especially after the dog has been running in long grass or brushy undergrowth. The usual colors of the coat are liver and white or black and white, with or without tan markings. The wide-set eyes are alert and oval in shape. The typical pendulous spaniel ears are well covered with hair. They are set quite low on the head and hang close to the face.

Breed Profile

Life expectancy:	11–12 years
Adult height at withers:	male 20in (51cm) female 19in (48cm)
Adult weight:	male 50lbs (22.5kg) female 40lbs (18kg)

Temperament: Friendly and quick to learn. Good with children, enjoy family life, but need space and time for exercise.

KNOWN HEALTH PROBLEMS

Progressive Retinal Atrophy (PRA) is an inherited progressive degeneration of the retina that can cause total blindness. There is no available treatment. The presence of the disease can be detected by testing, and affected dogs should not be used for breeding.

Retinal Dysplasia is an inherited eye defect causing folding of the retina. Its effects can vary from a negligible reduction in sight to total blindness.

Glaucoma, increased pressure of the fluid inside the eye, causes pain, inflammation, and excessive tear production. Surgical treatment is required. If left untreated, it leads eventually to blindness and loss of the affected eye.

Entropion (inturning eyelid) usually affects puppies. The eyelid turns in, causing the lashes to rub against the surface of the eye, and setting up irritation. The eye is sore and wet with tears, and is often kept closed. Surgical treatment is necessary.

Canine Fucidosis is a rare but progressive, and ultimately fatal, disease of the nervous system that affects young adult dogs. It is inherited in the English Springer Spaniel and has been seen in Great Britain and Australia. Symptoms, which include lack of coordination, loss of learned behavior, deafness, visual impairment, and depression, worsen over a period of several months. There is no effective treatment. Blood tests can identify carriers of the disease.

Hip Dysplasia, an inherited abnormality in one or both hip joints, may not be detected until the dog is a young adult. The usual symptoms are stiffness on getting up, a characteristic bunny-hopping gait, or lameness. Diagnosis is by a veterinary examination and X-ray. To avoid having an affected puppy, check the hip status of both parents, and restrict exercise during the first 6 months.

Achalasia, thickening of the muscle at the entrance of the stomach from the esophagus, causes regurgitation of food. The esophagus cannot empty fully into the stomach and gradually enlarges. Affected dogs have to be fed from a bowl in a raised position to prevent this. It is seen more often in the English Springer than many other breeds.

● *Every time we go out, Taylor, my Springer Spaniel, heads for water. He even does this when there is ice on the pond. Will he catch cold?*

This is normal Springer behavior. In warm weather there's no need to worry about drying him off, though it's a good idea to pat the insides of his ears gently with a towel. You should rub Taylor down in cold weather so he doesn't get chilled. Some people keep a "doggie bag" in the car. This is a loose terrycloth bag with a drawstring at the neck. You just put the dog inside, leaving his head and neck free at the top. Dogs seem to love it, and it warms them up very quickly.

● *I was out walking last summer with Rocket, my English Springer, when he suddenly started shaking his head violently. The vet examined him and found a grass seed in his ear that had to be removed under anesthetic. How do I avoid this happening again?*

This is a common problem. As the spaniel roots about in long grass, seeds such as wild barley get caught in the feathery hair on its long ear flaps. Tiny little barbs help move them deeper into the dog's coat. If one gets caught near the entrance to the ear, it sometimes moves into the ear canal and irritates the dog. He will make matters worse by shaking and scratching his ear, pushing the seed in deeper and deeper. Usually the ear is so tender that an anesthetic is needed to remove it. A seed imbedded in a paw can also have severe consequences. After walking in long grass or brushwood in summer, search your spaniel's coat, ears, and feet thoroughly for seeds and ticks.

● *When I went to choose an English Springer Spaniel, I was surprised to find the litter had long tails. I thought their tails were naturally short, as I've only ever seen them like that. Will my puppy's tail need shortening?*

No. The tradition used to be that Springer Spaniels' tails were docked at 3 days old to make them suitable as working dogs. Tails are very useful to dogs for communication, balance and for steering while swimming. As most dogs these days are family pets, there's no need to shorten them. Some kennel clubs still require docked tails for show purposes, though.

Staffordshire Bull Terrier

IN THE EARLY NINETEENTH CENTURY, BREEDERS in the English county of Staffordshire produced an excellent fighting dog by crossing Bulldogs with terriers to combine muscular strength with agility. "Staffies" were an instant success in and out of the ring. Dog fighting was banned in Britain in 1835, but the breed was already so popular that it survived the end of the sport for which it had been designed. With its terrier attributes, it proved useful as a ratter.

Since then selective breeding has minimized the Staffie's fighting instinct and emphasized its amiability to humans. The modern breed is fearless but people-oriented—gentle, friendly, and fond of children. Staffies are very bold and will come forward to investigate any strange or interesting noise without showing shyness or timidity. They will not tolerate the least challenge from other canines and have a reputation for being "scrappers." They may need to be kept on the leash when other dogs are around. The Staffie is best suited to an experienced handler, as firm training at an early age is essential.

Compact in build, Staffordshires are small enough to be kept in an apartment, but need plenty of exercise to keep them fit and sleek. The short coat requires only minimal grooming.

▲ *Reaching high. A Staffordshire Bull Terrier enjoys an energetic game with his owner. Exercise and the right diet will prevent the stocky frame from turning to fat.*

Breed Profile

Life expectancy:	10–12 years
Adult height at withers:	14–16in (36–41cm)
Adult weight:	male 28–38lbs (13–17kg)
	female 24–34lbs (11–15kg)

Temperament: Loyal and affectionate when properly socialized and trained. Good with children; enjoys family life, but needs space and time for exercise. Good watchdog, but not reliable with other dogs. Not a beginner's dog due to its temperament and strength.

KNOWN HEALTH PROBLEMS

Persistent Hyperplastic Primary Vitreous is a rare condition of the eye seen more in Staffordshires than other breeds. Some of the tissue present during development persists, causing a vision defect. There is an opacity at the back of the lens similar to a cataract, but with blood vessels present. Affected dogs are rarely completely blind, but there is no effective treatment for the complaint.

Cataracts are a progressive opacity of the lens in one or both eyes. The pupil appears gray to white instead of the normal black color. In advanced cases the lens looks like a pearl and the dog may be blind. In the Staffordshire Bull Terrier cataracts can occur as a hereditary problem, but they can also be due to other causes including infection, diabetes mellitus, and trauma. Surgery may be required.

A Solid Mass of Muscle

The entire appearance of the Staffordshire Bull Terrier suggests brute strength. This dog is a solid mass of bone and muscle, best described as "broad"—in the back, head, face, and chest. The coat is smooth and comes in many colors: red, fawn, blue, black, white, or brindle, or any of these colors and white. The head is fairly short, with a short foreface and strong, well-developed facial muscles. The eyes, which face forward, are dark and round, and the ears are small and half-pricked. The Staffordshire's jaws are very strong, and its teeth are large in proportion. Its straight tail is of medium length and tapers to a point.

The stocky build of the Staffordshire Bull Terrier makes it prone to put on weight. Prevent the problem by keeping rigorously to the recommended balanced diet for the dog's age and weight, and making sure that it is taken for at least one long daily run.

● *Winston, my Staffie, is just over a year old. He is very strong and tends to pull my arm off when he is on the leash. Would a harness be better for him than a collar?*

No, a harness would make things worse. You need a halter-style collar, with a noseband as well as a neck collar. The leash fits on the noseband and gently tightens it when you pull. This also turns the dog's face away from where he is pulling. Once he can't see where he is pulling, he will stop.

● *We'd like to get a Staffordshire Bull Terrier, but they have a reputation for terrorizing cats—we have two. What do you advise?*

Staffies do chase cats and can harm them—but they usually go for strangers rather than the family cat. The chase response is set off by the cat fleeing. If your Staffie puppy is aged 6 to 8 weeks when you acquire it, it will grow up with your cats and become habituated to them. The cats will not flee from it, so your Staffie should not be provoked to chase them.

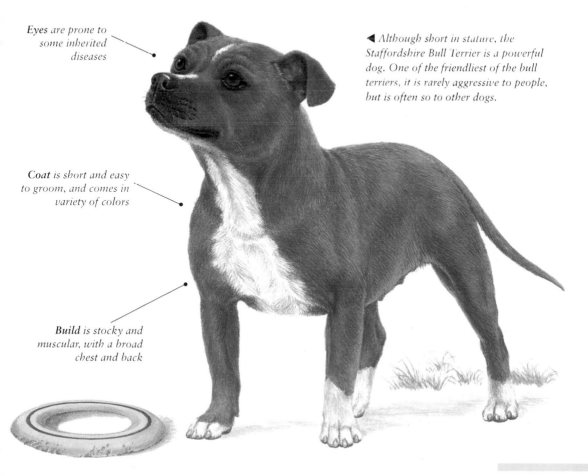

Eyes are prone to some inherited diseases

Coat is short and easy to groom, and comes in variety of colors

Build is stocky and muscular, with a broad chest and back

◀ *Although short in stature, the Staffordshire Bull Terrier is a powerful dog. One of the friendliest of the bull terriers, it is rarely aggressive to people, but is often so to other dogs.*

American and English Cocker Spaniel

THE SMALLEST OF THE WORKING SPANIELS, THE Cocker is also the most popular. As a hunting dog, its original purpose was to flush out woodcock. This was called "cocking," hence its name of Cocking Spaniel, later Cocker. There are two distinct varieties of Cocker Spaniel: the original English hunting dog and the American, recognized as a separate breed since 1946.

Cockers are usually fairly easy to train, but they require time and attention. They need lots of exercise, and their brains need to be occupied too, or else you will find they spend their time rounding up and retrieving household objects. If you can control their hyperactivity, they make affectionate, gentle pets and are usually good with children. Due to unwise breeding, Cocker Spaniels suffer from a range of health problems. Always ask for both parents' medical history before acquiring a puppy.

Two Very Similar Breeds

The two breeds are very similar in appearance, though the American Cocker is slightly smaller, with a shorter back and a more distinctly domed head. In both, the top body line slopes gently down from the shoulder to the base of the tail. The tail is well feathered and tapers gently from the base to the tip. The coat is flat and silky but not curly, and should be well feathered on the legs, body, and tail. There are many solid colors, including black, gold, red, and cream, and various mixed colors such as blue roan, orange and white, black and white. The muzzle is square with a distinct stop halfway between the tip of the nose and the top of the head. The alert eyes are usually brown and dark except in a few coat colors, where they may be dark hazel. The ears are set very low. The long, pendulous ear flaps are covered in straight, silky hair. Like all spaniels, Cockers pick up ear infections easily, so dry the ears well after swimming. Don't let the hair become matted. Trim (strip) the dead hair twice a year to keep the coat in condition.

Ear flaps are long and silky in both breeds

Coat is shorter in the English Cocker Spaniel

ENGLISH COCKER SPANIEL

● *My female Cocker Spaniel, Jodie, is 6 months old. I am planning to have her spayed soon, but her breeder says this will make her coat go fluffy. Is this true?*

For some reason, spaying does seem to have this effect on Cockers. The coat becomes finer to the touch, and may turn fluffy and curly. There is no way of knowing if it will happen or not. A fluffy coat will not be accepted by show judges, so if you are planning to show Jodie, you would be advised to delay spaying.

● *My 1-year-old English Cocker, Sunflower, suddenly snarled and snapped at me for no obvious reason—she was not ill or injured, and a minute later was back to normal. Can you explain it?*

Young adult English Cocker Spaniels, especially golden ones, are prone to "rage syndrome"—suddenly lashing out for no reason. The only warning sign is that their eyes glaze over. Sometimes they may threaten to, or actually bite their owner. Rage syndrome is not fully understood, but behavioral therapy appears to help.

Domed head with a shorter muzzle in the American Cocker

◀ *Cocker Spaniels are popular for their friendly, playful temperament. The American variety, which has been bred primarily as a companion rather than a hunting dog, is smaller than the English.*

Back is shorter than the English Cocker

Tail is well feathered in both breeds. It is carried straight and has an energetic motion

AMERICAN COCKER SPANIEL

Breed Profile

Life expectancy: 11–13 years

Adult height at withers
American: male 14½–15½in (37–39cm)
 female 13½–14½in (34–37cm)
English: male 16–17in (40.5–43cm)
 female 15–16in (38–40.5cm)

Adult weight
American: male 26–28lbs (12–13kg)
 female 24–26lbs (11–12kg)
English: male 28–34lbs (13–15.5kg)
 female 26–32lbs (12–14.5kg)

Temperament: Friendly and eager to please. Both make excellent family pets. Good with children. Need space and time for exercise. Generally fit and friendly, though there are a number of inherited breed problems, particularly of the eye.

KNOWN HEALTH PROBLEMS

Progressive Retinal Atrophy (PRA) is an inherited progressive degeneration of the retina of the eye that may lead to total blindness. It cannot be treat-ed. Tests will show if it is present, and affected dogs of either sex must not be used for breeding.

Entropion (inturning eyelid) is common in puppies. The edge of an eyelid rolls in and the lashes rub against the eye, which becomes sore and wet with tears, and is often kept closed. Surgery is necessary.

Persistent Pupillary Membrane occurs when tissue stays attached to the iris of the eye, affecting vision.

Glaucoma develops when fluid pressure inside the eye increases, causing pain, inflammation, and excessive tears. Surgical treatment is needed.

Distichiasis is caused by fine extra lashes growing along the edge of the eyelid. They rub against the surface of the eye, causing irritation.

Juvenile Nephropathy (premature kidney failure) occurs in some family lines. There is no effective treatment.

Rage Syndrome occasionally affects English Cockers as they reach maturity and seems to be most prevalent in the golden variety.

Beagle

Closely related to the foxhound, the Beagle has a 600-year history as a hunting pack hound, used for tracking and trapping hares. It has a characteristic exploring posture, with its nose close to the ground and its tail in the air, which suggests that it is permanently engaged in the hunt. The Beagle has a will of its own, and persuading it to obey its owner instead of its hunting instincts can be a real struggle. Once off the leash, it is likely to disappear over the horizon as it follows scents and investigates hedges and ditches. Early training and firm handling is necessary to instill obedience and ensure that your dog is not absent without leave for too long, returning to your shout or whistle.

Friendly, Playful, and Very Active

As a family pet, the Beagle is popular for its lack of aggression (both to people and to other dogs) and its playful, ready-for-anything disposition. However, it is not a dog for the fainthearted or those of sedentary habits. Vigorous daily exercise and frequent romps are essential outlets for its boundless energy, and the dog should not be confined to small indoor spaces for too long. It has a tendency to put on weight if it is overfed and underexercised.

They are excellent watchdogs. In common with most pack animals, however, Beagles have a tendency to mope and howl if left on their own. The Beagle's voice is less annoying than that of many dogs, but this tendency should not be encouraged—isolation is not good for the dog. If someone cannot be at home with it most of the day, the Beagle needs a canine companion.

The modern breed of Beagle is larger than its hunting ancestors. Previous generations of Beagles were sometimes as short as 11in (28cm)—small enough to fit into the capacious pocket of a hunting coat or in a saddlebag. When not carried in this way, they used to accompany the hunters on foot. Today the breed varies so greatly in size and appearance that many kennel clubs

recognize different varieties (the American Kennel Club recognizes two different sizes). The Beagle resembles a miniature Foxhound, with a look of solid robustness that reflects its ancestors' ability to remain all day in the hunting field, no matter how tough the conditions. Beagles are able to tolerate both hot and cold temperatures quite happily.

The Beagle's hard, thick coat is easy to groom. Most are white, black, and tan in color. The head is medium-sized with an attractive face, a slightly domed skull, and a fairly broad, pointed nose. The eyes are usually dark brown and large, and the ears are long and pendulous. A Beagle's tail is long and quite thick, with a visible white tip, and is carried high.

Breed Profile

Life expectancy:	10–13 years
Adult height at withers:	13–16in (33–41cm)
Adult weight:	18–30lbs (8–14kg)

Temperament: A good family dog for the experienced outdoor-loving family. Good with children. Takes up little room in the home or car. Not a beginner's dog—needs careful training to be obedient and under control.

Known Health Problems

Epilepsy is seen occasionally in the Beagle. The dog has a sudden, unexpected fit or convulsion, which lasts for a few minutes. Recovery is usually quick, although the dog may be quiet and look confused for a few hours. There is no cure, but treatment with anticonvulsant drugs is usually successful in controlling symptoms.

Glaucoma, a rare inherited disease in Beagles, develops when the pressure of the fluid inside the eye increases, causing pain, inflammation, and excessive tear production. If left untreated, it leads to blindness and loss of the affected eye.

Ear Infections occur in the Beagle because of the large pendulous ears, which block air circulation and encourage moisture.

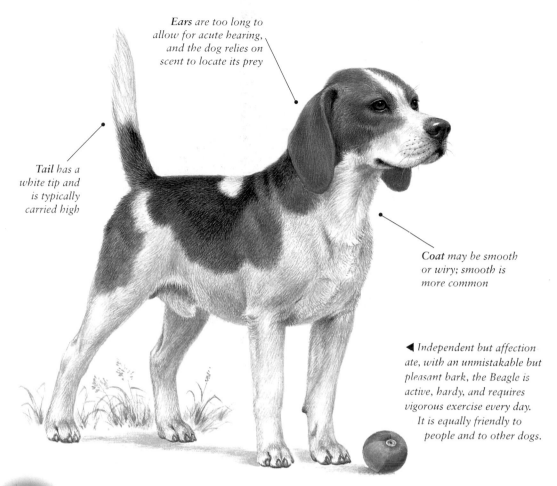

Ears are too long to allow for acute hearing, and the dog relies on scent to locate its prey

Tail has a white tip and is typically carried high

Coat may be smooth or wiry; smooth is more common

◄ *Independent but affectionate, with an unmistakable but pleasant bark, the Beagle is active, hardy, and requires vigorous exercise every day. It is equally friendly to people and to other dogs.*

● **Our Beagle, Muffin, is very greedy and even knocks food off the kitchen counter to get to it. What can I do about this?**

Beagles are often greedy, and food left out is a temptation for them. You can make life easier for yourself and the dog by making sure all food is put away and not leaving tasty snacks lying around, but you should also work hard to improve Muffin's obedience training. It might even be a good idea to enlist the help of a professional trainer.

● **Would you recommend a Beagle as a suitable pet for an active family? What are the pitfalls, if any?**

On the whole, Beagles make excellent family pets, particularly if you have owned a dog before and are prepared to work hard at training. Their biggest liability is that they tend to be unreliable off the leash and will dash after anything that moves, ignoring you when you call them back. Because Beagles are small dogs, they

are unlikely to cause major harm to other pets or wildlife, but undisciplined chasing should never be encouraged. However, if you pay particular attention to the "coming to call" aspect of obedience training when the puppy is very young, preferably from the time it is 8 weeks old, this behavior shouldn't become a problem.

● **We would like a companion for our 9-year-old Jack Russell Terrier, Scooter, both for his sake and for ours when we eventually lose him. Would a Beagle be a suitable choice?**

Definitely. Because they were originally bred as pack dogs, Beagles love company and are usually happier in a house with more than one dog than on their own. They are very gentle and will not normally challenge other dogs. However, you would be well advised to acquire a puppy, which will learn to respect the older terrier, otherwise Scooter may become jealous of the newcomer.

Poodle

MINIATURE

STANDARD

Coat does not molt, and requires daily grooming and regular clipping

TOY

▲ *The three types of Poodle contrast greatly in size. The Miniature shown here has the "lion clip," while the Standard and Toy have a more natural-looking shape.*

THE TINY, CLIPPED POODLES OF TODAY ARE FAR removed from the French retrieving dogs whose thick, curly coats suited them for working in water, from whom today's dogs have developed. Closest to them are the Standard Poodles, the largest of the modern poodles. Toy Poodles were being bred as companions for fashionable ladies in Paris as far back as the 16th century. Poodles were later used as performing dogs in circuses, and their popularity was boosted this century through their association with glamorous movie stars. As a result of unwise breeding to keep pace with the rising demand, the temperament of the breed suffered, giving rise to shrill, nervous dogs. Poodles lost their place as the world's favorite dogs to German Shepherds and Yorkshire Terriers. Responsible breeders are now attempting to correct the tendency to noisiness.

Three Sizes of Dog

The Poodle comes in three sizes: Toy, Miniature, and Standard. Naturally intelligent, friendly, and highly trainable, they make ideal family pets and good watchdogs. A peculiarity of the breed is that their hair grows continually so that they do not shed, making them suitable pets for people with allergies. However, the profuse wooly coat requires daily grooming and regular clipping to keep it in good condition. Many people choose an unfussy coat shape known as the "lamb clip," but for show purposes the coat is shaped into the elaborate "lion clip," in which fluffy pom-poms of fur on the feet, tail, and forequarters contrast with close-shaved areas on the legs, waist, and rump. The coat, which is always a single color, occurs in white, cream, silver, apricot, brown, blue, and black. The eyes are dark and almond-shaped, and the ears, which are long and pendulous, are well covered in fur. The tail is set high and usually angled up a little. It is thick at the base and well covered in fur. If left undocked, it tapers well to the base.

Breed Profile

Life expectancy:	11–14 years
Adult height at withers:	Standard, 15in and over (38.5cm)
	Miniature, 10–15in (28–38.5cm)
	Toy, 10in and under (25cm)
Adult weight:	Standard, 45–70lbs (20.5–32kg)
	Miniature, 26–30lbs (12–14kg)
	Toy, 12–16½lbs (5–7.5kg)

Temperament: Intelligent, playful, active, good with children. Suitable for a beginner who is willing to attend training classes.

KNOWN HEALTH PROBLEMS

Otitis, infection of the ear, seems to affect Poodles more than other breeds. The ear flaps are long and heavy, and hair grows in the ear canals, trapping moisture and wax, which attract bacteria.

Periodontal Disease of the gums is common in Poodles, possibly due to the saliva content. Home dental care, brushing, and a correct diet are important to maintain oral hygiene and avoid infection. Teeth may need to be scaled and polished by the vet.

Perthe's Disease affects the development of one or both hip joints in the Miniature and Toy Poodles. The top of the femur bone degenerates, producing severe pain and collapse of the hip joint. Although medical treatment may help in the early stages, an operation to remove the affected piece of bone is often needed.

Epilepsy is seen in the Miniature Poodle. The dog has a sudden, unexpected seizure or convulsion, lasting for a few minutes. Recovery is usually quick, although the dog may be quiet and look confused for a few hours. Anticonvulsant drugs usually control the problem.

Von Willebrand's Disease, an inherited disease of the blood platelets, is known to occur occasionally in the Miniature and Standard Poodle, leading to unexpected and unexplained bleeding.

Luxating Patella (dislocating kneecap) is seen in the Miniature Poodle, affecting one or both legs. Sometimes the kneecap slips in and out of position without causing the dog any discomfort or disability, but in other cases it remains out of place and the dog cannot straighten the leg. An operation can correct the joint structure and enable the patella to stay in its groove.

Progressive Retinal Atrophy (PRA) is a progressive degeneration of the retina of the eye that can lead to total blindness. It is seen in the Miniature and Toy Poodle. Affected dogs of either sex must not be used for breeding.

Entropion (inturning eyelid) is seen occasionally in the Standard Poodle, usually in puppies. The rim of an eyelid rolls in, causing the lashes to rub against the surface of the eye, irritating the eyeball. Surgery is necessary.

▲ *Poodles come in a variety of colors. An apricot coat is particularly attractive and popular with owners.*

● *Balzac, our 9-month-old Miniature Poodle, seems to have an extra canine tooth on each side of his upper jaw. Is this normal?*

Balzac has very likely retained his baby teeth, which should be shed at about 6 months of age. This condition is common in the smaller Poodles. There may be more of these baby teeth present than you have noticed. This will lead to overcrowding and dental problems later, so your vet will probably advise you to have the extra teeth removed.

● *We have Kristin, our Standard Poodle, regularly clipped, but I have noticed that she seems to have a lot of hair growing in the openings of her ears. Should we trim it?*

No, this will simply allow the hair to pack down in the ear canal. You will have to pluck the hair out regularly; otherwise it will become clogged with wax, increasing the likelihood of infection.

Shetland Sheepdog

THE SHETLAND SHEEPDOG (POPULARLY AND affectionately known as the Sheltie) is a native of the Shetland Islands, which lie just off the northern coast of Scotland. It is a small dog that resembles a miniature Rough Collie in shape of body, coat type, and color. The Shetland Islands are also home to a miniature breed of pony, the Shetland pony. Some experts hold that the bleak climate and sparse food reserves of the islands were factors in the miniaturization of both horse and dog. However, others believe that the Sheltie is a miniaturized form of the Collie, deliberately or accidentally produced.

Bred originally, as the name suggests, for herding sheep, the Sheltie is an intelligent, gentle dog, always alert, full of energy, and ready for work or play. Though there is a tendency toward shyness with strangers, once a Sheltie has come to accept you, it will prove a loyal and faithful companion. Because it is eager to please, it is usually an easy dog to train. Shelties make excellent family pets. Their small, compact size makes it possible for them to live happily in a town apartment and they can easily be lifted in and out of the car. However, they do need plenty of exercise. Potential owners should also note that the longish, fine coats that are such an outstanding feature of the breed require daily grooming.

▲ *A distinctive feature of the Shetland Sheepdog is its abundant mane of white hair. There is wide variation in body color, though the forelegs are usually white too. It is alert and eager for fun.*

Breed Profile

Life expectancy:	11–13 years
Adult height at withers:	male 14½in (37cm) female 14in (35.5cm)
Adult weight:	15–25lbs (7–11kg)

Temperament: A loyal, affectionate companion. Good with children and enjoys family life, though shy with strangers. Suited to living in town and country, but needs frequent walking. Longish hair needs daily grooming.

KNOWN HEALTH PROBLEMS

Collie Eye Anomaly (CEA), an inherited disease of Rough and Smooth Collies, is also found in the Shetland Sheepdog. It causes retinal hemorrhage or detached retina. In some affected dogs there may be no noticeable loss of vision, but a small proportion (about 5 percent) may incur partial or total blindness. There is no treatment. The defect can be detected at birth or shortly afterward by examination with an ophthalmoscope, and it is imperative that affected dogs are not used for breeding.

Progressive Retinal Atrophy (PRA) is a progressive degeneration of the retina of the eye that affects the light-sensitive cells and may lead to total blindness. Affected dogs of either sex must not be used for breeding.

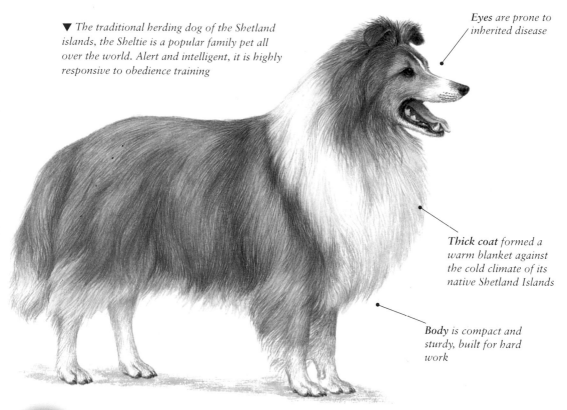

▼ *The traditional herding dog of the Shetland islands, the Sheltie is a popular family pet all over the world. Alert and intelligent, it is highly responsive to obedience training*

Eyes *are prone to inherited disease*

Thick coat *formed a warm blanket against the cold climate of its native Shetland Islands*

Body *is compact and sturdy, built for hard work*

● *My Sheltie, Colin, has an odd right eye. It's blue instead of brown. Does this mean he'll become blind?*

No. This is called a "wall eye" and is due to a lack of pigment in the iris. Colin is almost certainly a blue merle variety if he has this eye color.

● *I have a Sheltie puppy, Misty, who is now 4 months old. She loves to roll in all kinds of dirt and mud while out walking. Is it true you shouldn't bath sheepdogs?*

It is perfectly safe to bath Shelties, but make sure you use a shampoo that does not remove the natural oils or contains a conditioner.

● *Though we live in town, we are an active family. We want to keep a dog but haven't enough space for a Rough Collie, which is our favorite breed. Will a Shetland make an suitable substitute?*

Shelties have very much the appearance of a small Rough Collie, though the nose is shorter and they are much more compact. Provided you can find time to exercise a Sheltie at least twice a day, it will adapt happily to urban living. They benefit from company and are a good choice of family pet.

A Lean, Elegant Face

The Sheltie has a beautifully shaped head that tapers elegantly from the ears to the nose and is covered in smooth, short hair. When alert, the ears are carried vertically, with just the tips folding over forward. These, together with their dark-brown, gentle eyes, give Shelties a strikingly appealing expression. However, the small, deep-set eyes are easily irritated, and they suffer quite a lot from diseases of the eye.

In contrast to the smooth covering of the face, there is an outer coat of long, straight, harsh hair with an abundant mane and frill around the neck and pronounced feathering on the forelegs. There is a short, soft undercoat. The usual color is sable, either clear or shaded, ranging in tone from honey to dark russet, with white or tan markings. Tricolors of rich tan, black, and white also occur. Blue merle—a silvery blue coat with black splashes and marbling on it—is a particularly attractive variation. Other colors seen in the Shetland Sheepdog are black and white, and black and tan.

Miniature Schnauzer

THE MINIATURE SCHNAUZER IS THE SMALLEST and much the most popular of the German Schnauzer breeds ("schnauze" is the German for nose). It descends from the same root stock as the other Schnauzers, mixed with Affenpinscher and Miniature Pinscher. Like many of the most popular breeds, it has suffered from irresponsible breeding practices that have introduced some health problems. In spite of this, it remains an excellent choice for a family pet, though its lively, feisty character (it was originally bred to catch rats) means that is best suited to an owner or family that is used to dogs. However, it is not as snappy as the terrier breeds and has a calmer disposition. It is an enthusiastic guard dog. It will adapt happily to life in a city apartment and likes nothing better than to observe what's going on in the street from the window.

Despite their size, Schnauzers should never be thought of as lap dogs. Always alert and active, they are very tough and solidly built, and enjoy plenty of company and a good walk. They are very affectionate and respond quickly to training, which is always a good idea to ensure that their activity does not become hyperactivity.

▼ *The Miniature Schnauzer is an active, jaunty, friendly little dog. It is the ideal companion dog for the city dweller but needs plenty of stimulation to avoid destructive boredom.*

Coat *is coarse, hard, and wiry. It needs grooming but does not shed much*

Hips *should be checked for hereditary disease*

Whiskers *are abundant and bushy. They need regular grooming to keep them neat*

Legs *are medium to long, straight in front but angled at rear to give bursts of speed when running*

● *The whiskers on Pepper, our Miniature Schnauzer, are always brown and dirty-looking. He will not let us anywhere near his mouth. Could there be something wrong?*

Pepper has one of two problems. It may just be food and saliva staining. If he won't let you comb or wash his whiskers from day to day, you will have to train him to tolerate it. It may be, however, that he has a dental problem, so if you really cannot get anywhere near his mouth, you should ask your vet to examine him.

● *We have two teenage children and live in an apartment on the second floor. We are thinking of getting a Miniature Schnauzer, but I've been told they are noisy, especially with visitors. Is this likely to be a problem?*

Not if your dog is well trained. The modern Miniature Schnauzer has been bred for a century or more for companionship and is not aggressive by nature. Though they are natural guard dogs, with the right early socialization and training they can be taught to accept many different visitors.

● *Are Miniature Schnauzers reliable with children?*

Most miniature breeds are wary of children, and Miniature Schnauzers are no exception. It's probably because children are more unpredictable and less gentle than adults. Small dogs are more likely to feel bumps than larger ones. If hurt, they will snap. Young children should never be left on their own with a dog, even a small one.

Squared Off

A show-quality pedigree Miniature Schnauzer has a somewhat square shape, with its length equal to its height. The head is long, with a strong muzzle and well-developed nose, and a long, arched neck. The alert dark eyes are oval in shape, and the ears are high on the head and fold forward. The legs are of medium length, straight in the front, with the elbows close to the chest; the rear legs have strong bones and are slightly angled to give bursts of speed when running. The back slopes slightly toward the hind quarters. If left in its natural state, the tail is held high, but in show dogs it has customarily been docked at the third joint.

Miniature Schnauzers are one of the most elegant of the smaller breeds of dog. A soft undercoat underlies the coarse, hard top coat, which is short and wiry, and attractively colored in solid black, black and silver, or salt-and-pepper. The prominent whiskers and eyebrows, and the long hair on the chest, between the forelegs, and on the lower part of the legs, are always silver. These dogs shed very little hair but need grooming daily with a tough wire brush on the body and a comb on the whiskers and eyebrows. The whiskers need particular attention as they have a tendency to gather crumbs and bits of food when the dog is eating. Professional thinning (stripping) of the coat twice a year is advisable.

Breed Profile

Life expectancy:	12–14 years
Adult height at withers:	male 14in (36cm)
	female 12in (30cm)
Adult weight:	male 15lbs (7kg)
	female 13lbs (6kg)

Temperament: Lively, alert, tough, faithful. Good family dog that enjoys company. Sometimes nervous around children. Fairly vocal but not shrill. Will react to any noise nearby. A good choice for a family that is accustomed to keeping dogs.

KNOWN HEALTH PROBLEMS

Cataracts are progressive opacities of the lens in one or both eyes. The pupil becomes gray to white instead of the normal black color. In advanced cases the lens looks like a pearl and the dog may go blind. In the Miniature Schnauzer cataracts tend to be inherited, although, as in other breeds, they can be due to other causes including infection, diabetes, and trauma.

Von Willebrand's Disease, an inherited disease of the platelets (a blood component that helps in clotting), is not common, but when it occurs it leads to unexpected and unexplained bleeding. Transfusions may help control the problem.

Perthe's Disease is a disease affecting the development of one or both hip joints. It occurs when the bone of the head of the femur (leg bone) degenerates, producing severe pain and eventual collapse of the joint. Failure of the blood supply to this small piece of bone is thought to be the cause. Medical treatment can sometimes help in the early stages, but an operation is often needed to remove the affected piece of bone.

Jack Russell Terrier

A SMALL, LIVELY DOG, THE JACK RUSSELL TERRIER is probably one of the most numerous and popular breeds in the world. It was developed in the 1800s from a rough-coated strain of Fox Terrier by the Reverend (Parson) Jack Russell, an English clergyman who was an enthusiastic follower of hunting. Bred to go down holes to chase out foxes, it had to run with the huntsmen's horses and was longer in the leg than many of today's breed. Not many kennel clubs recognize the Jack Russell, so there are no official breed standards. The British Kennel Club has recently recognized the Parson Jack Russell Terrier as a separate breed, with a standard that aims to bring it closer to the original appearance.

A Feisty Ratter

The Jack Russell is a small, workmanlike, agile terrier who never seems to tire and is a master of the art of pest control. Quick, sharp-eyed, and sharp-witted, it will seize the speediest rat by the neck and shake it to death, and can clear a barn or granary in no time at all, piling the corpses up outside ready for disposal. Today Jack Russells are kept much more commonly as family pets.

Although they are affectionate and fun loving with people, especially children, they are sometimes snappy with other dogs and animals.

There is little point in keeping a Jack Russell if you do not enjoy long walks, preferably in the country, where the dog will spend hours sniffing around in ditches and undergrowth for wildlife to chase. Jack Russells need to be kept occupied and should not be left on their own for too long. If bored, they will find an alternative activity to amuse themselves with, normally chewing up your house and favorite possessions.

Jack Russells are both smooth and wirehaired. The coat of both types is harsh and rough, giving it protection from weather and thorns. The color of the coat is usually, but not always, white with some black, lemon, or tan markings. There is a considerable variation in height, and the body is generally longer than it is tall. The muzzle is long and usually rather pointed. The ears, which are high-set, normally drop forward but are sometimes held erect. In the past the tail was traditionally docked at 3 days, but this practice is beginning to die out. The Jack Russell is generally robust, with few known health problems.

Breed Profile

Life expectancy:	12–15 years
Adult height at withers:	10–14in (25–35cm)
Adult weight:	9–16lbs (4–7kg)

Temperament: Very active, bold, and willing. A good family dog, friendly with people, but may drive off other dogs and chase strange cats. Needs plenty of exercise. Rarely ill.

KNOWN HEALTH PROBLEMS

Lens Luxation occurs when the lens of the eye dislocates from its normal position behind the pupil and moves into the anterior chamber of the eye, where it blocks the drainage of the eye and causes acute glaucoma. It is an emergency situation requiring immediate surgery. There appears to be an inherited tendency in Jack Russells.

Luxating Patella (dislocating kneecap) occurs sometimes in Jack Russells, particularly the smaller, short-legged type. In some dogs the kneecaps slip in and out of position without causing any discomfort or disability, but sometimes a kneecap remains out of place and the dog cannot straighten the leg. An operation is usually necessary to correct the joint structure and fix the kneecap in its groove.

Perthe's Disease affects the development of one or both hip joints. It is seen most commonly in small terriers such as the Jack Russell. The bone of the head of the femur degenerates, producing severe pain. Eventually, the joint collapses. Medical treatment may help to alleviate symptoms in the early stages, but an operation is often needed to remove the affected piece of bone.

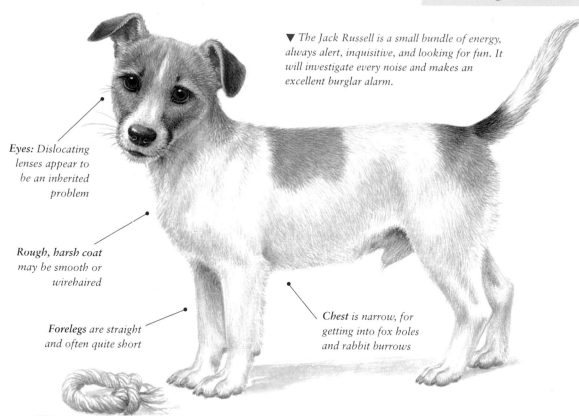

▼ *The Jack Russell is a small bundle of energy, always alert, inquisitive, and looking for fun. It will investigate every noise and makes an excellent burglar alarm.*

Eyes: Dislocating lenses appear to be an inherited problem

Rough, harsh coat may be smooth or wirehaired

Forelegs are straight and often quite short

Chest is narrow, for getting into fox holes and rabbit burrows

Q&A...

● **How do I stop my 3-year-old Jack Russell, Finn, from barking when visitors arrive?**

Jack Russells have noisy guarding instincts, and it will take some time to change Finn's behavior at this age. Encourage Finn to learn the command "stay" by giving him a food reward when he obeys you. When he has thoroughly grasped this, ask a friend to arrive at the door at a prearranged time. Just before, restrain Finn on a leash at the far end of the hall and tell him to "stay" in a lying position. When the bell rings, tell him to "stay" again, and if he does, give him a reward. Repeat this exercise many times, and in time the problem should subside.

● *Ever since my children saw a Jack Russell Terrier on a television show, they have constantly asked me for one. As we live in a small apartment and Jack Russells are small dogs, I'm tempted to agree. What do you think?*

It depends how much time and commitment you and your children are able to give. Jack Russells are actually big dogs in small bodies. They are very active and outgoing, and require lots of exercise and training if they are to make good city pets.

▲ *Jack Russells were essentially farm dogs, kept for their ratting skills. They make active, healthy companions, but retain many of their terrier instincts.*

Cavalier King Charles Spaniel

Tail *is long and silky. It is in almost constant motion when the dog is active*

Hair *on the ears should be combed and trimmed often to keep the ear canals free from infection*

Heart *murmur is common; check before buying a puppy*

THIS LIVELY LITTLE SPANIEL IS ONE OF THE MOST loving, reliable, and adaptable of all breeds. The adult dogs are small enough to pick up and carry around, and may easily be taken anywhere in the car, yet they also enjoy good long walks and strenuous romps outdoors. But it is their temperament that makes them popular. Cavaliers always seem happy; they are friendly and nonaggressive, and have little tendency toward nervousness or shyness. With their open, trusting expressions and big, gentle brown eyes, they make appealing and lovable companions. The breed is the perfect first dog for a family with young children or an elderly person who is looking for a devoted friend.

Due to its great popularity, the Cavalier King Charles Spaniel has been the object of intensive inbreeding. As a result, there is a quite considerable incidence of inherited heart disease, and the breed's life expectancy can be as low as 9 years. By 5 years of age, up to 50 percent of males, and only a slightly smaller number of females, have developed heart murmurs.

● *I have been told that Cavalier King Charles Spaniels suffer from heart murmurs. How can I avoid choosing one with this condition?*

The problem seems to occur more often in some bloodlines or families than others, so ask the breeder whether the parents or grandparents of the pups have been affected. If there is a high incidence in the litter's ancestry, go elsewhere. Make sure that the parents are over 2 years old, as many Cavaliers do not begin to show the symptoms of heart disease before that age.

● *My Cavalier, Manhattan, has developed a most peculiar habit of snapping at imaginary flies. Why does she do this, and how can I stop her?*

This behavior in dogs is thought to be linked to a type of epilepsy and will sometimes respond to treatment with anticonvulsant drugs prescribed by your veterinarian. When Manhattan starts behaving like this, don't try to stop her by making a fuss of her; this could make the condition worse. Instead, try to divert her attention with an interesting toy or game.

New Look for an Old Breed

The Cavalier King Charles was developed some 50 years ago as a separate breed from the King Charles Spaniel, whose origins date back several centuries. The chief difference is the Cavalier's longer muzzle, which gives it a closer appearance to the spaniels that the Flemish artist Van Dyck included in his famous portrait of King Charles II of England (1630–85), hence their name. The Cavalier is also somewhat larger than its cousin. Seen from the front, it has the same appealing flat-faced look as the Pekingese, though the eyes, which are large and round, are not so prominent. The ears are typical of spaniels—pendulous, high on the head, and covered with long, wavy hair. The tail, seldom still, is rarely carried above the level of the back. The long silky coat may be slightly wavy but never curly.

There are four distinct color types. The Black and Tan is solid black with tan markings above the eyes, on the cheeks, inside the ears, on the chest and legs, and under the tail. There should

◀ *The Cavalier King Charles Spaniel was selectively bred from the 1920s to remove puglike characteristics and restore those of 17th-century spaniels.*

▶ *Cavaliers have larger heads and longer muzzles than their relatives, the puglike King Charles Spaniels. Their vision and sense of smell are both excellent.*

be no white marks. The Ruby Cavalier is a solid rich copper color. White markings are undesirable. The coloring of the Blenheim consists of chestnut markings on a white background. The head is half-and-half, with both ears and eyes included, and white down the center. There is often a chestnut mark between the ears. The Tricolor has well-spaced patches of black and white, with tan markings over the eyes, cheeks, inside the ears, and under the tail.

Breed Profile

Life expectancy:	9–13 years
Adult height at withers:	12–13in (30.5–33cm)
Adult weight:	12–18lbs (5.5–8kg)

Temperament: Completely reliable and nonaggressive; very good with children. Equally at home in town or country, will live happily in an apartment with access to walks, and is an ideal urban companion. Excellent for beginners.

KNOWN HEALTH PROBLEMS

Early Onset Endocardiosis (heart murmur), as the name suggests, often occurs early in life. It is a degenerative disease affecting the valves of the heart. When the heart beats, some blood, instead of leaving the heart chambers and moving on round the arterial system, leaks back into the heart because the valves fail to close fully. This turbulence causes a characteristic sound, known as a heart murmur, which can be heard through a stethoscope. As the valves become more affected, the heart becomes much less efficient and enlarges in an attempt to compensate. Eventually congestive heart failure occurs. It is usually symptomless in the initial stages, but with advancing age, especially if the dog is overweight, signs of heart disease develop— a chronic cough, panting, weakness, and even fainting. Treatment with diuretics and heart drugs can prolong the dog's active life.

Cataracts are a slowly progressive opacity of the lens in one or both eyes. The normally dark pupil turns gray or white as the lens gradually hardens and becomes obscured. In advanced cases the lens looks like a pearl and the dog can become blind. Cataracts can be inherited in the Cavalier King Charles, though other causes such as infection, diabetes mellitus, or injury may also be responsible.

Miniature Pinscher

ALTHOUGH THE MINIATURE PINSCHER LOOKS like a tiny replica of a Doberman Pinscher, the relationship between the two breeds is only a distant one. The Miniature Pinscher probably originated at least 200 years before the Doberman, and its original ancestor was the German or Standard Pinscher. Miniature Pinschers did not appear outside their native Germany until the end of World War II (1939–45). Well suited to urban living, these attractive little dogs have grown steadily in popularity since.

The breed, affectionately known as the Min Pin, has a lively, fearless spirit that makes it anything but a lap dog. It was originally developed for ratting (a skill it has retained) and will take on all comers regardless of size. Its boldness, coupled with its acute hearing, make it an excellent guard dog. It should not be kept in an outdoor kennel except in a very warm climate as it tolerates heat much better than cold. Vigorous exercise is not a requirement, but it will always respond enthusiastically to an invitation for a walk and will benefit from frequent romps.

Miniature Pinschers are usually very friendly with people, though they can be a little wary of children. Early socialization and training are vital to counteract the breed's tendency to snappishness. For this reason, this breed is not the best choice for a first-time dog owner. It should also be avoided by those with small children, as they may be tempted to pick up and tease the dog, which is no bigger than a cat, and provoke an incident. But for those experienced in training puppies and those with older children, it is an excellent choice of family pet. There is a very low incidence of breed-related health problems.

Small but Sturdy

Selective breeding has refined the breed's original appearance as well as reducing it in size. Though small, Miniature Pinschers are sturdily built, with a strong muzzle. When walking, they have a characteristic high-stepping gait. This is often

● We have been to look at a litter of Miniature Pinschers, and the one we really liked the look of seemed to stay quietly at the back while the other three came to us. My children tried to pick this one up, but even at 6 weeks old he growled at them. They felt sorry for him and really want him. Would this be sensible?

Definitely not. If you must have one of this litter, choose a lively puppy that is not afraid of you. The frightened little one needs a quiet home with one person, where it will learn with time and experience to feel more secure. With children, you are probably better off with another breed that is more outgoing, such as a Yorkshire or Border Terrier, or a Miniature Schnauzer.

● Squeak, our 6-year-old Miniature Pinscher, has gum disease. The vet says she needs to have her teeth polished and scaled. This has to be done under a general anesthetic. I'm so worried that Squeak may not come round from the operation because she is such a small dog. Do you think I've cause for concern?

Though there is always a small risk involved in any surgical procedure, anesthesia is very safe nowadays. The vet may do a blood test first to make sure Squeak is in good health. If you do not let the vet clean her teeth, Squeak will be in pain for the rest of her life, so I strongly advise you to go ahead.

● I'm planning to collect my new Min Pin puppy next week. She's less than 2 months old and really tiny. Friends tell me I should start training right away, but surely it's too early?

Little dogs, especially those developed from the guard breeds, need training just as much as larger ones. Miniature Pinschers have a tendency to seek a dominant role unless they are made aware as early as possible of their position in the family. They respond well to training, provided it starts early. About 8 weeks is ideal, and certainly not too soon. Get your puppy used to being with your family and its activities, and then continue with puppy training classes.

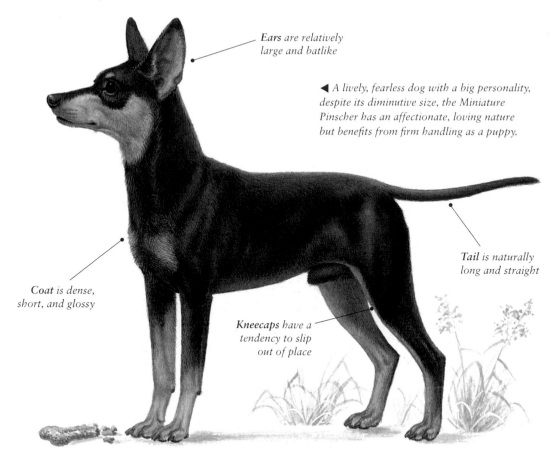

Ears *are relatively large and batlike*

◄ *A lively, fearless dog with a big personality, despite its diminutive size, the Miniature Pinscher has an affectionate, loving nature but benefits from firm handling as a puppy.*

Tail *is naturally long and straight*

Coat *is dense, short, and glossy*

Kneecaps *have a tendency to slip out of place*

called the hackney gait, after an old-fashioned type of horse-drawn carriage.

The head, while not short, is not as long in proportion to the body as that of a Doberman. The coat, which is short, smooth, and glossy, is almost self-grooming, requiring only the minimum of attention. It can be black, chocolate, or blue in color, with tan markings on the cheeks, lips, lower jaw, throat, and lower legs, and twin spots above the eyes and chest. A solid red color is also sometimes seen. The eyes are black, and the batlike ears can be erect or folded. Like a number of German breeds, Miniature Pinschers traditionally had their ears cropped at a young age so that they stood erect. This was supposed to give them a fiercer expression. This practice, which has been banned in many countries on grounds of cruelty, is becoming increasingly unacceptable throughout the world. In the past, too, the tail was always docked, but this custom is also beginning to disappear.

Breed Profile

Life expectancy:	13–15 years
Adult height at withers:	male 12in (30cm) female 10in (25cm)
Adult weight:	male 11lbs (5kg) female 9lbs (4kg)

Temperament: Lively, tough, faithful companion. Alert, vocal, and will react to any noise nearby. Ideal for apartment life as it can get sufficient exercise in a very small space.

KNOWN HEALTH PROBLEMS

Luxating Patella (dislocating kneecap) occurs occasionally in the Miniature Pinscher, aggravated by its distinctive high-stepping gait. In many cases the kneecap just slips in and out of position without causing the dog any discomfort or disability, but sometimes the kneecap remains out of place and the dog cannot straighten its leg. An operation is usually necessary to correct the structure of the joint and enable the kneecap to stay in its groove.

West Highland White Terrier

Head is thickly coated with hair. The ears are small, pointed, and erect

Coat is pure white, harsh, and thick. It needs regular brushing

Tail is covered with harsh hair but not feathered

Feet have black nails and pads, protecting its feet in its native rocky highlands

ORIGINATING FROM THE WEST HIGHLANDS OF Scotland, "Westies" (as they are affectionately known) are deservedly one of the most popular small breeds. Extroverted, lively characters, with a well-developed sense of fun, they are always ready for a walk and are virtually tireless. The Westie's great appeal is that it is small enough to pick up and take anywhere, and will live as happily in an apartment as in a house with a yard, provided that it gets enough exercise.

A Compact Dog with "Drive"

Westies are small but compact, with a deep chest and level back. The forefeet are larger than the hind feet, well covered in hair, and all the claws and pads of the feet are black. The hindquarters should be strong and wide. When they move, the gait should be free and straight, with the front legs extended forward from the shoulder. Hind movement should be free, strong, and close, with the stifles (knees) and hocks (ankles) well flexed to give the dog "drive."

The pure-white double coat is harsh and thick. It needs regular brushing and should be thinned by hand (stripped) by a professional groomer twice a year. The slightly domed head, covered with hair, is carried upright to the neck. The jet-black nose is large but not projecting. Westies have very dark, wide-set eyes, which give them a piercing, intelligent expression. Their teeth are large, and the mouth should have a regular scissor bite. Short ears, covered in velvety hair, are held erect and terminate in sharp points. The tail, which is 5–6in (12.5–16cm) long, is covered with harsh, unfeathered hair. It is carried jauntily, not too high or over the back.

Breed Profile

Life expectancy:	11–14 years
Adult size at the withers:	11in (28cm)
Adult weight:	male 19lbs (8.5kg)
	female 16½lbs (7.5kg)

Temperament: An ideal family dog and companion for children. Easy to train, suitable for urban or rural lifestyles.

KNOWN HEALTH PROBLEMS

Perthe's Disease is an inherited condition in small terriers, affecting one or both hip joints. It is a developmental disease, first noticeable in young dogs. The head of the femur degenerates, causing pain, lameness, and collapse of the joint.

Cranio-Mandibular Osteopathy (Lion-Head Disease) causes bony enlargements in the skull and lower jaw. It is hereditary (but rare) in Westies, and is almost always seen during puppy growth. The early stages are painful. The puppy is feverish, salivates excessively, and lacks appetite. Pain-killing drugs can relieve the symptoms during the active stage of the disease. When the puppy is fully grown, at about 9 months, the pain ceases, leaving the dog with painless bony lumps on the skull and jaw.

Atopy, an allergic skin disease particularly common in Westies, causes severe itchiness. It can start as early as 6 months and is provoked by inhaling pollen, house dust mites, or other allergens. Intradermal skin tests can determine the precise cause of the allergy.

Keratoconjunctivitis Sicca (Dry Eye) is an inherited autoimmune disease that is seen more often in the West Highland than in other breeds. One (sometimes both) of the eyes fails to produce tears, causing the cornea to become dried out. It is then invaded by blood vessels attempting to heal it. Symptoms of the condition include pigmentation of the eye(s) and a sticky, grayish discharge. If left untreated, the disease can cause severe pain and lead eventually to total blindness.

"Little White Shaker Syndrome" affects older puppies and young adults. All four legs and the head go into tremor. It usually resolves itself after seven days. The Maltese is also affected.

▲ *The Westie is a friendly, companionable dog that thrives on affection and attention. It is usually very reliable with children. Westies are small enough to live in an apartment but should have access to a small yard. Its bravery and sharp ears make it a good watchdog.*

Q & A...

● *My Westie, Krystal, has sticky mucus in one eye, and she rubs it a lot. What is causing this?*

One likely cause is that she has injured her eye and needs medical attention, so you should ask your vet to examine her as soon as possible. If no injury is apparent, your vet will look for the early signs of dry eye—the common name for keratoconjunctivitis sicca, an eye condition often seen in Westies.

● *My Westie, Scottie, has started to scratch himself and to lick and bite his feet. The skin on these parts is red, and he has developed some bald patches. I can't find any fleas or mites on him. Is this a behavior problem?*

Although there are many different causes of itchy skin in dogs, including fleas and mites, Westies are particularly prone to atopy, a canine allergy that inflames the skin. If you have eliminated parasites as the cause of itching, your vet can run tests to pinpoint atopy or another cause and then suggest appropriate treatment. It is quite likely that Scottie is allergic to dust or dust mites. If this is the case, you should consider buying a special antiallergy vacuum cleaner to keep his environment as free of irritants as possible.

Pomeranian

THE POMERANIAN IS THE SMALLEST OF THE Spitz family of dogs, which evolved throughout the Arctic regions of the world. Originally from Germany, the breed was popularized by Britain's Queen Victoria in the 19th century, when it was larger than its present tiny size, weighing up to 30lbs (13kg). Selective breeding has brought it down in size and altered its color from predominantly white to the orange and sable that is usually seen today. Bright and lively, and with plenty of self-confidence, Pomeranians make ideal companion dogs but are an unsuitable family pet for those with small children. They do not see themselves as small dogs and have a tendency to bark noisily at intruders.

A Small Fluffy Fox

With its pointed face, bushy tail, and tawny coloring, the Pomeranian has the look of a miniature fox. The fluffy tail is carried back and high over its body. Its small ears are upright and alert. The eyes are slightly oval and dark, and in some colors have attractive black rims to the eyelids. A fluffy double coat covers the body and provides good insulation. The undercoat is soft, while the profuse, long, straight outer coat forms a thick mane or ruff at the neck.

▲ *Pomeranians are not usually considered the most trainable of dogs, but there has to be an exception to every rule. This one shows keenness and alertness as it takes part in an agility competition.*

Breed Profile

Life expectancy:	13–15 years
Adult height at withers:	8½–11in (22–28cm)
Adult weight:	male 4–4½lbs (1.8–2kg)
	female 4½–5½lbs (2–2.5kg)

Temperament: Lively, faithful, confident. A good companion for the less active; also a good watchdog. Not ideal for first-time owners, as it needs an experienced hand for early training.

KNOWN HEALTH PROBLEMS

Luxating Patella (dislocating kneecap) can occur in the Pomeranian, affecting one or both joints. Sometimes the kneecap slips in and out of position without appearing to cause the dog any discomfort or disability. Sometimes, however, it stays out of place, and the dog cannot straighten its leg. An operation is usually necessary to correct the joint structure and keep the kneecap in its groove.

Patent Ductus Arteriosus (PDA) occurs in the Pomeranian. A fetal blood vessel that connects the aorta, the main artery from the heart, with the pulmonary artery, the major vessel to the lungs, fails to close after birth. As a result, the aorta cannot transport oxygen efficiently to the major body organs, diverting it instead to the lungs. Some puppies die of circulatory failure shortly after birth. Others develop symptoms such as a heart murmur, chronic cough, or breathing difficulties in later life.

Head reflects the Spitz ancestry, being wide and flat with a rather narrow, pointed muzzle

Tail has profuse hair. It lies flat and straight

Coat is long but straight and requires dedicated grooming

Q&A...

● I live in a third-floor apartment and am looking for a small dog as a companion pet. I suffer from arthritis in my hands. Would a Pomeranian make a good choice?

I'm afraid I cannot recommend it. The Pomeranian's thick coat requires vigorous grooming with a wire brush to stop tangles and matting, and this may prove difficult for you. A small dog with a short, smooth coat, such as a Chihuahua or Miniature Pinscher, would be more suitable.

● How is it you never see a pure white Pomeranian? I'd dearly love to have one.

When the breed became popular outside Germany, more than 100 years ago, it closely resembled the all-white Samoyed, to which it is related. The demand for a smaller dog meant that the all-white coloration was lost through selective breeding. Some breeders today are trying to bring the white dog back in the miniature form, but without great success. Though white puppies are often born, by the time they are 6 or 7 months old, they have grown larger than the breed standard.

▲ *Though today's dog is dainty looking and compact in build, the Pomeranian was originally much larger. It remains highly active and needs more living space than some of the other smaller breeds.*

● My children keep asking for a Pomeranian after they fell in love with one they saw at a friend's house. They are lovely dogs, but look so delicate and fragile, I'm quite nervous about keeping one in our rambunctious household. Do you think it is a good idea?

Due to miniaturization, Pomeranians have smaller and thinner bones than some of the larger breeds of dog. As a consequence, they do break quite easily, especially if the dog is accidentally dropped by a child or it gets caught up in the rough and tumble of family life. Although they are very friendly, Pomeranians are also highly excitable and bark noisily when roused (they make excellent burglar alarms). For all these reasons, you would probably be advised not to consider keeping one while your family is still young.

Dachshund

WITH THEIR ELONGATED, LOW-SLUNG BODIES and short legs, Dachshunds are unmistakable in appearance. The characteristic body shape was originally bred for hunting small animals: the Dachshund was put down holes after badgers and foxes ("Dachshund" is the German for badger dog). Miniature varieties of the breed were used to hunt rabbits. Sometimes still used as working dogs, especially in Germany, they are today one of the best-known breeds of family dog, enjoying great popularity throughout the world. The Dachshund is known for its courageous spirit and makes an extremely good guard dog, guaranteed to alert the family to visitors.

A Small, Powerful Machine

Dachshunds come in two sizes, standard and miniature. The standard is about twice as large as the miniature. As evidence of their hunting past, both types have a keen-nose for prey and possess a powerful, long set of jaws. The chest, which was developed for working down holes and burrows, is deep and robust, with a prominent breastbone that gives the front profile a markedly curved appearance. The size of the adult dog is customarily measured by the circumference of the chest. The long trunk is very straight, and the tail, which tapers gradually, follows the line of the spine. The eyes, beneath their prominent bridges, are dark, intelligent, and alert in expression. The nose is black (brown in some colors of coat), and the ears are set high and quite far back on the head. The rounded ear flaps fold down and cover the ear canals, the front edges touching the cheeks.

There are three types of coat. The smooth-haired is thick, short, and sleek. It does not shed much and requires the minimum of grooming to keep it in good condition. The long-haired variety is soft, straight or slightly wavy, and long,

▶ *The Dachshund is an alert, intelligent family dog with well-developed senses. A firm hand is needed in training to keep its lively hunting spirit in check.*

Length of tapering *muzzle exceeds that of skull*

Coat *may be longhaired (as here), smooth, or wirehaired. There is a wide range of colors*

Long trunk, *which lends the Dachshund mobility, is the cause of frequent back problems*

with feathering on the ears, under the neck, on the underparts of the body, and underneath the tail. It requires regular brushing. The wirehaired has a short, harsh, and straight outer coat, with a dense undercoat. It has distinctive bushy eyebrows and a small beard, but the hairs on the ears are smooth. The dead hair needs thinning (stripping) regularly from the coat. Almost any color is possible. Smooth and longhairs are often red, but black and tan, chocolate and tan, and dapple (an even mixture of white and tan, chocolate, or black) are all common. Brindle (black or brown streaked with a lighter color) is the most usual color for wirehairs.

As a result of their elongated body shape and short legs, Dachshunds have a tendency to suffer from back problems. In particular, they are prone to "slipped disk," which causes acute pain and can result in partial or total paralysis of the hindlegs. The Dachshund's long jaws, designed to help it flush out prey, also give rise to a considerable number of problems.

● *My neighbors have started to complain that my 2-year-old Dachshund, Zola, barks a lot while I am out. What can I do?*

Dachshunds are very alert dogs. Zola may be responding to every little sound she hears, especially if she is bored, or she may just miss you a lot. When you have to go out, try leaving a few lights on, and the radio or TV playing, and provide her with plenty of toys. If she carries on barking, ask your veterinarian to refer you to an animal behaviorist.

● *Ollie, our Miniature Wirehaired Dachshund, has just had his first booster shot at age 15 months. The vet weighed him and said he is too fat at 15lbs (7kg). He is very fit, so why does this matter?*

Miniature Dachshunds should weigh only about 10lbs (4.5kg). Ollie is far too heavy and is highly likely to suffer a disk problem, so you must slim him down. Dachshunds enjoy their food and will eat almost anything offered, so it is important to get advice on the correct feeding regime.

Breed Profile

Life expectancy:	11–14 years
Adult chest measurement:	Standard, over 14in (35cm) Miniature 12–14in (31–35cm)
Adult weight:	Standard 16–32lbs (7–14.5kg) Miniature 10–11lbs (4.5–5kg)

Temperament: Completely reliable, provided a firm hand is used in training. A good family pet, behaves well with children, and is equally at home in town or country. Will live happily in an apartment with access to walks.

KNOWN HEALTH PROBLEMS

Intervertebral Disk Disease occurs more often in the Dachshund than other breeds because of the long back, and possibly the nature of the intervertebral disks. When an excess movement of the spine occurs, the cartilage roof of a disk ruptures, usually mid spine, and some of its contents escape upward and press on the spinal cord. Similar ruptures can occur in the disks of the chest or neck. Medical treatment and total rest will often reverse the symptoms, but the dog may be left with a weak back. Surgical correction may be necessary. Some dogs suffer permanent paralysis of the hind legs.

Prognathia is an overdevelopment of the naturally long upper jaw of the Dachshund. It means that it is so overshot, the upper teeth do not fit neatly with those of the shorter lower jaw. Surgical correction may be necessary.

Retention of the temporary (baby) teeth occurs in the Dachshund, probably because of a mild or serious prognathia (see above). The baby teeth should normally have all been replaced by adult teeth by the time the dog is 6 months old. If they are still there when the adult teeth appear, the jaw becomes overcrowded, leading to severe dental problems. Any baby teeth left in the mouth after the age of 6 months will have to be extracted by the vet under general anesthetic.

Distichiasis is an inherited defect of the Dachshund in which fine extra lashes grow along the edge of the eyelid and rub against the surface of the eye. Plucking them out improves the situation temporarily, but surgery may be necessary to resolve it.

Progressive Retinal Degeneration is an inherited disease of the eye that causes gradual loss of vision. All dogs should be checked and cleared before being used for breeding.

Von Willebrand's Disease, an inherited disease of the blood platelets, is known to occur occasionally in the Dachshund. It leads to unexpected and unexplained bleeding.

Yorkshire Terrier

Eyes are dark and alert. They are prone to cataracts

Tail is medium long but not easy to spot when carried down

Facial hair has a tendency to get in the dog's way if not kept short

Coat has been trimmed back to minimize grooming

CLASSIFIED AS A TOY BREED, THE YORKSHIRE Terrier, or Yorkie as it is affectionately known, is the world's most popular small terrier. Elegant but feisty, it is equally at home whether out in the woods hunting rats or rabbits or parading with a red bow in its topknot at a dog show.

The Yorkie was originally bred by miners in the industrial heartland of northern England to hunt down the rats that infested the mine shafts. It is thought to be descended from the Maltese, the Black-and-Tan Terrier, and the now-extinct Clydesdale Terrier. It has retained the powerful instinct for ratting that is typical of terriers.

For such a tiny creature, the Yorkshire Terrier is alert and surprisingly audacious. It loves nothing better than a good romp in the park or country. Because of their size, many Yorkies are kept in city apartments, but they are too adventurous

▲ *When presented for showing, Yorkshire Terriers have a decorative appearance that belies their hardy origins— they were bred originally as ratters, not lap dogs, and retain a spirited, inquisitive personality.*

to be real "lap dogs" and need plenty of exercise to burn off some of their energy. If you haven't a large backyard, your Yorkie will need frequent trips to the park.

The Yorkshire Terrier is easily picked up and carried, and can be taken anywhere. It makes an ideal family pet as it is generally good-tempered and enjoys playing games. However, if harassed by very small, undisciplined children, a Yorkie, like almost any other dog, may be provoked to bite. The Yorkie is fearless and curious, making it an excellent watchdog. It is more intelligent than most people give it credit for, though few

Breed Profile

Life expectancy:	12–15 years
Adult height at withers:	9in (23cm)
Adult weight:	5–7lbs (2.5–3.5kg)

Temperament: Alert, active, brave. Can be yappy but therefore a good guard dog—it will investigate every noise. A good family dog, likes people, but may not get along with other dogs. Not ideal for very small children, but fine for senior citizens as the dogs are easy to lift and carry.

KNOWN HEALTH PROBLEMS

Luxating Patella (dislocating kneecap) occurs occasionally in the Yorkshire Terrier, affecting either one or both legs. Sometimes this causes lameness, but often the kneecap slips in and out of place without evident pain. Surgery will correct the joint structure, enabling the kneecap to stay in its groove.

Tracheal Collapse occurs when the cartilage rings that keep the trachea (windpipe) open so that air can pass through become weak and collapse. This narrows the windpipe severely so that the dog has difficulty in breathing, producing heavy, labored breaths. The dog becomes weak, often staggers, and death can occur. The problem is associated with miniaturization. Surgery is usually unsuccessful.

Retention of the milk teeth after the adult teeth have come through is a problem of the Yorkie. Overcrowding leads to severe dental problems as food is packed between the temporary and the permanent teeth. Periodontal disease quickly follows. Any temporary teeth left in the mouth after the age of 6 months should be extracted by the vet.

Cataracts are a progressive opacity of the lens in one or both eyes, causing the pupil to appear gray or white instead of black. In advanced cases the lens looks like a pearl and the dog may be blind. Cataracts are hereditary in the Yorkie; the onset is usually late in life.

---

owners bother to train their Yorkie. This is a pity, as it will fully repay the trouble taken to teach it, in common with all dogs.

A Walking Coat

A tiny dog, the Yorkshire Terrier usually weighs no more than 7lbs (3.5kg). It has a distinctive silky coat that is steel-blue from the base of its skull to the root of its tail and light tan on the underside of its neck and chest. Puppies are born nearly black and develop the colored coat in their first year. The nails are black. In show condition, the straight coat is very long and sleek, but this takes hours of grooming to achieve. As an outdoor pet, its coat will be much wavier, but still requires a lot of grooming. Many owners prefer to cut it short, and a woolen coat should be put on when the dog goes outside in winter as Yorkies are prone to feel the cold.

Under the long topknot, the Yorkie's eyes are dark and bright, and look directly forward. The small, tan-colored, V-shaped ears stand upright. It has been customary to dock Yorkies' tails, but this practice is rapidly dying out. The tail cannot easily be seen beneath the long body hair, even when full length. Nor, indeed, can the rest of the body, which is compact, with straight, thin legs and a level back.

● *My male Yorkie, Dale Boy, can hardly see because his hair is so long. My husband refuses to let me tie it back with a ribbon. Is it all right to trim it?*

If you don't plan on showing your dog, you should certainly trim the excess hair carefully with blunt-ended scissors. Dale Boy will be delighted—Yorkies hate getting their overly long hair in their mouths.

● *I have a 2-year-old female Yorkshire Terrier, Mona, and would love to breed from her. She is bigger than the breed standard, about 11lbs (5kg), but not fat. Should I use her for breeding nevertheless?*

Yes. Some Yorkie females are so tiny that they can only give birth by Caesarean section. It is far better to use a bigger female and choose a small male to father the litter. This way the birth should be easier, but the final adult size of the offspring should not be too large for the breed standard.

● *We are an active, retired couple who love long walks in the country. We are looking for a small dog (we live in an apartment). Could a Yorkie keep up?*

Don't be fooled by its size—a Yorkie would almost certainly outdistance you. It would be an ideal dog for you—small enough to live happily in an apartment but full of energy and stamina.

Chihuahua

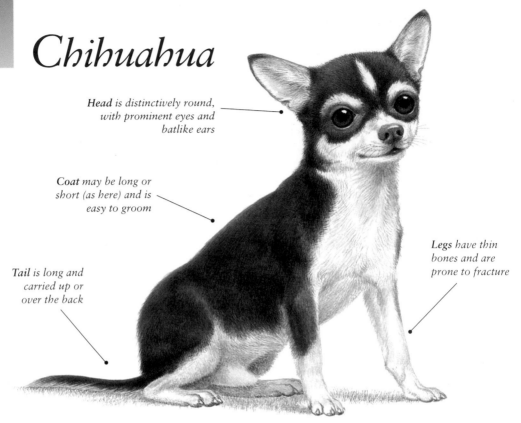

Head is distinctively round, with prominent eyes and batlike ears

Coat may be long or short (as here) and is easy to groom

Legs have thin bones and are prone to fracture

Tail is long and carried up or over the back

THE CHIHUAHUA COMES ORIGINALLY FROM Mexico and is the oldest breed on the American continent. It was probably brought to the Americas by Spanish conquistadors, though this is not known for certain. The name is derived from the Mexican state from which the dogs were exported to the United States in the mid-19th century.

Chihuahuas are the smallest dog breed in the world, smaller than most domestic cats. Despite their size, they are assertive, high-spirited, and mischievous. Convinced that they are much bigger than they are, Chihuahuas will tackle anyone on their own territory. Lively and alert, they make good indoor guard dogs. Though they have a tendency to shiver at the slightest breeze, they are generally resilient and active, and enjoy plenty of exercise. They were bred originally as lap dogs, and their small appetites are in proportion to their size; they can be fussy eaters. Their affectionate, loyal nature makes them the ideal companion for an elderly owner, but their assertiveness means that they may not be a good choice for a family with small children.

▲ *The ultimate "lapdog," the Chihuahua is highly affectionate. It does not get along well with other breeds. You might expect it to run and hide, but it will not hesitate to challenge a much larger dog.*

A Tiny Dog with Big Eyes

Chihuahuas may be either smooth-coated, with short, glossy hair, or long-coated, with a silky coat and more hair on the ears, legs, and tail, which is full and plumed. The long-coated variety is rarer than the smooth. It is more tolerant of cool conditions. Both types have thicker hair around the neck, forming a ruff. They come in several colors or mixtures of colors, ranging from light fawn and chestnut to silver or steel blue, and are easy to groom. The Chihuahua's compact body is longer than it is tall, with thin front legs. The head is round and nearly apple-shaped, with a narrow, pointed muzzle, large erect ears that slope outward, and a strong neck. The forward-facing eyes are large, round, black, and very alert, giving the Chihuahua its typical appealing and intelligent expression.

● *My year-old Chihuahua pup, Chandler, loves lying in my lap, but has started to snap at me if I try to move him. Should I be worried?*

Chandler is at an age when he feels confident enough to challenge you. Even tiny dogs can become aggressive and bite quite hard, so it is important that you train him out of this behavior, mainly by cooling your relationship with him and making sure he stays at ground level for a while.

● *My elderly mother, who is still very active, lives alone in a small apartment. I'd like to buy her a dog as a companion. Would a Chihuahua suit her?*

As long as your mother provides lots of interesting toys to play with indoors and is able to give it regular exercise, a Chihuahua is an excellent choice. Because they are so small, elderly people can easily pick them up and carry them around. Chihuahuas do have shrill barks, so your mother must be prepared to train her dog to be quiet, especially when left on its own.

▶ *A longhaired Chihuahua has a much more pronounced ruff around its neck than the shorthaired variety, and the tail is feathered. Both have small mouths and tend to lose teeth easily.*

Breed Profile

Life expectancy:	11–13 years
Adult height at withers:	6–9in (15–23cm)
Adult weight:	2–6lbs (1–3kg)

Temperament: Courageous, extremely loyal, affectionate, and intelligent. They enjoy being walked but are ideal for people living in an apartment. Not recommended for people with small children.

KNOWN HEALTH PROBLEMS

Hydrocephalus (water on the brain), a common congenital condition in Chihuahuas, occurs when increased fluid in the brain chambers presses on the brain cells. The pressure may be so severe that only a narrow rim of brain tissue is left. Symptoms include dullness, weakness, and fits. In some cases, surgical drainage may relieve the pressure and allow a fairly normal life, but in others no treatment is possible.

Molera is a soft spot at the center of the top of the skull that occurs when the developing bones fail to meet, leaving the brain unprotected in that area. Chihuahua breeders have had some success in eliminating it by selective breeding.

Pulmonic Stenosis (narrowing of the pulmonary artery) is a rare inherited disease in the Chihuahua. The artery is narrow where it leaves the heart, and so the heart has to work very hard to pump blood to the lungs, leading eventually to heart failure. It is sometimes possible to correct this defect by surgery.

Primary Glaucoma, an inherited disease in Chihuahuas, develops when the pressure of the fluid inside the eye increases due to failure of a drainage system. It causes pain, inflammation, and excessive tear production. Surgery is needed to correct it.

Luxating Patella (dislocating kneecap) is known to occur in the Chihuahua, affecting one or both joints. Sometimes the kneecap slips in and out of position without causing the dog any discomfort or disability, but a displaced kneecap may result in the dog being unable to straighten its leg. In such cases, an operation can usually correct the joint structure and enable the kneecap to stay in its groove.

Hemophilia A is a failure of certain clotting mechanisms of the blood, leading to virtually uncontrollable hemorrhage. Although uncommon, it is seen occasionally in the Chihuahua.

The Crossbreed

Not everyone wants to keep a pedigree dog. Many people choose to own a crossbreed or mixed-breed dog instead. There are good reasons for doing so. Most crossbreeds make fine, healthy, affectionate pets. By and large, they are well-balanced, trainable dogs and, if socialized properly as puppies, fit happily into the rough and tumble of family life. They have an average life expectancy of 10–15 years and often avoid many of the health problems that affect their purer bred cousins.

The term crossbreed applies to puppies from purebred parents of different breeds or from parents of two mixed but known breeds, as well as to puppies whose ancestry is very mixed or unknown—in other words, mongrels. Though very many crossbreeds result from accidental matings, they can also be deliberately bred.

Because crossbreeds are not the product of the inbreeding required to produce a pure pedigree bloodline, they possess a quality that is known as "hybrid vigor." Outbreeding (breeding from an unrestricted gene pool) ensures that genetic characteristics are drawn from many strains of dog. As a result, crossbreeds tend to be tougher, more robust, and more resistant to disease than most pedigree animals, and their chances of avoiding inherited defects and diseases are therefore much higher.

For many, the delight of taking a crossbred or mixed puppy into the family is the mystery of not knowing quite how it will turn out. Will it have long or short hair? Will it alter in color as it grows older? Will it stay small, or will it grow to catch up with the size of its disproportionately large feet? A good clue to a crossbreed's ancestry is whether it seems to have some of the looks of a particular breed.

Choosing Your Crossbreed

Crossbreeds can be acquired from many different sources. Very often they will be given away by a friend or neighbor whose female dog has mated inadvertently with an unknown male and produced a litter of mixed, often very appealing pups. If possible, try to meet the mother before accepting the puppy as this will enable you to find out about the puppy's ancestry, especially if the father is known to the owner. Take the opportunity to observe the mother's behavior toward her puppies, as this should offer a clue to the way your puppy's temperament and character is likely to develop as it grows up.

▶ These adorable 8-week-old Collie–Tibetan Terrier crosses are already well socialized and ready for new homes. Though they won't win prizes, they'll make excellent family pets.

Should I Choose a Crossbreed?

Pros

✓ Hybrid vigor usually produces a robust, healthy dog with fewer genetic diseases.

✓ A crossbreed will give as much loyalty and affection as other breeds if properly socialized and trained.

✓ It is usually much cheaper to buy.

✓ It often comes with free or reduced-cost vaccination and neutering (if the dog is acquired from a rescue center).

Cons

✗ There is no guarantee of what size or type of dog you are acquiring if parentage is unknown.

✗ No guarantee of temperament or behavior.

✗ An animal shelter may insist on neutering the dog before you take it home or make sure you agree to have it neutered after you have adopted it.

● *I am a 70-year-old widow and have just lost my faithful canine companion of many years. I am still fit and really miss having a pet. Would you advise me to take on another dog at my age?*

Having another dog is often the best way to recover from the loss of a previous pet. You may find a puppy too much for you, but why not see if your local animal shelter has a calm, friendly, middle-aged crossbreed that will welcome all the affection you can give it?

● *We want to acquire a family dog for our kids who are 8 and 10. We can't afford the high fees charged by pedigree breeders and have been considering a small crossbreed. What do you think?*

Go ahead—crossbreeds often make the best family pets. Try to find a puppy that is between 8 and 12 weeks old. That way, you can be sure of educating it yourself (see pages 108–109) and ensuring that it has proper temperament and obedience training.

● *I like the idea of adopting a crossbreed from a shelter, but am worried that it may have behavior problems. Is this so?*

Behavioral problems tend to arise quite frequently in rescued dogs because of their early history of mistreatment and abandonment and because they have spent much of their lives in shelters. However, crossbreeds are likely to have fewer inherited problems than purebred dogs, and if you choose a puppy, all should be well.

Many crossbreeds come from animal shelters and dog pounds. Veterinary hospitals often keep lists of puppies and adult dogs that need new homes. Try to check the dog's previous history as thoroughly as you can before acquiring a pet this way. If you are choosing a puppy, ask the staff for any information they may have about its background. Was it born in the shelter or did it come in with its mother? Does it have brothers and sisters? Everything you are able to discover about the puppy will help you build up a picture of its character and future development. But though your puppy's temperament will to some degree have been forged by its ancestry, the way it is handled and trained in the first few months of life will be at least as, if not more, important in determining its adult character and behavior. This rule applies to crossbreeds just as much as it does to pedigree dogs.

Glossary

Acaracidal A medical treatment that kills PARASITES that are members of the spider family—e.g. mites and/or ticks.

Acute Describes a disease that is sudden in onset and runs a short course.

Alpha dog The highest ranking dog in the pack.

Anal sacs Scent glands each side of the anus.

Antibody A protein formed by the body and found in the blood to kill invading infections.

Atopy An itchy skin disease caused by allergic reaction to an inhaled substance.

Autoimmune A destructive immunity developed against part of the dog's own body.

Benign A TUMOR that is not MALIGNANT, recurring, or spreading.

Biopsy A sample of tissue taken from the living animal for purposes of diagnosis.

Bloat Dilation of the stomach by trapped gas, often leading to gastric torsion. Affects mainly deep-chested breeds. Often fatal.

Blue merle Blue and gray coat color mixed with black.

Brachycephalic Short nosed.

Breed PUREBRED dogs, more or less uniform in size and structure, as produced and maintained by man.

Breed standard Description of the ideal specimen in each breed set by national kennel associations.

Brindle Black oat color streaked with brown, tawny, or other color.

Brisket The part of the body below the chest between the forelegs.

Carpus The equivalent joint to the human wrist joint, between the elbow and the toes of the forelimb, that acts like a hinge.

Castration Surgical removal of the testes of the male dog.

Cataract A permanent opacity in the lens of the eye that interferes with vision.

Chronic Describes a disease that is gradual in onset and runs a long course.

Congenital A condition that is present at birth.

Cropping The surgical trimming of the ear flap of some breeds to make the ear more erect (a practice banned in many countries).

Crossbreed A dog of mixed parentage—either two distinct breeds or a mixture of many breeds.

Cruciate ligament One of two important ligaments—the anterior and posterior—that stabilize the STIFLE joint.

Cyst An abnormal fluid-filled cavity that may occur in any body tissue.

Dentition The arrangement of the teeth in the mouth.

Dew claw The first toe, on the inside of the paw, not in contact with the ground. In many breeds, they are often missing from the hind limbs.

Diabetes insipidus A hormonal disease causing increased thirst as the result of failure of the kidneys to concentrate urine.

Diabetes mellitus A disease characterized by high blood glucose.

Distemper A deadly viral disease of dogs. It is prevented by vaccination.

Docking The surgical removal of the tail. Usually done for cosmetic reasons in young puppies.

Dolichocephalic Long nosed.

Double coat A coat consisting of a weather-resistant outer GUARD HAIRS and an undercoat of softer hairs.

Dry eye Failure to produce adequate tears, resulting in desiccation of the surface of the eye.

Dysplasia Abnormal development, for example of the hip.

Elizabethan collar A conical collar fitted around the neck to prevent the dog from biting its body, stitches etc., or scratching the head and ears.

Epulis A hard lump on the gums; usually BENIGN.

Estrus The period in the female HEAT cycle when she is fertile and will mate, if an opportunity occurs.

False pregnancy Hormone-induced state following an unproductive HEAT period causing signs that mimic pregnancy. The female may lactate, have an enlarged abdomen, and treat toys as if they were pups.

Feathering A fringe of longer hairs found on the ears, legs, tail, or body of an otherwise shorter haired dog.

Gait The pattern of steps the dog takes at different speeds.

Guard hairs The longer, usually stiffer hairs in the coat.

Habituation The process by which an animal becomes familiar with its environment.

Hackles Long hairs on the back and neck, often raised in anger or fright.

Head collar (halti) A nonpunitive, nose-led training device to improve control while the dog is on the leash.

Heat Usually refers to the 21-day period twice a year when the female is able to breed.

Hereditary Usually related to a disease or defect that is passed on from one or both parents to some or all of their offspring. Not necessarily present or obvious at birth.

Hock Hinged joint in the hindleg, equivalent to the human ankle, between the toes and the STIFLE.

Hot spot A red, moist area of infected skin; intensely painful.

Inbreeding The mating of closely related dogs, e.g. father and daughter.

Insulin A hormone produced by the pancreas that causes absorption of glucose in the bloodstream.

Intact A dog that has not been NEUTERED (also called **entire**).

Invertebral disk The small cartilage "shock absorber" between each vertebra in the spine.

Knee Joint of the hindleg, also known as the STIFLE.

Larva An immature stage in the life cycle of a PARASITE.

Level bite When the front teeth of the upper and lower jaws meet exactly; also known as pincer bite.

Lick granuloma A callus or swelling that develops on the dog's skin when it habitually chews a particular area.

Lipoma A BENIGN TUMOR of fat cells.

Luxation Dislocation of a joint. One bone becomes displaced from its normal articulation with another.

Malignant A TUMOR that has potential to spread throughout the body.

Metabolic disorder An abnormality of the chemical processes that normally keep the body in balance, such as DIABETES.

Molt The seasonal shedding of the coat hairs.

Muzzle The part of the head in front of the eyes: the nose and jaws. Also, a device to prevent the dog biting that fits around the above.

Neuter To sterilize a male or female dog by surgical removal of the testes or ovaries.

Obesity Excessive weight: more than 15% above the average weight for the dog's size and age.

Overshot jaw The result of an overlong upper jaw that causes the upper front teeth to overlap the lower.

Pads Tough, thickened skin on the undersides of the feet.

Parasite An animal living on and deriving food from another animal, usually to its detriment.

Patella (kneecap)—a small movable bone that acts like a pulley on the front of the STIFLE joint.

Pedigree The written record of a dog's ancestry.

Platelet A small blood component responsible for blood clotting.

Prepuce The lined sheath of skin in which the penis is normally located.

Prognosis The expected outcome of a disease, condition, or surgical procedure.

Purebred A dog whose parents belong to the same breed and are themselves of unmixed descent.

Puzzle feeder An activity toy designed to stimulate the dog mentally by releasing food at a rate that it determines itself.

Pyometra A life-threatening infection of the uterus, usually seen in middle aged or older females.

Rabies A fatal central nervous system disease of mammals, including dogs and humans, passed on in the saliva of an infected animal.

Rage syndrome Severe, recurrent, unpredictable aggression, often unprovoked and short lived.

Renal Relating to or located in the region of the kidneys.

Roundworm A long spaghettilike worm living in the small intestine. Most common in puppies.

Sable Black-tipped hairs overlaid on a gold, silver, gray, fawn, or tan coat.

Scent marking Using body scents (in urine, feces, or anal sac fluid) to leave a message for other dogs.

Scissor bite A perfect, regular mouth closure in which the upper teeth closely overlap the lower teeth.

Separation anxiety State of anxiety caused by separation from a person or other dog to which the dog is attached.

Socialization The process by which a dog becomes familiar with other animals, including humans.

Spay The NEUTERING of females by surgical removal of both ovaries and the uterus.

Stifle The equivalent of the human knee joint. The hind limb joint between the thigh bone and shin.

Stop The step up from the MUZZLE to skull; the indentation between the eyes where the nasal bone and the skull meet.

Stopper pad The highest pad of the forelimb, positioned on the back of the CARPUS. It may come into contact with the ground when the forepaws are extended during a sudden stop.

Stripping A grooming procedure by which long, thick hair is removed by hand or with a serrated blade.

Stud A male dog used for breeding.

Submission Deference to a more dominant individual.

Syndrome A group of symptoms that occur together, indicating a particular condition or disease.

Terrier A dog originally bred for hunting vermin.

Topline The dog's outline from behind the WITHERS to the tail.

Trauma An injury or wound to the body.

Tricolor A three-color coat of black, white, and tan.

Tumor An abnormal mass or swelling of body tissue that may be BENIGN or MALIGNANT.

Undershot jaw The result of an overlong lower jaw that causes the lower front teeth to overlap those on the upper jaw.

Ulcer An open sore on an external or internal surface of the body.

Vaccination Stimulation of the immune system to protect against infectious disease.

Vertebrae The individual bones of the spine.

Virus A submicroscopic organism that infects animals.

Wall eye A pale blue eye, affecting all or part of the iris.

Whelping The act of giving birth to puppies.

Whelps Unweaned puppies.

Withers The highest point of the body, immediately behind the neck.

CONTRIBUTORS

Caroline Bower BVM&S MRCVS: What Breed Should I Choose, Taking in a Rescued Dog, Choosing Your Puppy, Your New Puppy at Home, Housebreaking, Traveling with Your Dog, and part 3: Training and Behavior Problems

John Bower BVSc MRCVS: Death of a Pet, Common Infectious Diseases, Common Parasites, First Aid and Emergencies, and part 4: Dog Breeds

Adam Coulson BVMS CertVR MRCVS: Your Dog and the Law, Your Puppy's Diet, Your Puppy's Health, Feeding Your Adult Dog, Your Healthy Dog, The Older Dog, Structure of the Dog, Getting the Most from Your Vet, Loss of Balance, Increased Appetite, Increased Thirst, Urinary Problems, Lameness, Eye Problems

Philip Hunt BVSc MRCVS: Mouth and Teeth Problems

Hilary O'Dair BVetMed CertSAD CertSAM MRCVS: Fits and Seizures

Stephen O'Shea MA VetMB CertVC MRCVS: Coughing, Breathing Difficulties and Choking, Sudden Weakness and Collapse

Neil Slater BVSc MRCVS: Vomiting, Diarrhea and Other Bowel Problems

Alix Turnbull BSc BVMS MRCVS: Responsibilities of Owning a Dog, Grooming, Going On Vacation and Moving, Tumors and Cysts, Neutering: the Male Dog, The Female Dog, Mating and Breeding

Kevin Watts BSc BVetMed CertVD MRCVS: Itchy Skin Conditions, Non-itchy Skin Conditions, Hair and Coat Problems, Paw Problems, Ear Problems

Nigel Bray MA VetMB MRCVS: Consultant Editor (USA)

Stephanie Robinson, formerly Associate Director of Canine Legislation, the American Kennel Club, gave help with Your Dog and the Law.
The Kennel Club's Illustrated Breed Standards book was a useful source of information.

PICTURES

ABBREVIATIONS

AOL	Andromeda Oxford Ltd	IF	Isabelle Francais
AP	Animal Photography	US	Ulrike Schanz
BCL	Bruce Coleman Ltd	TSM	The Stock Market, UK
JB	Jane Burton	AL	Ardea London

1 John Daniels/Shoot Photographic; 2 JB/AOL; 4 AOL; 7 John Daniels/AL; 9 TSM; 10 IF; 11 R. Drury/TRIP; 14–15 IF; 16–17 E.A. Janes; 18l JB; 18r AOL; 19c Sally Anne Thompson/AP; 19b AOL; 20, 22, 23, 24, 25 IF; 26t AOL; 26b US; 27 JB; 28t Your Dog Magazine; 28b TSM; 29 Jorg & Petra Wegner/BCL; 30 US; 31t Sally Anne Thompson/AP; 31b AOL; 32t Barnaby's Picture Library; 32b Spectrum Colour Library; 33 Hi-Craft; 34 JB; 35 US; 37 John Daniels/AL; 39 Heather Angel/Biofotos; 41 Your Dog Magazine; 45 TSM; 46t Dr. H. Thompson/University of Glasgow Veterinary School; 46b Chandoha Photography; 48 with kind permission of Bayer AG, Germany; 49l A. van den Broek; 49c Dr. K.L. Thoday/Royal School of Veterinary Studies, Edinburgh; 49r A. van den Broek; 50tl Sherley's Ltd; 50cl Novartis Animal Health; 50tr David Scharf/Science Photo Library; 52t Chandoha Photography; 52b Dr. Janet Littlewood/Animal Health Trust; 55t JB; 55b Dr. Janet Littlewood/Animal Health Trust; 56 Angela Hampton/RSPCA; 57 Barnaby's Picture Library; 57cr Dr. Janet Littlewood/Animal Health Trust; 58 JB; 59 IF; 60 Barnaby's Picture Library; 61 Sally Anne Thompson/AP; 62 JB; 63 James E. McKay; 64 M.J. Brearley/Animal Health Trust; 65 Hans Reinhard/BCL; 66 Dr. K.L. Thoday/Royal School of Veterinary Studies, Edinburgh; 67, 68 US; 69 The Veterinary Hospital, Estover, Plymouth; 70l JB; 70r JB/BCL; 71 AOL; 72 IF; 73 JB; 73bl AOL; 74–75 Hilly Hoar; 76 Urolithiasis Laboratory, Inc.; 77 AOL, hand model Mary Hammond; 78, 79c Professor Andrew Nash/University of Glasgow Veterinary School; 79t J. Howard/Sylvia Cordaiy Photo Library; 81t The Veterinary Hospital, Estover, Plymouth; 81b J. Howard/Sylvia Cordaiy Photo Library; 82t Sally Anne Thompson/AP; 82b Simon Everett/Pet Dogs; 83 L. Trickey/RSPCA; 84 John G.A. Robinson B.D.S.; 85 JB; 87tl Wayland Publishers; 87tr Dr. Janet Littlewood/Animal Health Trust; 87b Sally Anne Thompson/AP; 88tl, tr, br Dr. Dan Lavach/ Eye Clinic for Animals, California; 88bl Dr. Jane Sansom/Animal Health Trust; 91 Your Dog Magazine; 92, 95, 96, 97 JB/BCL; 99 JB; 100 Sally Anne Thompson/AP; 101 John Daniels/Shoot Photographic; 103 Bob Glover/BCL; 105 Stephen J. Krasemann/ BCL; 106 J. Howard/Sylvia Cordaiy Photo Library; 107 JB; 108, 109 IF; 110 TSM; 111 John Daniels/Shoot Photographic; 112l, 112r, 113l, 113r JB/AOL; 114 TSM; 114–115 AOL; 115 JB; 116 Chandoha Photography; 118 John Daniels/AL; 119 TSM; 120 JB/ BCL; 121 E.A. Janes; 122 J.P. Ferrero/AL; 123 Hans Reinhard/ BCL; 124 IF; 127 Hilly Hoar; 129t US; 129b, 130 JB; 131 US; 132 TSM; 133 Your Dog Magazine; 134 TSM; 135 John Daniels/Shoot Photographic; 136–137 JB/BCL; 137 AOL; 138–139 Your Dog Magazine; 141 R.T. Willbie/AP; 143 C. Seddon/RSPCA; 144 David Dalton/Frank Lane Picture Agency; 145 IF; 147 J.M. Labat/AL; 149 IF; 153 Barnaby's Picture Library; 159, 172 IF; 179 US; 180 IF; 185 Sally Anne Thompson/AP; 187 IF; 191 US/Aquila; 192 Daniele Robotti; 199 J.M. Labat/AL; 200–201 Jorg & Petra Wegner/BCL; **Equipment photography** by Mark Mason Studios

Artwork
Priscilla Barrett 42l, 107t, 204–208; Lizzie Harper 42c; Richard Lewington 48; Ruth Lindsay 51, 59, 61, 67, 76, 80, 89, 90; Denys Ovenden 43, 104, 109, 111, 117, 125, 126, 128, 131, 133, 137, 139, 140, 143, 148–199; Graham Rosewarne 85, 95

The publishers would like to thank Rosewood Pet Products and Money and Friend pet shop, Abingdon, for their assistance in this project.

Index

Italic page numbers refer to picture captions.